Anyone Can Be Saved

Anyone Can Be Saved

A Defense of "Traditional" Southern Baptist Soteriology

Edited by
DAVID L. ALLEN,
ERIC HANKINS,
and
ADAM HARWOOD

WIPF & STOCK · Eugene, Oregon

ANYONE CAN BE SAVED
A Defense of "Traditional" Southern Baptist Soteriology

Copyright © 2016 Wipf and Stock Publishers. All rights reserved. Except for brief quotations in critical publications or reviews, no part of this book may be reproduced in any manner without prior written permission from the publisher. Write: Permissions, Wipf and Stock Publishers, 199 W. 8th Ave., Suite 3, Eugene, OR 97401.

Wipf & Stock
An Imprint of Wipf and Stock Publishers
199 W. 8th Ave., Suite 3
Eugene, OR 97401

www.wipfandstock.com

PAPERBACK ISBN: 978-1-4982-8515-5
HARDCOVER ISBN: 978-1-4982-8707-4
EBOOK ISBN: 978-1-4982-8516-2

Manufactured in the U.S.A. 09/09/16

Scripture quotations marked ESV are taken from the ESV® Bible (The Holy Bible, English Standard Version®), Copyright © 2001 by Crossway, a publishing ministry of Good News Publishers. Used by permission. All rights reserved.

Scripture quotations marked HCSB are taken from the Holman Christian Standard Bible®, Copyright © 1999, 2000, 2002, 2003, 2009 by Holman Bible Publishers. Used by permission. HCSB® is a federally registered trademark of Holman Bible Publishers.

Scripture quotations marked NASB are taken from the New American Standard Bible®, Copyright © 1960, 1962, 1963, 1968, 1971, 1972, 1973, 1975, 1977, 1995 by The Lockman Foundation. Used by permission.

Scripture quotations marked NKJV are taken from the New King James Version®. Copyright © 1982 by Thomas Nelson. Used by permission. All rights reserved.

Contents

List of Contributors | vii
Introduction | ix
  —Adam Harwood

The Current SBC Calvinism Debate: Observations,
Clarifications, and Suggestions | 1
  —David L. Allen

Savability: Southern Baptists' Core Soteriological Conviction
and Contribution | 9
  —Eric Hankins

A Statement of the Traditional Southern Baptist Understanding
of God's Plan of Salvation | 16
  —Eric Hankins

Commentary on Article 1: The Gospel | 25
  —David Hankins

Commentary on Article 2: The Sinfulness of Man | 37
  —Adam Harwood

Commentary on Article 3: The Atonement of Christ | 55
  —David L. Allen

Commentary on Article 4: The Grace of God | 66
  —Brad Reynolds

Commentary on Article 5: The Regeneration of the Sinner | 77
  —Ronnie W. Rogers

Commentary on Article 6: Election to Salvation | 90
  —Eric Hankins

Commentary on Article 7: The Sovereignty of God | 103
—STEVE W. LEMKE

Commentary on Article 8: The Free Will of Man | 119
—BRAXTON HUNTER

Commentary on Article 9: The Security of the Believer | 133
—STEVE HORN

Commentary on Article 10: The Great Commission | 143
—PRESTON NIX

Is the Traditional Statement Semi-Pelagian? | 157
—ADAM HARWOOD

Five Theological Models Relating Determinism, Divine Sovereignty, and Human Freedom | 169
—STEVE W. LEMKE

Suject Index | 179
Name Index | 183
Scripture Index | 187

List of Contributors

David L. Allen (PhD, University of Texas at Arlington), dean of the School of Preaching at Southwestern Baptist Theological Seminary, Fort Worth. His publications include *Hebrews*, *Lukan Authorship of Hebrews*, *Text-Driven Preaching*, *Whosoever Will*, *1–3 John*, and *The Extent of the Atonement*.

David Hankins (PhD, Southwestern Baptist Theological Seminary), executive director of the Louisiana Baptist Convention, Alexandria. He is the author of *One Sacred Effort*.

Eric Hankins (PhD, Southwestern Baptist Theological Seminary), pastor of First Baptist Church, Oxford, Mississippi. He is the primary author of A Statement of the Traditional Southern Baptist Understanding of God's Plan of Salvation.

Adam Harwood (PhD, Southwestern Baptist Theological Seminary), associate professor of theology, McFarland Chair of Theology, and editor of *Journal of Baptist Theology & Ministry* at New Orleans Baptist Theological Seminary. His publications include *The Spiritual Condition of Infants* and *Born Guilty?*.

Steve Horn (PhD, New Orleans Baptist Theological Seminary), pastor of First Baptist Church, Lafayette, Louisiana.

Braxton Hunter (PhD, Trinity Theological Seminary), president and professor of philosophy and apologetics at Trinity College of the Bible and Theological Seminary, Newburgh, Indiana. His publications include *Death is a Doorway*, *Blinding Lights*, *CORE Facts*, and *Evangelistic Apologetics*.

List of Contributors

Steve W. Lemke (PhD, Southwestern Baptist Theological Seminary), provost and professor of philosophy and ethics at New Orleans Baptist Theological Seminary. His publications include *The Return of Christ* and *Whosoever Will*.

Preston Nix (PhD, Southwestern Baptist Theological Seminary), professor of evangelism and evangelistic preaching and Roland Q. Leavell Chair of Evangelism at New Orleans Baptist Theological Seminary.

Brad Reynolds (PhD, College of William and Mary), vice president for Academic Services and professor of Christian Studies at Truett-McConnell University, Cleveland, Georgia.

Ronnie W. Rogers (MS, Henderson State University), senior pastor of Trinity Baptist Church, Norman, Oklahoma. His publications include *Undermining the Gospel, The Death of Man as Man, Reflections of a Disenchanted Calvinist,* and *The Equipping Church*.

Introduction

Adam Harwood

THE ESSAYS IN THIS book were prompted by the overwhelming response to a soteriological statement drafted by Mississippi pastor Eric Hankins titled A Statement of the Traditional Southern Baptist Understanding of God's Plan of Salvation. Hankins authored the document, also known as the Traditional Statement (TS), in consultation with a group of pastors and professors. After being affirmed by several past presidents of the Southern Baptist Convention (SBC) and other denominational leaders, the TS was circulated among the SBC state executive-directors in May of 2012. Within the first few weeks of its release, the TS elicited online replies from Roger Olson and Albert Mohler, an e-book from Founders Ministries, and two articles in *Christianity Today*. The website featuring the statement, sbctoday.com, was ranked in June 2012 by Technorati as the #2 religion blog in the world.

Most articles and books which critique Calvinism do so while affirming particular commitments shared by both Calvinists and Arminians. For that reason, most soteriological discussions employ theological definitions and categories informed by the Canons of Dort (1618–19). Most of the contributors to this book reject as unhelpful the theological commitments distinctive to the Calvinist-Arminian debate. Instead, we attempt to construct a doctrine of salvation from the Bible alone while appealing to statements from the Baptist Faith and Message, and consciously rejecting the Calvinist-Arminian presuppositions that have framed this debate in western theology for centuries.

Introduction

The contributors to this book are unified in their conviction that any person who hears the gospel can be saved. These essays reflect a desire by Southern Baptists to provide a positive articulation for the non-Calvinist Baptist tradition which might be called the General Baptist or the Sandy Creek or the Mullins-Hobbs-Rogers tradition. The other theological tradition, which is more Calvinistic, is known as the Particular Baptist or the Charleston tradition.

The subtitle clarifies that this book is a defense of "Traditional" Southern Baptist soteriology, or doctrine of salvation. As Hankins explains in the preamble to the TS, the word "Traditional" is not meant to imply that this is the *only* theological tradition in the SBC and among Baptists. Rather, the word "Traditional" is an attempt to apply a label to a specific theological tradition affirmed among Baptists. The terms "Traditional Baptist" and "Traditionalist" were used by Baptist theologians to distinguish this non-Calvinist viewpoint several years before Hankins used it as a descriptor for this statement.[1]

In the opening essay, David Allen, dean of the School of Preaching and distinguished professor of preaching at Southwestern Baptist Theological Seminary in Fort Worth, Texas, provides general observations on the convention-wide discussion and offers particular suggestions for fostering greater understanding, clarity, and unity. Next, Eric Hankins, pastor of First Baptist Church, Oxford, Mississippi, outlines his theological and missiological motivations for drafting the TS. The next chapter provides the preamble and text of the Traditional Statement.

The next ten essays provide the content and commentary on each of the articles in the TS. David Hankins, executive director of the Louisiana Baptist Convention, defends the claim from Article 1 that any person can be saved. Next, I affirm from Article 2 the full sinfulness of man, deny that Adam's sin renders people guilty before they sin, and affirm that all people who hear the gospel are capable of making a Spirit-enabled response. David Allen explains the significance of the affirmation in Article 3 of universal, or general, atonement.

Brad Reynolds, vice president for Academic Services and professor of Christian Studies at Truett-McConnell University in Cleveland, Georgia, affirms in his essay on Article 4 that God's grace is necessary for salvation and asserts that God's grace can be resisted. Ronnie Rogers, senior pastor

---

1. See, as examples, Humphreys and Robertson, *God So Loved the World* and Dockery, *Southern Baptist Consensus and Renewal*, 11.

Introduction

of Trinity Baptist Church in Norman, Oklahoma, argues from Article 5 that people are regenerated, or saved, at the moment—and because—they believe; Rogers argues against the view that people are regenerated *before* they believe. In his essay on Article 6, Eric Hankins eschews a decretal view of election for one that is covenantal, Christocentric, categorical, concurrent, and corporate. Steve Lemke, provost and professor of philosophy and ethics at New Orleans Baptist Theological Seminary, demonstrates that the claims in Article 7 regarding God's sovereignty and knowledge of future events are consistent with the freedom of individuals.

In his essay on Article 8, Braxton Hunter, evangelist with Trinity Crusades for Christ and president and professor of philosophy and apologetics at Trinity College of the Bible and Theological Seminary in Newburgh, Indiana, advocates for a model of soft-libertarian rather than compatibilist freedom. Steve Horn, pastor of First Baptist Church, Lafayette, Louisiana, affirms eternal security as stated in Article 9 and distinguishes this view from perseverance of the saints. Preston Nix, the Roland Q. Leavell professor of Evangelism and director of the Leavell Center for Evangelism and Church Health at New Orleans Baptist Theological Seminary, focuses his attention on the affirmation in Article 10 of the Great Commission. In the next chapter, I address the inaccurate charge that the Traditional Statement is semi-Pelagian. The book closes with a chapter in which Steve Lemke identifies five models for understanding the various approaches to divine determinism, divine sovereignty, and human freedom.

These essays appeared in the Fall 2012 and Spring 2013 issues of the *Journal of Baptist Theology and Ministry* and are reprinted with permission. All of the contributors serve the Lord in a variety of ways, including the local church, denominational service, and the academy. I am thankful for their investment of time and energy in this effort, especially the efforts of David Allen and Eric Hankins, who served with me as co-editors on this project. The work of Patrick Cochran, Hoyt Denton, and Brandon Langley on proofreading the book as well as compiling the indices is appreciated. Finally, this book would not be in print without the skillful work of editors at Wipf & Stock.

This book is not meant to be the final word on Southern Baptist soteriology. Rather, it is offered as a contribution to the peaceable, on-going, convention-wide conversation on the doctrine of salvation. May God be glorified as we continue this discussion of God's work of saving lowly sinners through the matchless person, work, and name of his Son, Jesus Christ.

Introduction

BIBLIOGRAPHY

Dockery, David S. *Southern Baptist Consensus and Renewal: A Biblical, Historical, and Theological Proposal.* Nashville: B&H Academic, 2008.

Humphreys, Fisher, and Paul E. Robertson. *God So Loved the World: Traditional Baptists and Calvinism.* Covington, LA: Insight Press, 2000.

The Current SBC Calvinism Debate
Observations, Clarifications, and Suggestions

David L. Allen

THE RELEASE OF A Statement of the Traditional Southern Baptist Understanding of God's Plan of Salvation in the summer of 2012 engendered a convention-wide discussion and made nation-wide news. Tongues wagged and fingers pecked computer keyboards ceaselessly in subsequent weeks. This document, referred to in the present work as the Traditional Statement (TS), has received both acclaim and criticism. In reflecting on the tsunami of words, and as a conversation partner along with my fellow brothers and sisters in Christ, I have asked the Lord to help me be wise as a serpent and harmless as a dove. I hope the following thoughts will be helpful as we continue the conversation in the days ahead. By way of brief personal background, I served in the local church for twenty-six years; twenty-one of those years as a senior pastor of two churches. I have served two theological institutions in the classroom since 1985. In addition, I served on the board of trustees at one of our Southern Baptist Convention (SBC) seminaries for twelve years. In my current role, I preach regularly in SBC churches.

Two things are crystal clear. The issue of Calvinism in the SBC is not going away, and finding our way forward is not going to be easy. Calvinism is viewed through many prisms in the SBC. Some see it as absolutely vital to the health and prosperity, both theological and otherwise, of the SBC. Others view it as theologically flawed, a niggling nuisance spawning various levels of problems, including divisiveness, in the churches. Regardless of which camp you are in, or somewhere in the middle, Southern Baptists need to proceed with caution in the days ahead. When it comes to Calvinism in the SBC, a fair amount of misinformation, misinterpretation, misunderstanding, and misrepresentation characterizes the current climate. This makes it difficult for most to cut through the discrepant fog.

The first place to begin, it seems to me, is with our common ground. As Southern Baptists, our agreements outnumber or disagreements. We agree: 1) on the BFM 2000; 2) on the Lordship of Christ; 3) on the inerrancy and sufficiency of Scripture; 4) on the exclusivity of the gospel and the lostness of humanity; and 5) that salvation is by grace alone through faith alone in Christ alone, not to mention a host of other issues on which we agree. Virtually all of us recognize that Southern Baptists are not going to agree on Calvinism. However, that does not mean that this discussion should not happen! While the debate about Calvinism is necessary, it is absolutely essential that all involved desire, speak, and work for unity. There is a difference between union and unity. Two cats with their tails tied together have union. They sure don't have unity! Southern Baptists generally agree that our unifying doctrinal statement is the BFM 2000. It is sufficiently broad in latitude that we can all live, breathe, and work under its umbrella. In fact, Calvinists and Traditionalists, for the most part, have been doing that already for quite a number of decades.

Second, because of this common ground in the BFM 2000, we should avoid at all costs the Scylla of attempting to run all Calvinists out of Dodge and the Charybdis of attempting to return us as a convention to the Calvinistic theology of some of our founding fathers. Neither of these will bring us together. In fact, both approaches will foster division. I have on rare occasion sought to correct overzealous Traditionalists who have questioned the place of Calvinists in the SBC. It is any and every Baptist's right to be persuaded that a Calvinistic soteriology reflects the teaching of Scripture. Being a Calvinist should not be a Convention crime. Calvinists have and should always be free to have a place at the SBC table. Any church that feels led of God to call a Calvinist pastor should do so without hesitation. I serve a seminary that has some Calvinists on the faculty, some of whom I myself recommended to the administration for hiring. I have on occasion recommended other Calvinist faculty members to other SBC colleges and seminaries. I have and continue to work side-by-side with Calvinist brothers and sisters in the churches I pastored, in the seminary I serve, and in the broader Southern Baptist Convention of which I am a part.

The Current SBC Calvinism Debate

On the other hand, Calvinism should not be a convention cause either. The publication of an article by a Southern Baptist professor in recent years entitled "Why Your Next Pastor Should Be a Calvinist" is an example of one aspect of the current problem in the convention. Dr. Danny Akin said in 2007: "I have Calvinist friends who say they hope and pray for the day when all of our seminaries have presidents and faculties that are five-point Calvinists."[1] Dr. Akin rightfully eschews such a sentiment, but this validates the concern of many Southern Baptists that some Calvinists in the SBC do indeed believe we would be better off if we reverted to Calvinism unilaterally in the seminaries. If there are Calvinists who feel this way about the seminaries, perhaps many of them feel this way about SBC churches as well. Of course this is a recipe for disaster. As long as Calvinists, individually or as groups, continue to seek to make it a cause with the intention of moving the SBC towards Calvinism, then we will continue to have a problem.

If we are to come together in unity, we must do so *as Baptists*, not as Calvinists and Traditionalists. We must unite around *Baptist distinctives* which includes the only glue that can hold us together: a biblical, Baptist theology wedded to a Great Commission-resurgence of evangelism and missions. We don't have to cease to be Calvinists or Traditionalists to be Baptists. We've had both from day one. Let us debate the theology of Calvinism and let the chips fall where they may, but deliver us from attempting to Calvinize or de-Calvinize the SBC.

Third, we need to love and respect one another even though we are not in complete agreement on every theological point. This is the clear mandate of Scripture. We should speak the truth in love and avoid strident, emotive language. May we not allow the opinions of others about us, whether positive or negative, to cause us to reciprocate in kind (the negative that is!) to our fellow brothers and sisters or cloud our assessment of their doctrinal positions. One of my favorite stories about General Robert E. Lee concerns the time he was asked by Confederate President Davis his opinion of one of his officers in the Confederate army. Lee responded that he thought the gentleman was a good man and a fine officer. Someone nearby reminded Lee that this particular officer had been critical of the great general. Lee's response was classic: "Yes, that's true. But the president asked my opinion of him, not his opinion of me."[2]

---

1. Akin, "Answering the Call," 253.
2. This story is told in Lutzer, *When You've Been Wronged*, 162.

Deep-seated convictions usually breed deep-seated emotions. Deep-seated emotions, left unguarded, can breed deep-seated sin. Fair-mindedness coupled with plainspokenness scores a direct hit. A thick head and thin skin is a bad combination for theological dialogue. Scrappy, sarcastic, sardonic speech and writing chills the air quickly. It is incumbent on all of us to engage the concerns and questions that come our way in a straightforward manner, rather than appearing to evade and dissimulate. We're not here to hornswoggle anyone. On a related note, those on both sides of the issue should refrain from drive-by verbal "shootings." We don't need innocent casualties via collateral damage. Failure to be careful in these areas will not exculpate us at the Judgment Seat of Christ. Remember, the enemy is the devil, not each other.

Fourth, we need to be reminded that the truth of a given position is in no way related to who or how many hold that position. Positions should be evaluated on their merits and ultimately according to their comportment with Scripture, not because high profile leaders and/or churches or groups hold them or don't hold them. The fact that the majority of Southern Baptists do not adhere to Calvinism is no argument against whether it is true or false. The fact that some of the early Southern Baptist leaders were Calvinists is no argument that Calvinism is true or false nor is it an argument that Calvinism should be embraced today. Neither the popularity nor unpopularity of something should play into the discussion of whether that something is true or false. Each of us should take to heart the approach of the Bereans, who "searched the Scriptures daily to find out whether these things were so" (Acts 17:11, NKJV).

Fifth, generally speaking, all Southern Baptists are concerned about theology. With respect to the current discussion, some of my Calvinist friends as well as some of my Traditionalist friends need to become better and more careful theologians and historians. Some Traditionalists need to be aware of and respect the Calvinistic heritage of the SBC. Some Traditionalists need to read more broadly in the area of Calvinism in order to understand its theology and why Scripture is interpreted the way it is in a Reformed soteriological framework. On the other hand, some of my Calvinist friends need to shore up their theologizing as well. I have observed through the years that some Calvinists, especially young Calvinists, make two mistakes. One mistake is to simply take their theology from Calvinist writers, especially modern writers, without filtering it through the New Testament. None should be a theological epigone. A second mistake is that they read predominately, if not exclusively, contemporary Calvinist authors and neglect the writings of the earliest generations among the Reformers and the Reformation, Calvinist or otherwise. Calvinism is not monolithic. In fact, it never has been. Disagreement among Calvinists themselves exists over many issues, chiefly limited atonement, since the Reformation. The TULIP acrostic is itself a twentieth-century construct.[3] Many Calvinists, especially young Calvinists, simply equate Calvinism with TULIP. This is a serious historical error that leads to serious theological distortion.

In this vein, all of us are prone to a number of errors which we should heartily strive to avoid: 1) subsuming one set of Scripture passages under another set of Scripture passages in order to maintain a particular doctrine or belief system; 2) prejudicing that which is logical over that which is paradoxical in the Scripture; 3) succumbing to logical fallacies in an attempt to maintain our particular theology; 4) doing systematic theology before one does biblical theology and/or allowing systematic theology to trump biblical theology; 5) confusing one's theological system with the gospel and reacting as if a critique of the system is a challenge to the gospel; 6) confusing a critique of someone's doctrine as a critique of that individual personally; 7) engaging in *ad hominem* attacks; and 8) questioning one's motives (which are often wrongly judged and can only be surmised at best unless one directly speaks to his/her motives for what he says and does). I suppose, at one time or another, each of us has fallen into one or more of these or similar traps. Ted Williams ended the 1941 baseball season with an extraordinary .406 average. But even with this remarkable feat, he still grounded out, flied out, or struck out roughly six times out of every ten at bats. No one bats a thousand. We need to cut each other a little slack along the way.

Sixth, it is crucial that we avoid misrepresenting someone's theology. I have found that when this happens, it is usually the result of a lack of understanding the specifics of a position, or of overzealous rhetoric. There have been times in the past when Calvinists and their theology have been misrepresented by those who disagree with them. Anyone deliberately misrepresenting Calvinism is wrong, should repent of such misrepresentation of the views of fellow Christians, and immediately cease and desist in such behavior. Those who in the past have misrepresented Calvinism from a lack of understanding Calvinist doctrine should take steps necessary to

---

3. TULIP represents: total depravity, unconditional election, limited atonement, irresistible grace, and perseverance of the saints.

rightly understand Calvinism before they speak critically of it. Our Calvinist brothers and sisters have every right to expect those of us who disagree with them to accurately represent their doctrines. Likewise, Traditionalists have every right to expect the same from their counterparts, including the right to critique Calvinism without being accused of denying cardinal doctrines of the faith. We actually do believe in the sovereignty of God, election, total depravity, etc.; we just do not believe in your interpretation of them. We must learn to distinguish between Scripture and our interpretation of Scripture. The former is inerrant; the latter is not. I hope my Calvinist friends will acknowledge that the reason I and other Traditionalists are not Calvinists is not because we don't understand Calvinism, but because we actually *do* understand it, and find aspects of it inconsistent with Scripture. Without a reciprocal acknowledgment of these and similar factors, dialogue and progress in the debate is ultimately an exercise in futility.

Furthermore, and this is crucial, we must distinguish between a belief system and our inferences or implications that we draw from that system. When we say that something "implies" such and such, we mean that if you affirm doctrine x, then said doctrine implies y. When doctrine x is critiqued by arguing that it implies y, sometimes those who adhere to doctrine x assume doctrine x is being denied or distorted, willfully or not. It is the difference in logic between saying "A is B" and saying "A implies B." Sometimes we are unclear in our discussions and false conclusions are drawn because we fail to make this crucial distinction. This failure leads to mischaracterization, misrepresentation, misinterpretation, and hence, misunderstanding.

Thus, the current SBC discussion on Calvinism is sometimes hindered by the failure: 1) to accurately describe what the other side believes; 2) to accurately describe what the other side is attempting to do (that is, disprove a particular doctrinal point via use of a *reductio ad absurdum* argument); and 3) to accurately distinguish between what one believes from what one thinks might be inferred from that belief (in other words, to use a "straw man" argument). When these kinds of things happen, it becomes virtually impossible to read what others write or listen to what others say without partiality. Emotive language and emotive thinking are often slippery slopes to straw men arguments and generally erect signs that read "Dead End Street."

This, I believe, describes some of the misunderstanding surrounding the debate concerning the TS. Some in the press, on blogs, and in comment threads have accused the statement of "distorting" Calvinism, setting up "straw men" arguments, and "inaccurately" describing the theology of Calvinism. I do not believe this charge is accurate. For example, I have seen several occasions where the TS has been criticized for "saying" or "implying" that Calvinists believe a person can be saved apart from repentance and faith. The TS neither says nor implies such. Some have apparently wrongly inferred this from the TS. There is a huge difference in "implying" and "inferring." Implication is in the mind and pen of the writer; inference is in the mind of the reader. Writers/speakers imply; readers/hearers infer. Most Traditionalists are well aware that Calvinists don't believe anyone is saved apart from repentance and faith (with the exception of infants and mentally disabled people, who are regarded as exceptions). The real difference between Calvinists and Traditionalists here is the nature and function of the will in salvation. Traditionalists believe that compatibilism implies a denial of genuine freedom. Calvinists don't. But both groups affirm the necessity of repentance and faith for salvation. Mischaracterization is one thing. Disagreement with someone's critique of your position should not *ipso facto* place the one who disagrees under condemnation of mischaracterization. One person's mischaracterization is sometimes merely another person's critique. May God help us to be less shrill in our rhetoric, less sloppy in our understanding and use of history, theology, and language, and may he help us make every argument and counter-argument biblically tethered.

Seventh, is the TS divisive? Division, like most things, occurs in varying degrees and is not always unhealthy or wrong. One degree of division is the simple fact that some believe Calvinistic doctrines but others don't. Although some Calvinists believe in limited atonement, other Calvinists and all Traditionalists don't. Calvinists believe in irresistible grace, but Traditionalists don't. This kind or level of division is not at all unhealthy. Another kind of division occurs when people of a like theological mind tend to pal together. They spend more time talking, texting, and emailing one another than they do those in the other group. Again, this kind of division is not unhealthy. A third kind of division is when people in one theological camp think, speak, and act in ways that promote their theological convictions. They sponsor conferences and join together to produce books. These actions naturally divide them from those who hold differing theological convictions. This kind of division is likewise to be expected and is not necessarily unhealthy.

But there are unhealthy divisions as well. When people think, speak, and act in ways that seek to promote their theological convictions with an agenda, stated or unstated, to marginalize those who differ with them theologically, this kind of division is unhealthy. When people fail to be courteous and respectful in their discussions with those who disagree with their theology; when they engage in emotive language, straw-man arguments, and misrepresentation; this kind of division is unhealthy. It is divisive when people insist that their view is the only possible correct reading of Scripture or even to insist that those who disagree with them are heretical. (I am speaking only about the discussion of Calvinism within the SBC.) If leaders unfairly favor one group over another in hiring practices, service opportunities, committee representation, book and literature production, etc., this creates unhealthy division. This is especially egregious if the favored group is in the statistical minority in the organization.

In daily life, healthy division is unavoidable. Theological disagreement need not be divisive, need not entail unhealthy division, and need not result in disunity. To preserve unity will require focused effort on the part of all parties in this discussion. May God help us to keep in step with the Holy Spirit, who is our source of unity.

Finally, the entire enterprise calls for a healthy dose of humility and prayer. The worm of pride is ever threatening to eat into the fruit of the Spirit. Adrian Rogers used to talk about preachers who could strut sitting down. God deliver us from ourselves and a tin God complex in this debate. To reflect God's light, we shouldn't seek the limelight. As Southern Baptist missionary Miss Bertha Smith used to say: "Even the donkey that brought Jesus into Jerusalem knew that the applause was not for him." The goal in this dialogue should not be to win at all costs. The goal should be to win the world for Christ at all costs. May God grant it for his glory.

Let the dialogue continue.

BIBLIOGRAPHY

Akin, Daniel L. "Answering the Call to a Great Commission Resurgence." In *Calvinism: A Southern Baptist Dialogue*, edited by E. Ray Clendenen and Brad J. Waggoner, 247–60. Nashville: B&H Academic, 2008.

Lutzer, Erwin W. *When You've Been Wronged: Moving from Bitterness to Forgiveness*. Chicago: Moody, 2007.

Savability

Southern Baptists' Core Soteriological Conviction and Contribution

Eric Hankins

THE SOUTHERN BAPTIST CONVENTION was formed in 1845 and is comprised of forty-five thousand churches, fifteen million members, ten thousand home and international missionaries, and six large seminaries with ten thousand students preparing for ministry. More than three hundred thousand people are baptized in Southern Baptists churches and ministries in the United States annually.[1] The SBC has survived and thrived in a kaleidoscopic and increasingly secular American culture. While mainline denominations are collapsing under the weight of modernism's flight from biblical authority,[2] Southern Baptists' unique identity, polity, and theology have seen us through difficult days in unparalleled fashion.[3] All of these

---

1. In 2014, the SBC had 15,499,173 members and 305,301 baptisms among 46,499 churches in the United States. Executive Committee, "Annual," 134. For comparison, the Presbyterian Church in America (PCA) in 2014 had 358,516 members and 9,425 professions of faith (which is comparable to baptisms in SBC churches) among 1,771 churches. Presbyterian Church, "PCA Statistics." Yet the PCA has a very distinctive theological tradition which exerts an influence on American evangelical theology that far exceeds its size. Note the output and impact of pastors and theologians such as R. C. Sproul, J. Ligon Duncan, Timothy J. Keller, Philip G. Ryken, Bryan Chapell, and John M. Frame.

2. McGrath, *The Future*, 100. McGrath essentially makes the point that the future of Christianity will not include the mainline denominations.

3. *Contra* Dockery, *Southern Baptist*, 9, who believes that Southern Baptist laypeople

reasons and more provide a sufficient warrant for the articulation of a theological perspective that is uniquely our own. Not a Baptist theology, for we do not speak for all Baptists, but a *Southern Baptist* theology. This needs to be done not for the purposes of separating ourselves from others or demonstrating our superiority. Rather, it is right for us to codify and contribute to the wider Christian world what we understand to be the basis for the sustained cooperative kingdom reach that is unique to us. Moreover, because the SBC is being challenged by the threats of fragmentation and decline, it is needful to understand clearly what it is about our identity that should be maintained as we seek to make our message meaningful in an ever-changing world.[4] Finally, because no theological paradigm is perfect or eternal, ours needs to be publicly articulated so that it may be evaluated, improved, and retooled for future generations.

Within the broad sweep of systematic theology, soteriology has been the most contested doctrine over the last fifteen hundred years. While Calvinism and Arminianism have dominated the discussion within Protestantism, neither system has prevailed in Southern Baptist life.[5] The contention here is that our reluctance to identify with either system is actually a clue to our effectiveness: we believe very simply but very deeply that *anyone can be saved and, once saved, is secure forever*. Anyone is "sovereignly savable." In a technical theological sense, savability seeks to convey the idea that the salvation of every sinner is the object of God's sovereign love and Christ's saving work. Savability means that anyone who hears the gospel is the object of the Spirit's saving ministrations and can respond with repentance and faith or rebellion and unbelief. This response of faith results

---

were ill-equipped for modernism's challenge to biblical authority, I think it is clear that they were quite adequately equipped. Through the consistent and biblical simplicity of Hershel Hobbs's Sunday school literature and the leadership of preachers like W. A. Criswell, Adrian Rogers, Jerry Vines, Charles Stanley, and Jimmy Draper, Southern Baptists believed that biblical inerrancy, soul winning, and missions were core values. When they discovered that these values were not shared at their agencies, local church autonomy empowered them to bring radical change.

4. Before Wayne Grudem's *Systematic Theology*, which is strongly Calvinistic, became the dominant theology textbook at Southern Baptist seminaries, Millard Erickson's *Christian Theology* was the standard. While encyclopedic and conservative, its moderate Calvinism is not particularly distinctive, creative, or compelling. Certainly, it never produced the sort of convictional commitment to a particular theological system that Grudem's has. Erickson's text is more of a reference book for general theological parameters rather than a resource book for constructive Southern Baptist theological engagement.

5. Allen et al., "Neither Calvinists." See also Dockery, *Southern Baptist*, 60–62.

in the sealing of the Spirit and eternal security in the accomplished work of Christ. Savability also insists that every sinner is in desperate need of salvation; it takes as axiomatic each sinner's absolute need for rescue and redemption. Savability speaks not of one's ability to save himself (the term itself is fundamentally passive) but of God's ability to save anyone, even the "vilest offender who truly believes."[6] In a sense, the ten articles of A Statement of the Traditional Southern Baptist Understanding of God's Plan of Salvation are simply an expression of the various implications of the belief that anyone can be saved forever.

Now, all Southern Baptist Calvinists want to speak of the gospel, salvation, and God's love as being for all, but their own theology works against the intelligibility of such a claim. If Christ died only for the sins of some, then no provision has been made for others, making their salvation *impossible*. If some are chosen without respect to their response of faith, then *no hope* of salvation ever existed for others. If saving grace is irresistible for some, then saving grace is *unavailable* for others. If there is no hope for some, if salvation is impossible and saving grace is unavailable for some, then the Calvinists' claim that the gospel is for all is, ultimately, self-contradictory.[7]

Because of our unique commitment to biblical authority, to simplicity and praxis, and to passion for missions, Southern Baptists must make clear what we mean when we say that the gospel is for all. For the vast majority of us, *we mean that anyone can be saved*, and we are intentionally not speaking the language of consistent Calvinism when we say it. A theological tradition running from Carroll and Scarborough through Mullins, Conner, Hobbs, Criswell, Rogers, and Patterson is a distinct and sufficient basis on which to construct such a soteriology. The Traditional Statement (TS) is a first attempt at a programmatic description of Southern Baptist soteriology, and it is made in hope that a Southern Baptist systematic theology might someday be forged that is reflective of the totality of Southern Baptist witness both historically and at present.

To be sure, this soteriological tradition has its weaknesses. The simplicity and practicality of the conviction that anyone can be saved makes it easy to truncate and manipulate. Constructive theology should be critical theology, and Southern Baptists must be willing to let our tradition be

6. Crosby, "To God Be the Glory," hymn 4.

7. Nettles, *By His Grace*, 281: "All are invited indiscriminately to share in Christ, Christ is open to all and displayed to all. It is clear, however, that only those who believe receive the promised benefits. How does anyone believe? By special operation of God's power on the word of truth, a benefit given only to the elect."

challenged by the word and by the wider *communion sanctorum*. This is why the Calvinist critique of Southern Baptist soteriology has often been significant and salient. It has exposed the need for coherence, depth, spiritual formation, true community, and substantive cultural engagement in our theology. Indeed, Southern Baptist theology has always had a deep, intimate connection with Calvinism that has kept it grounded in the superiority of Scripture, the sovereignty of God, the sufficiency of Christ, and the severity of sin. It has provided a critical counterweight to the revivalism that mediates to us our belief in savability but sometimes falls into man-centered excess. While this critical evaluation is beneficial, Calvinism has never been the dominant voice. Despite the claims of a Southern Baptist theological golden age of Calvinism to which we must return,[8] there is simply no denying that most Southern Baptists do not think of themselves as Calvinists and that the prospect of such an identity is disconcerting.[9] The proponents of the TS believe that, while Calvinism is a major contributor to Southern Baptist self-understanding, its logical implications are ultimately at cross-purposes with our core soteriological conviction that anyone can be saved.

The TS was written to make clear the places where Southern Baptist thinking departs from Calvinism while acknowledging that, indeed, "non-Calvinism" is a poor descriptor of what we believe. Therefore, we are arguing for the term "Traditionalist" to define Southern Baptists who reject Calvinist soteriology. "Traditionalist" intends to convey that Southern Baptist soteriology from the very beginning has stood in appreciative but critical relationship with Calvinism. This tradition of modification of certain tenets of Calvinism is seen in all of our founding denominational documents including the Abstract of Principles, which does not include limited atonement or irresistible grace.[10]

---

8. Malone, "Misery Loves Company," 138. Cf. Leland, "Letter of Valediction," 172. Leland believed that the best preaching is characterized by "the doctrine of sovereign grace in the salvation of men's souls, mixed with a little of what is called Arminianism." Original is italicized.

9. Rankin, "SBC Pastors Polled," para. 8. More than sixty percent of SBC pastors are "concerned about the impact of Calvinism" in the convention.

10. Wills writes, "[In the time of James P. Boyce] Few Southern Baptists were Arminians—perhaps none of the clergy—but many held 'lax views' on the doctrine of election, most commonly by teaching that God elected persons because he foresaw that they would repent and believe." Wills, *Southern*, 92–93. William Broaddus, an advocate for Southern Seminary at that time in Virginia, opposed Arminianism, "but he also knew that some Virginia Baptists might find an unqualified statement of the faculty's

Savability

The TS is written not only to challenge some of the specific components of Calvinism but also ultimately to challenge it at the deepest level. What holds Calvinism together, what provides its grid and filter for the biblical text, is its commitment to compatibilism, which is the idea that all events are unchangeably foreordained in such a way that people do not have the power to choose otherwise. This "soft-determinism" colors every aspect of the system. Theistic determinism necessarily undoes any regular understanding of humanity's interaction with the world and with God. On this view, claims that God loves everyone and wants to save everyone are simply untenable.[11] While Calvinists sincerely reject such evaluations, the necessary implication is, unfortunately, unavoidable: God unconditionally causes certain people to spend eternity in hell.[12] Therefore, what is fundamental to Calvinism is quite problematic for Southern Baptist soteriology: we believe in savability; we believe that anyone can be saved.

To say that we are rejecting consistent Calvinism is, however, not an innovation, it is a theological tradition. The TS simply makes explicit what has always been the case for Southern Baptists. Our evangelism and missions have been driven by the conviction that it is God's sovereign desire for all people to hear and respond to the gospel. Many will never hear the gospel; many will hear and reject it. This is not due to any deficiency in God's plan or the power of the gospel. God, who is certainly powerful enough to create any possible world he wants, wanted a world of uncoerced relationships, and so the free response of people really matters. Yet, because of his great grace, anyone who hears the gospel may come and, believing, may have everlasting life. To abandon this for anything else is to trade in that which has made Southern Baptists so useful to God's kingdom for so long.[13]

Calvinism troubling." Wills, *Southern*, 93.

11. Craig, *Only Wise God*; Himes, "When a Christian Sins," 329–44; Keathley, *Salvation and Sovereignty*; Lamb, "Proof," 20–35; Plantinga, *God, Freedom, and Evil*, 48–53; Inwagen, "Incompatibility," 185–99; Walls, "Classical Theist," 75–104; Walker, "Freedom of Judgment," 63–92.

12. Little writes, "At the end of the day, if they (Calvinists) wish to hold to their view of sovereignty (theistic determinism), they should be willing to accept the logical conclusion of their position and acknowledge that God is morally responsible for evil." Little, "Evil," 297.

13. As a principle contributor to "Truth, Trust, and Testimony in a Time of Tension," the report from the Calvinism Advisory Committee presented to the SBC at the annual meeting in 2013, I want to make clear that this essay and all the others here dealing with the TS are intended to work within the spirit of critically constructive interaction that is called for in the document. Unity does not demand unanimity, and we look forward to

BIBLIOGRAPHY

Allen, David L., et al. "Neither Calvinists nor Arminians but Baptists." White Paper 36. The Center for Theological Research (September 2010). http://www.baptisttheology.org/white-papers/neither-calvinists-nor-arminians-but-baptists/.

Calvinism Advisory Committee. "Truth, Trust, and Testimony in a Time of Tension." http://www.sbclife.org/Articles/2013/06/sla5.asp.

Craig, William Lane. *Only Wise God*. Grand Rapids: Baker, 1987; Reprint, Eugene, OR: Wipf & Stock, 2000.

Crosby, Fanny J. "To God Be the Glory." In *The Baptist Hymnal*. Edited by Wesley Forbis. Nashville: Convention, 1991.

Dockery, David S. *Southern Baptist Consensus and Renewal: A Biblical, Historical, and Theological Proposal*. Nashville: B&H Academic, 2008.

Erickson, Millard J. *Christian Theology*. Three editions. Grand Rapids: Baker, 1986, 1998, 2013.

Executive Committee, Southern Baptist Convention. "Annual of the 2015 Southern Baptist Convention." http://www.sbcec.org/bor/2015/2015SBCAnnual.pdf.

Grudem, Wayne. *Systematic Theology: An Introduction to Biblical Doctrine*. Grand Rapids: Zondervan, 1994.

Himes, Paul. "When a Christian Sins: 1 Corinthians 10:13 and the Power of Contrary Choice in Relation to the Compatibilist-Libertarian Debate." *Journal of the Evangelical Theological Society* 54 (June 2011) 329–44.

Inwagen, Peter van. "The Incompatibility of Free Will and Determinism." *Philosophical Studies* 27 (1975) 185–99.

Keathley, Kenneth. *Salvation and Sovereignty: A Molinist Approach*. Nashville: B&H Academic, 2010.

Lamb, James W. "On a Proof of Incompatibilism." *Philosophical Review* 86 (January 1977) 20–35.

Leland, John. "Letter of Valediction, on Leaving Virginia, in 1791." In *The Writings of the Late Elder John Leland*, 171–75, edited by L. F. Greene. New York: G. W. Wood, 1845. Reprint, Religion in America 23, edited by Edwin S. Gaustad. New York: Arno, 1969.

Little, Bruce A. "Evil and God's Sovereignty." In *Whosoever Will: A Biblical-Theological Critique of Five-Point Calvinism*, edited by David L. Allen and Steve W. Lemke, 275–98. Nashville: B&H Academic, 2010.

Malone, Fred A. "Misery Loves Company: A Presbyterian Pastor Comes Home." In *Why I Am a Baptist*, edited by Tom J. Nettles and Russell D. Moore, 134–42. Nashville: B&H, 2001.

McGrath, Alister E. *The Future of Christianity*. Blackwell Manifestos. Oxford: Blackwell, 2002.

Nettles, Tom. *By His Grace and for His Glory*. Rev. ed. Cape Coral, FL: Founder's, 2006.

Plantinga, Alvin. *God, Freedom, and Evil*. New York: Harper & Row, 1974. Reprint, Grand Rapids: Eerdmans, 1977.

Presbyterian Church in America Administrative Committee. "PCA Statistics Five Year Summary." http://www.pcaac.org/resources/pca-statistics-five-year-summary/.

Rankin, Russ. "SBC Pastors Polled on Calvinism and Its Effect." http://www.lifeway.com/Article/research-sbc-pastors-polled-on-calvinism-affect-on-convention.

---

the ongoing conversation concerning Calvinism that will make us better together.

Walker, Mark Thomas. "The Freedom of Judgment." *International Journal of Philosophical Studies* 11 (2003) 63–92.

Walls, Jerry. "Why No Classical Theist, Let Alone Orthodox Christian, Should Ever be a Compatibilist." *Philosophia Christi* 13.1 (2011) 75–104.

Wills, Gregory A. *Southern Baptist Theological Seminary, 1859–2009*. New York: Oxford University Press, 2009.

A Statement of the Traditional Southern Baptist Understanding of God's Plan of Salvation

Eric Hankins

PREAMBLE

EVERY GENERATION OF SOUTHERN Baptists has the duty to articulate the truths of its faith with particular attention to the issues that are impacting contemporary mission and ministry. The precipitating issue for this statement is the rise of a movement called New Calvinism among Southern Baptists. This movement is committed to advancing in the churches an exclusively Calvinistic understanding of salvation, characterized by an aggressive insistence on the "doctrines of grace" (TULIP), and to the goal of making Calvinism the central Southern Baptist position on God's plan of salvation.

While Calvinists have been present in Southern Baptist life from its earliest days and have made very important contributions to our history and theology, the majority of Southern Baptists do not embrace Calvinism. Even the minority of Southern Baptists who have identified themselves as Calvinists generally modify its teachings in order to mitigate certain unacceptable conclusions (e.g., anti-missionism, hyper-Calvinism, double predestination, limited atonement, etc.). The very fact that there is a plurality

A Statement of the Traditional Southern Baptist Understanding

of views on Calvinism designed to deal with these weaknesses (variously described as 3-point, 4-point, moderate, etc.) would seem to call for circumspection and humility with respect to the system and to those who disagree with it. For the most part, Southern Baptists have been glad to relegate disagreements over Calvinism to secondary status along with other important but non-essential theological matters. The Southern Baptist majority has fellowshipped happily with its Calvinist brethren while kindly resisting Calvinism itself. And, to their credit, most Southern Baptist Calvinists have not demanded the adoption of their view as the standard. We would be fine if this consensus continued, but some New Calvinists seem to be pushing for a radical alteration of this long-standing arrangement.

We propose that what most Southern Baptists believe about salvation can rightly be called "Traditional" Southern Baptist soteriology, which should be understood in distinction to "Calvinist" soteriology. Traditional Southern Baptist soteriology is articulated in a general way in Article 4 of the Baptist Faith and Message. While some earlier Baptist confessions were shaped by Calvinism, the clear trajectory of the BFM since 1925 is away from Calvinism. For almost a century, Southern Baptists have found that a sound, biblical soteriology can be taught, maintained, and defended without subscribing to Calvinism. Traditional Southern Baptist soteriology is grounded in the conviction that every person can and must be saved by a personal and free decision to respond to the gospel by trusting in Christ Jesus alone as Savior and Lord. Without ascribing to Calvinism, Southern Baptists have reached around the world with the gospel message of salvation by grace through faith in Christ alone. Baptists have been well-served by a straightforward soteriology rooted in the fact that Christ is willing and able to save any and every sinner.

New Calvinism presents us with a duty and an opportunity to more carefully express what is generally believed by Southern Baptists about salvation. It is no longer helpful to identify ourselves by how many points of convergence we have with Calvinism. While we are not insisting that every Southern Baptist affirm the soteriological statement below in order to have a place in the Southern Baptist family, we are asserting that the vast majority of Southern Baptists are not Calvinists and that they do not want Calvinism to become the standard view in Southern Baptist life. We believe it is time to move beyond Calvinism as a reference point for Baptist soteriology.

Below is what we believe to be the essence of a Traditional Southern Baptist Understanding of God's Plan of Salvation. We believe that most Southern Baptists, regardless of how they have described their personal understanding of the doctrine of salvation, will find the following statement consistent with what the Bible teaches and what Southern Baptists have generally believed about the nature of salvation by grace through faith in Jesus Christ.

Article One: The Gospel

We affirm that the gospel is the good news that God has made a way of salvation through the life, death, and resurrection of the Lord Jesus Christ for any person. This is in keeping with God's desire for every person to be saved.

We deny that only a select few are capable of responding to the gospel while the rest are predestined to an eternity in hell.

Genesis 3:15; Psalm 2:1–12; Ezekiel 18:23, 32; Luke 19:10; 24:45–49; John 1:1–18; 3:16; Romans 1:1–6; 5:8; 8:34; 2 Corinthians 5:17–21; Galatians 4:4–7; Colossians 1:21–23; 1 Timothy 2:3–4; Hebrews 1:1–3; 4:14–16; 2 Peter 3:9.

Article Two: The Sinfulness of Man

We affirm that, because of the fall of Adam, every person inherits a nature and environment inclined toward sin and that every person who is capable of moral action will sin. Each person's sin alone brings the wrath of a holy God, broken fellowship with him, ever-worsening selfishness and destructiveness, death, and condemnation to an eternity in hell.

We deny that Adam's sin resulted in the incapacitation of any person's free will or rendered any person guilty before he has personally sinned. While no sinner is remotely capable of achieving salvation through his own effort, we deny that any sinner is saved apart from a free response to the Holy Spirit's drawing through the gospel.

Genesis 3:15–24; 6:5; Deuteronomy 1:39; Isaiah 6:5; 7:15–16; 53:6; Jeremiah 17:5, 9; 31:29–30; Ezekiel 18:19–20; Matthew 7:21–23; Romans 1:18–32; 3:9–18; 5:12; 6:23; 7:9; 1 Corinthians 1:18–25; 6:9–10; 15:22; 2 Corinthians 5:10; Hebrews 9:27–28; Revelation 20:11–15.

Article Three: The Atonement of Christ

We affirm that the penal substitution of Christ is the only available and effective sacrifice for the sins of every person.

We deny that this atonement results in salvation without a person's free response of repentance and faith. We deny that God imposes or withholds this atonement without respect to an act of the person's free will. We deny that Christ died only for the sins of those who will be saved.

Psalm 22:1-31; Isaiah 53:1-12; John 12:32, 14:6; Acts 10:39-43; 16:30-32; Romans 3:21-26; 2 Corinthians 5:21; Galatians 3:10-14; Philippians 2:5-11; Colossians 1:13-20; 1 Timothy 2:5-6; Hebrews 9:12-15, 24-28; 10:1-18; 1 John 1:7; 2:2.

Article Four: The Grace of God

We affirm that grace is God's generous decision to provide salvation for any person by taking all of the initiative in providing atonement, in freely offering the gospel in the power of the Holy Spirit, and in uniting the believer to Christ through the Holy Spirit by faith.

We deny that grace negates the necessity of a free response of faith or that it cannot be resisted. We deny that the response of faith is in any way a meritorious work that earns salvation.

Ezra 9:8; Proverbs 3:34; Zechariah 12:10; Matthew 19:16-30, 23:37; Luke 10:1-12; Acts 15:11; 20:24; Romans 3:24, 27-28; 5:6, 8, 15-21; Galatians 1:6; 2:21; 5; Ephesians 2:8-10; Philippians 3:2-9; Colossians 2:13-17; Hebrews 4:16; 9:28; 1 John 4:19.

Article Five: The Regeneration of the Sinner

We affirm that any person who responds to the gospel with repentance and faith is born again through the power of the Holy Spirit. He is a new creation in Christ and enters, at the moment he believes, into eternal life.

A Statement of the Traditional Southern Baptist Understanding

We deny that any person is regenerated prior to or apart from hearing and responding to the gospel.

Luke 15:24; John 3:3; 7:37–39; 10:10; 16:7–14; Acts 2:37–39; Romans 6:4–11; 10:14; 1 Corinthians 15:22; 2 Corinthians 5:17; Galatians 2:20; 6:15; Colossians 2:13.

Article Six: Election to Salvation

We affirm that, in reference to salvation, election speaks of God's eternal, gracious, and certain plan in Christ to have a people who are his by repentance and faith.

We deny that election means that, from eternity, God predestined certain people for salvation and others for condemnation.

Genesis 1:26–28; 12:1–3; Exodus 19:6; Jeremiah 31:31–33; Matthew 24:31; 25:34; John 6:70; 15:16; Romans 8:29–30, 33; 9:6–8; 11:7; 1 Corinthians 1:1–2; Ephesians 1:4–6; 2:11–22; 3:1–11; 4:4–13; 1 Timothy 2:3–4; 1 Peter 1:1–2; 2:9; 2 Peter 3:9; Revelation 7:9–10.

Article Seven: The Sovereignty of God

We affirm God's eternal knowledge of and sovereignty over every person's salvation or condemnation.

We deny that God's sovereignty and knowledge require him to cause a person's acceptance or rejection of faith in Christ.

Genesis 1:1; 6:5–8; 18:16–33; 22; 2 Samuel 24:13–14; 1 Chronicles 29:10–20; 2 Chronicles 7:14; Psalm 23; 51:4; 139:1–6; Proverbs 15:3; Joel 2:32; John 6:44; Romans 11:3; Titus 3:3–7; Hebrews 11:6; 12:28; James 1:13–15; 1 Peter 1:17.

Article Eight: The Free Will of Man

We affirm that God, as an expression of his sovereignty, endows each person with actual free will (the ability to choose between two options), which must be exercised in accepting or rejecting God's gracious call to salvation by the Holy Spirit through the gospel.

We deny that the decision of faith is an act of God rather than a response of the person. We deny that there is an "effectual call" for certain people that is different from a "general call" to any person who hears and understands the gospel.

Genesis 1:26–28; Numbers 21:8–9; Deuteronomy 30:19; Joshua 24:15; 1 Samuel 8:1–22; 2 Samuel 24:13–14; Esther 3:12–14; Matthew 7:13–14; 11:20–24; Mark 10:17–22; Luke 9:23–24; 13:34; 15:17–20; Romans 10:9–10; Titus 2:12; Revelation 22:17.

Article Nine: The Security of the Believer

We affirm that when a person responds in faith to the gospel, God promises to complete the process of salvation in the believer into eternity. This process begins with justification, whereby the sinner is immediately acquitted of all sin and granted peace with God; continues in sanctification, whereby the saved are progressively conformed to the image of Christ by the indwelling Holy Spirit; and concludes in glorification, whereby the saint enjoys life with Christ in heaven forever.

We deny that this Holy Spirit-sealed relationship can ever be broken. We deny even the possibility of apostasy.

John 10:28–29; 14:1–4; Romans 3:21–26; 8:29–30, 35–39; 2 Corinthians 4:17; Ephesians 1:13–14; Philippians 1:6; 3:12; Colossians 1:21–22; 2 Timothy 1:12; Hebrews 13:5; James 1:12; 1 John 2:19; 3:2; 5:13–15; Jude 24–25.

A Statement of the Traditional Southern Baptist Understanding

Article Ten: The Great Commission

We affirm that the Lord Jesus Christ commissioned his church to preach the good news of salvation to all people to the ends of the earth. We affirm that the proclamation of the gospel is God's means of bringing any person to salvation.

We deny that salvation is possible outside of a faith response to the gospel of Jesus Christ.

Psalm 51:13; Proverbs 11:30; Isaiah 52:7; Matthew 28:19-20; John 14:6; Acts 1:8; 4:12; 10:42-43; Romans 1:16; 10:13-15; 1 Corinthians 1:17-21; Ephesians 3:7-9; 6:19-20; Philippians 1:12-14; 1 Thessalonians 1:8; 1 Timothy 2:5; 2 Timothy 4:1-5.

Article 1: The Gospel

We affirm that the gospel is the good news that God has made a way of salvation through the life, death, and resurrection of the Lord Jesus Christ for any person. This is in keeping with God's desire for every person to be saved.

We deny that only a select few are capable of responding to the gospel while the rest are predestined to an eternity in hell.

Genesis 3:15; Psalm 2:1–12; Ezekiel 18:23, 32; Luke 19:10; 24:45–49; John 1:1–18; 3:16; Romans 1:1–6; 5:8; 8:34; 2 Corinthians 5:17–21; Galatians 4:4–7; Colossians 1:21–23; 1 Timothy 2:3–4; Hebrews 1:1–3; 4:14–16; 2 Peter 3:9.

COMMENTARY ON
Article 1: The Gospel

David Hankins

IS THE GOSPEL "GOOD NEWS" FOR EVERY SINNER?

EVERY PERSON IS SAVABLE. This is the central claim of the first article in the Traditional Statement entitled "The Gospel." I have been a gospel preacher for forty-five years. From my youth, shortly after my commitment to follow Christ, I have pursued the calling to proclaim to all people that God has made a way for them to find forgiveness by sending his only Son, Jesus of Nazareth, to die for their sins. This wonderful, astounding message is the gospel which literally means "good news." There was never any lack of clarity in those who taught me or any doubt in my mind that the message was intended for everyone. This meant more than that it should be preached to everyone. It also meant that everyone—any morally responsible person who heard it—could respond to and receive the saving provision the gospel announces.

I assert that this traditional understanding of Southern Baptists about the salvation of sinners includes this proposition: God meant for the gospel of Jesus Christ to be good news for everyone; God meant for it to be bad news for no one.

THE GOSPEL IS GOOD NEWS

I write these words a few days into the New Year, having just completed an extensive and enjoyable celebration of the Christmas holidays. Although many allow the message of the first advent to get lost in secular celebration, I am always blessed by the seasonal emphasis with its pageants and carols and preaching on the birth of Jesus. The message of Christmas is cause for celebration for the likes of us, sinners one and all. We ought to be as thrilled as the shepherds who first heard the amazing announcement from the angel: "Do not be afraid; for behold, I bring you *good news* of great joy which will be for *all the people*; for today in the city of David there has been born for you a Savior, who is Christ the Lord" (Luke 2:10–11, emphasis mine).[1] The gospel is the story of God's plan for his creature, man. It is a story of everlasting love. It is a story of eternal planning. It is a story of waiting and watching, and sacrificial giving. It is a story of redemption. It is good news. It is *the* good news.

The gospel story began in eternity past, when God according to his own counsels decided to have a race of creatures with whom he could express covenant love. He placed them in an environment completely suitable for them where they might create with him, reign with him, and fellowship with him. He knew they would be tempted to sin and would succumb. He knew this rebellion would corrupt them and his creation. He knew it would seem to Satan and sinners that evil had ruined it all. But before the foundation of the world, he had a plan that would overturn the blight of sin, defeat Satan and evil, and make his beloved creatures fit for life in an unsullied, incorruptible kingdom.

The gospel story centers in Jesus Christ, God's one and only Son. His coming had been prophesied for centuries. By the time the angel announced his birth, the people had been languishing a long time. Now, in the fullness of time, the one whose name means "God saves" had come to save his people from their sins. The price of salvation was his own horrific death. But through that death, God's justice was satisfied, and Jesus was raised to life. The good news that was announced to the shepherds was now to be announced to the whole earth: "For God so loved the world, that He gave His only begotten Son, that whoever believes in Him shall not perish, but have eternal life" (John 3:16).

---

1. All Bible quotations in this chapter are from the New American Standard Bible.

Commentary on Article 1: The Gospel

Euangelion is the New Testament word generally translated "gospel." It literally means good news. It is the message sinners everywhere need to hear. In the words of the "gospel" hymn:

> Sinners Jesus will receive: Sound this word of grace to all / Who the heavenly pathway leave, All who linger, all who fall. / Come, and He will give you rest; Trust Him, for His word is plain; / He will take the sinfulest; Christ receiveth sinful men![2]

We must begin our conversation about soteriology, the doctrine of salvation, with the declaration that this subject is good news for Adam's race. This good news of salvation in Christ is objective, sufficient, exclusive, and available to all.

THE GOSPEL IS GOOD NEWS FOR EVERYONE

The additional and pivotal claim we are making is that this gospel, this good news, is for *everyone*. It is in the heart of God to desire the salvation of every person he created. I expect no objections from the Christian community to Article 1 for its centering the gospel in the person and work of Jesus. But the further point of this affirmation and denial is that the salvation proclaimed by this gospel, though not finally received by all, is in fact available to *all*. When God made provision in Christ, he had a universal scope in mind. All persons were potential recipients of this magnanimous, magnificent salvation. Are we justified in making such a claim? Can we really know the mind of God on this matter? Is it more than a gesture toward equity or a sentimental view of God? I submit that this view is the *plain* teaching of Scripture and is foundational to the plan of God for redemption. The gospel is not the gospel if it is not for everyone.

God's Word Declares It

Note three of the texts from the list of supporting passages. Because New Testament scholars have made the case extensively in numerous works that these verses declare that the gospel is for everyone, I will offer only a brief review.

---

2. Neumeister, "Christ Receiveth Sinful Men," hymn 563.

Anyone Can Be Saved

John 3:16

There is a prevailing opinion that John 3:16 is the most significant verse in the Bible. It has been memorized, quoted, placarded, distributed, translated, and preached perhaps more than any other single verse of Scripture. It has been called the gospel in superlatives, the Bible in miniature, the little gospel, and the gospel in a nutshell.[3] It deserves all this attention because it succinctly declares what the gospel is (eternal life made possible through faith alone in God's only Son) and who the gospel is for (the world). If there were no other verse to appeal to regarding the intention of God toward sinners, John 3:16 would be sufficient to make it clear. The verse teaches:

1. God loves the world. He is not disinterested, dispassionate, or spiteful regarding people. He loves them enough to sacrifice his Son for them.

2. He loves the *whole* world. The word for world in the Greek is *kosmos*, that is "the whole human race."[4] God's love and resultant offer of eternal life is for all humans.

3. The verse further asserts the universality of the gospel's intent by the word "whoever," translating the word *pas* which is used in the New Testament 1,228 times and is regularly translated whoever, all, and every. In John 3:16, "The best translation is: 'Anyone who believes.' The idea is non-restrictive. The idea is anyone . . . anywhere . . . anytime."[5]

1 Timothy 2:3–4 and 2 Peter 3:9

Added to the remarkable salvation invitation for all people in the verse above is the clear declaration of God's intent as expressed in 1 Tim 2:3–4 and 2 Pet 3:9:

> "This is good and acceptable in the sight of God our Savior, who desires all men to be saved and to come to the knowledge of the truth." (1 Tim 2:3–4)

---

3. Vines, "Sermon," 13–14.
4. Robertson, *Word Pictures*, 50.
5. David Allen, correspondence, in Vines, "Sermon," 24.

Commentary on Article 1: The Gospel

> "The Lord is not slow about His promise, as some count slowness, but is patient toward you, not wishing for any to perish but for all to come to repentance." (2 Pet 3:9)

Only by the most tortured eisegesis can one avoid the profound truth that God desires all sinners to be saved. Some interpreters, in order to maintain that God does not intend the gospel for everyone, suggest that the "all" in these verses means "all of the elect" or "all kinds of people" or something less than every individual human being. Timothy George writes, "This is a strained exegesis that is hard to justify in every case. Unless the context requires a different interpretation, it is better to say that 'all means all.'"[6]

God's Covenant Displays It

It is not only individual Scriptures like those above that teach the gospel is good news for everyone, but also the whole trajectory of Scripture points to the universal design of God for all people to benefit from his love. God is not a localized deity who cares for only one tribe. He is the Creator of all men and calls all to himself.

This is noted early in God's call to Abraham. It begins with "I will make you a great nation" but ends with ". . . in you all the families of the earth will be blessed" (see Gen 12:2–3). Although the nation of Israel often believed that the blessings were just for them, God always intended that they would be his servants so that all the world could be reached for his glory. As the prophet Isaiah declares:

> He says, "It is too small a thing that You should be My Servant
> To raise up the tribes of Jacob and to restore the preserved ones of Israel;
> I will also make You a light of the nations
> So that My salvation may reach to the end of the earth." (Isa 49:6)

Jesus was challenged by the Pharisees because they thought the Messiah was just to benefit them. And the Apostle Paul had to counter the Judaizers who didn't understand that the wall of partition (Eph 2:14) had been broken in Christ and that the mystery had been unveiled that salvation is for the Gentiles, too (Col 1:26–27). In too many instances, the Jews, the Pharisees, and the Judaizers said to certain people, "God's plan is not for you," but Jesus along with the rest of the writers of the NT roundly

---

6. George, *Amazing Grace*, 94.

condemned such thinking. How can the church conclude from the providential sweep of God's plan for the ages that the gospel is not for everyone?

God's Gospel Demonstrates It

When we say the gospel is good news for everyone, we do not mean that everyone will be saved. We are simply declaring that because of God's offer in Jesus Christ, everyone could be saved. Romans 1:16 is instructive on this issue:

> "For I am not ashamed of the gospel, for it is the power of God for salvation to everyone who believes, to the Jew first and also to the Greek." (Rom 1:16)

The enabling act in the sovereign design of God, which makes it possible for anyone and everyone to come to salvation, is the gospel (its particulars and its proclamation). When the gospel is heard, its inherent power makes all sinful hearers able to respond. The failure of some sinful hearers to be saved is solely because of their refusal to believe. John 3:18 tells us that those who believe are not condemned, but those who do not believe are condemned already. There is no deficiency in the power of the gospel or in the willingness of God to save.

The New Hampshire Confession of Faith (1833/1853) reads: "We believe that the blessings of salvation are made free to all by the Gospel; that it is the immediate duty of all to accept them by a cordial, penitent, and obedient faith; and that nothing prevents the salvation of the greatest sinner on earth except his own inherent depravity and voluntary rejection of the gospel; which rejection involves him in an aggravated condemnation."[7]

In the gospel, God has done all that is necessary to bring otherwise helpless sinners to the point of salvation. With that being done, sinners must receive or reject the gospel offer. God, in his sovereign plan, has chosen neither to coerce nor prohibit the sinner's choice in salvation. Only God (and the sinner himself) knows why sinners, having been enabled by the gospel to believe, choose as they do. As we try to understand why some are saved and others are lost, we must be careful that we do not misinterpret Scripture, malign the character of God, or minimize the love of God by

---

7. Lumpkin, *Baptist Confessions*, 363. See pp. 360–67 for The New Hampshire Confession of Faith (1833) with 1853 revisions.

suggesting that his desire for some sinners is to simply ignore them or to damn them instead of to redeem them.

WHEN THE GOOD NEWS IS BAD NEWS

Is there any scenario in which the gospel (which is good news) would be bad news to anyone? If they were excluded by God from being afforded the gospel's provision and, from the day of their birth, were only passing time until a sure and certain consignment to an eternity in hell, then indeed, that is bad news.

The implication of Calvinism is just that. God's salvific intent was always only for a select number. He picked them out before time began (unconditional election), caused events so that they would with certainty be redeemed, and left all other human beings to just as certainly perish in their sins. This interpretation of soteriology is good news for some and bad news for the rest.

Do Calvinists really teach that the gospel was always only intended by God for some sinners and that decision was made by God prior to creation? Consider the following comments by Reformed theologian Loraine Boettner: "The Reformed Faith has held to the existence of an eternal, divine decree which, antecedently to any difference or desert in men themselves, separates the human race into two portions and ordains one to everlasting life and the other to everlasting death [hell]." Boettner goes on to say that Calvinists "believe that from all eternity God has intended to leave some of Adam's posterity in their sins, and that the decisive factor in the life of each is to be found only in God's will."[8]

According to T. H. L. Parker in *A Dictionary of Christian Theology*, Augustine is the father of these views. Parker explains:

> The conclusion, to which Augustine was not afraid to go, is that mankind is from all eternity divided into two classes of elect and non-elect. The elect, of whom there are from all eternity a fixed number (known only to God) will in time believe and at last be saved.... The non-elect are so because God has rejected them on account of their sin, and they are justly, as sinners, condemned to eternal punishment.... God was in no sense a passive spectator before the event, but as the sovereign Lord determined the eternal

---

8. Boettner, *Predestination*, 83, 104. Olson, *Against Calvinism*, 103, concludes that this view "is crucial to all true Calvinists; it is the heart of their system of soteriology."

lot of each man and therefore foresaw how he would deal with each man and what should become of him.[9]

Augustine was unmoved by the apparent arbitrariness of God's actions. He thought that it was impertinence to question the goodness of God on these matters. He pled ignorance on one hand because God's purposes are unsearchable; then, on the other hand, proceeded to give an answer to the dilemma, declaring it is a good thing for God to give sinners what they deserve even as he shows other sinners his mercy.

Subsequent theologians adopted Augustine's views, but none was more prominent than John Calvin. Parker writes, "We turn to Calvin, with whose name predestination is popularly linked. Yet Calvin himself thought that he was merely reproducing Augustine's doctrine."[10] Parker, appealing to quotations from a translation of Calvin's 1559 edition of *Institutes*, continues,

> Calvin's definition, it will be remembered, stated that "eternal life is foreordained for some, eternal damnation for others" (iii.21.5). There is no question here of a mere taking out of the elect from the mass of mankind and of overlooking the rest. Calvin will certainly speak of "passing over" and "setting apart," but he sees the passing over as a deliberate excluding by God, determined in eternity: "those whom God passes over, he condemns; and this for no other reason than that he wills to exclude them from the inheritance which he predestines for his own children" (iii.23.1). This he determined, therefore, before the sin for which the reprobate would in time be condemned had been committed. More, God willed the fall of man: "man falls, the providence of God so ordaining" (iii.23.8).[11]

James P. Boyce, the oft-cited founder of Southern Seminary, says this regarding the Decree of Reprobation in his *Abstract of Theology*:

> The Scriptural statements as to Reprobation are that God, in eternity, when he elected some, did likewise not elect others; that as resulting from this non-election, but not as efficiently caused by it, he passes by these in the bestowment of the special favors shown to the Elect, and, as in like manner yet further resulting, condemns men because of sin to everlasting destruction, and while they are

---

9. *A Dictionary of Christian Theology*, s.v. "Predestination."
10. Ibid.
11. Ibid.

in the state of sin and condemnation, he effects or permits the hardening of their hearts, so that his truth is not appreciated, but actually rejected.[12]

The preceding survey illustrates that Calvinism, at least in its historic and standard form, does not teach that everyone is savable. Those holding this view do not concur with Article 1 of the Traditional Statement. They affirm the position that God pre-temporally elected certain individuals for eternal life, which makes their faith response inevitable, while not electing all others, which makes their faith response impossible.

It is well known, however, that Calvinism (like many other theological systems) has within in its ranks numerous variations of belief. Chief among these variations is the attempt to salvage the idea that "God desires to save every sinner" from the ravages of the "horrible decree" of double predestination.

One such view is commonly referred to as "single predestination." This was the position of Charles Haddon Spurgeon. A self-described Calvinist and hero to most Southern Baptists, including me, Spurgeon goes to great lengths to separate the decree to elect and the decree to pass by. In a sermon on Rom 9:13, Spurgeon begins with this strong disclaimer about his understanding of this subject: "Do not imagine for an instant that I pretend to be able thoroughly to elucidate the great mysteries of predestination." Instead, he is willing to "give you what I think to be a scriptural statement of the fact, that some men are chosen, other men are left."[13]

Spurgeon basically argues that God's decision to elect is alone causative for salvation but his decision not to elect is not in any way causative for condemnation. He writes, "All the glory to God in salvation; all the blame to men in damnation." He insists it is not possible or necessary to reconcile the two arguments and deflects objections to his view with an appeal to mystery and to some sort of fideism. He adds, "It is not a matter of understanding; it is a matter of faith."[14]

The "single predestination" view is widely held among people who self-identify as Calvinists.[15] They believe it permits the concept that God really desires the salvation of all, even though he does not elect all which is a prerequisite for being able to respond to the gospel. This stripe of Cal-

12. Boyce, *Abstract of Theology*, 356.
13. Spurgeon, "Jacob and Esau," par. 1-2.
14. Ibid., par. 17-19.
15. George, *Amazing Grace*, 88-89.

vinist appeals to mystery, as did Spurgeon. But isn't this really a case of clear contradiction? The logical result of electing only some is the certain condemnation of the rest.[16] In other words, the result to the non-elect is the same whether you style God's activity as "double predestination" or "single predestination." It is God's choice alone that rescues sinners from hell or leaves them in their sin to face eternal judgment. According to these views, God has chosen for only some to be rescued.[17]

Another variation of Calvinism that attempts to affirm God's love for all sinners and his desire to save everyone posits that God has two wills, his hidden (or secret) will and his revealed will. They assert that while it is God's revealed will to desire the salvation of all, his hidden will is that only some (the elect) be saved.[18]

The hidden/revealed wills theory is flawed in numerous ways, including a destruction of confidence in the revealed will. How can one be assured of God's revelation in Christ, the truth of gospel claims, or salvation for anyone in particular if these may be secretly countermanded by God's hidden will? Additionally, this theory doesn't solve the problem its proponents have with the question of God's desire to save everyone. The revealed will (God desires to see all saved) is trumped by God's hidden will (only some are intended for salvation). This makes the claim that God desires to save all a mere charade.

Because we deny the notion that the Bible teaches that only some humans are the objects of God's desire to save, we reject the theological interpretations described above as Calvinism. We applaud the attempt of some Calvinists to try to hold to their understanding of election and, at the same time, to affirm that God desires to save all. However, those attempts that just appeal to mystery or paradox are puzzling because they want to affirm simultaneously two contradictory claims. Those proposals for a hidden/secret will are more troubling because they claim to affirm God's desire to save all but do not believe he really does. If these views do not make the

---

16. Olson, *Against Calvinism*, 104–10.

17. Ware affirms "single predestination." He writes, "As this relates to unconditional election, yes it is absolutely true that the elect most surely and certainly will be saved, and that the non-elect are just as certainly left in their sinful condition to experience the consequences of their sin." Ware, "Divine Election," 39.

18. See Keathley, *Sovereignty and Salvation*, 42–62, for his chapter which summarizes how theologians have tried to manage the question, "Does God Desire the Salvation of All?" For a similar treatment, see Keathley, "The Work of God," 557–86.

affirmation that God desires the salvation of everyone a central tenet, then they have diminished the good news of the gospel.

CONCLUSION

By God's design, everyone is savable. We affirm that the gospel is for everyone. We reject the concept that only a select few are capable of responding to the gospel while the rest are predestined to an eternity in hell.

The article on the gospel is first in the Traditional Statement because it sets the boundaries for the further discussion of the doctrine of salvation. Subsequent chapters will address the implications of the belief that God desires to save everyone on subjects such as grace, election, and sovereignty. Whatever conclusions one makes of the various aspects of God's plan of salvation, if it cannot be maintained that everyone is savable, then the good news for all has become bad news for most.

BIBLIOGRAPHY

Boettner, Loraine. *The Reformed Doctrine of Predestination*, 6th ed. Grand Rapids: Eerdmans, 1948.

Boyce, James P. *Abstract of Theology*. 1887. Reprint, Cape Coral, FL: Founders, 2006.

George, Timothy. *Amazing Grace: God's Initiative—Our Response*. Nashville: LifeWay, 2000.

Keathley, Kenneth. *Sovereignty and Salvation: A Molinist Approach*. Nashville: B&H Academic, 2011.

———. "The Work of God: Salvation." In *A Theology for the Church*, rev. ed., edited by Daniel Akin, 543–600. Nashville: B&H Academic, 2014.

Lumpkin, William L. *Baptist Confessions of Faith*. Rev. ed. Valley Forge: Judson, 1969.

Neumeister, Erdmann. "Christ Receiveth Sinful Men." Translated by Emma Bevan. In *The Baptist Hymnal*, edited by Wesley L. Forbis. Nashville: Convention, 1991.

Olson, Roger E. *Against Calvinism*. Grand Rapids: Zondervan, 2011.

Robertson, A. T. *Word Pictures in the New Testament*, vol. V: The Fourth Gospel and the Epistle to the Hebrews. Nashville: Broadman, 1932.

Spurgeon, Charles. "Jacob and Esau." Sermon 239, delivered on January 16, 1859. http://www.ccel.org/ccel/spurgeon/sermons05.xvi.html.

Vines, Jerry. "Sermon on John 3:16." In *Whosoever Will: A Biblical-Theological Critique of Five-Point Calvinism*, edited by David L. Allen and Steve W. Lemke, 13–28. Nashville: B&H Academic, 2010.

Ware, Bruce A. "Divine Election to Salvation: Unconditional, Individual, and Infralapsarian." In *Perspectives on Election*, edited by Chad Owen Brand, 1–58. Nashville: B&H, 2006.

Article 2: The Sinfulness of Man

We affirm that, because of the fall of Adam, every person inherits a nature and environment inclined toward sin and that every person who is capable of moral action will sin. Each person's sin alone brings the wrath of a holy God, broken fellowship with him, ever-worsening selfishness and destructiveness, death, and condemnation to an eternity in hell.

We deny that Adam's sin resulted in the incapacitation of any person's free will or rendered any person guilty before he has personally sinned. While no sinner is remotely capable of achieving salvation through his own effort, we deny that any sinner is saved apart from a free response to the Holy Spirit's drawing through the gospel.

Genesis 3:15–24; 6:5; Deuteronomy 1:39; Isaiah 6:5; 7:15–16; 53:6; Jeremiah 17:5, 9; 31:29–30; Ezekiel 18:19–20; Matthew 7:21–23; Romans 1:18–32; 3:9–18; 5:12; 6:23; 7:9; 1 Corinthians 1:18–25; 6:9–10; 15:22; 2 Corinthians 5:10; Hebrews 9:27–28; Revelation 20:11–15.

Commentary on
Article 2: The Sinfulness of Man

Adam Harwood

SOUTHERN BAPTISTS AFFIRM THAT Adam's single act of disobedience in the garden was an egregious rebellion against a holy God. His judgment against sin is visible throughout the Old Testament atonement motif, culminates at the cross of Christ, and will be fully realized at the return of the Lord Jesus Christ. Questions concerning Article 2 of the Traditional Statement (TS) are justified because one's doctrine of sin informs one's doctrine of salvation. Jesus came to seek and save the lost (Luke 19:10). Jesus came to die in order to offer himself as a ransom for many (Mark 10:45). Any rejection of our lost and sinful condition is a rejection of his stated mission. The TS affirms both man's lost condition and God's gracious provision of salvation by grace through faith in Christ (Eph 2:8–9) as the only way by which people may be saved from their hopeless and helpless condition.

Of the ten articles, the strongest objections to the TS have centered on Article 2, entitled "The Sinfulness of Man." Specifically, the article denies both incapacitated will and inherited guilt. Rather than address the points on which there is agreement, this chapter will focus on those points of disagreement. Because Article 8 in the TS addresses free will, this chapter will deal briefly with incapacitated will and at length with inherited guilt.

DOES ARTICLE 2 AFFIRM THAT PEOPLE CAN RESIST GOD'S SAVING GRACE?

Yes. After providing two qualifications, Article 2 affirms that people can resist God's saving grace. First, Article 2 affirms that "no sinner is remotely capable of achieving salvation through his own effort." Second, it denies "that any sinner is saved apart from a free response to the Holy Spirit's drawing through the gospel." With those qualifications stated explicitly, Article 2 declares, "We deny that Adam's sin resulted in the incapacitation of any person's free will." Chapter 8 deals with free will in greater detail. In summary, Article 2 denies the Calvinistic view that sinners are unable to repent and confess faith in Christ until they are first regenerated by God. Instead, the TS affirms that people who are saved by grace alone are called and enabled to exert their will by placing their faith or trust in Christ alone.

The Bible describes the sinful and lost condition of humanity (John 3:36; Rom 3:9–20). The Bible also declares that God loves the world (John 3:16), Christ died for the sins of the world (John 1:29; 1 John 2:2), and all people in every place are called to repent (Mark 6:12; Acts 2:38; 17:30). Will God hold people accountable for failing to do what they are unable to do? If God calls all people to repent and there are open invitations for people to respond in faith to Christ, then it follows that people are able to repent and place faith in Christ.[1]

The denial of an incapacitated will in Article 2 is a denial of Calvinism's doctrine of irresistible grace. Roger Olson rejects irresistible grace, but explains the view is biblically and logically *necessary* if one accepts total depravity, unconditional election, and limited atonement. Olson writes,

> As for logic, the argument is that because people are totally depraved and dead in trespasses and sins, unless God elects him or her, the person will never respond to the internal calling of the Holy Spirit. So, the Holy Spirit has to change the person inwardly in an effectual manner, which is regeneration. Then the born again person desires to come to Christ, in which case he or she is given repentance and faith (conversion) and justification (forgiveness and imputation of Christ's righteousness). This process is called "monergistic grace" or just "monergism."[2]

---

1. Calvinists distinguish between natural and moral inability. For more on this internal discussion, see the works of Jonathan Edwards, Andrew Fuller, A. A. Hodge, and William Shedd.

2. Olson, *Against Calvinism*, 156.

Commentary on Article 2: The Sinfulness of Man

Steve Lemke denies the doctrine of irresistible grace, which Olson also calls monergism. While rejecting the idea that any person "can achieve salvation apart from God," Lemke identifies the theological debate as "whether humans have any role at all in accepting or receiving their own salvation."[3] Calvinists explain that God does not violate a lost person's will; rather, God changes their will through regeneration so they are drawn to Christ. Compatibilism is the Calvinist view that a lost person's will is irresistibly changed through regeneration so they now desire Christ. Lemke explains that compatibilism is not a solution because there is no opportunity for a person to choose otherwise.

Lemke presents a robust argument from Scripture that God's saving grace is *resistible*. After noting several Old Testament texts on the topic, Lemke turns his attention to the New Testament. Stephen declared his accusers were "resisting the Holy Spirit" (Acts 7:51, HCSB). Jesus lamented over Jerusalem; he wanted to gather them to himself but they "were not willing" (Matt 23:37, HCSB). The rich young ruler appears unwilling to follow Jesus' instructions about inheriting eternal life (Luke 18:18–23). Other examples of resistible grace in the parables of Jesus include the two sons (Matt 21:28–32), the vineyard (Matt 21:33–44), and the soils (Matt 13:1–23).[4]

Lemke also notes the "all-inclusive invitations" in Scripture. He writes, "The key issue, then, is whether salvation is genuinely open to all persons or merely just to a few who receive irresistible grace." He notes God's desire for the salvation of all people (Matt 18:14; 1 Tim 2:4; 2 Pet 3:9; 1 John 2:2) and traces all-inclusive invitations throughout the Bible (Joel 2:32; Matt 7:24; 10:32–33; 11:6; 11:28; 12:50; Luke 9:23–24; John 1:7; 3:15–16; 4:13–14; 6:40; 6:51; 7:17; 7:37; 8:51; 11:26; 12:46; Acts 2:21; 10:43; Rom 9:33; 10:11; 1 John 2:23; 4:15; 5:1; Rev 3:20; 22:17).[5]

Richard Swinburne, professor emeritus of philosophy at Oriel College, the University of Oxford, writes, "My assessment of the Christian theological tradition is that all Christian theologians of the first four centuries believed in human free will in the libertarian sense, as did all subsequent Eastern Orthodox theologians, and most Western Catholic traditions from

---

3. Lemke, "Irresistible Grace," 114.
4. Ibid., 117–22.
5. Ibid., 122–27. Quotation from 123.

Duns Scotus (in the fourteenth century) onwards."[6] Likewise, the TS resists monergism and affirms libertarian free will.

DOES ARTICLE 2 DENY THAT PEOPLE INHERIT ADAM'S GUILT?

Yes. Article 2 makes two particular claims regarding our inheritance from the first Adam. First, Article 2 affirms that all people inherit "a nature and environment inclined toward sin." Second, it denies that Adam's sin renders "any person guilty before he has personally sinned." This view that people inherit from Adam a sinful nature only (or inclination to sin) appears to be more consistent with a plain reading of the Bible than the view that people inherit Adam's guilt. Also, the verbiage for Article 2 of the TS was taken from Article 3 of the Baptist Faith and Message (BFM), both the 1963 and 2000 editions. By approving the BFM in 1963 and 2000, the SBC excluded from the convention's confession any notion of inheriting the guilt of Adam's sin.

The BFM affirms that people inherit a nature inclined toward sin. (See the single-underlined words in the table below.) Article 2 of the TS attempts to clarify Article 3 of the BFM, which provides this explanation concerning Adam's posterity: "as soon as they are capable of moral action, they become transgressors and are under condemnation." The TS restates the view as follows: "every person who is capable of moral action will sin." The TS then denies explicitly that people are born with the guilt of the first Adam's sin. We regard this to be an implication of the BFM: "*We deny* that Adam's sin . . . rendered any person guilty before he has personally sinned." (See the double-underlined words in the table below.)

---

6. Swinburne, *Providence*, 35. This claim is explored in Eppling, "Free Will."

Commentary on Article 2: The Sinfulness of Man

COMPARISON OF THE BAPTIST FAITH AND MESSAGE AND THE TRADITIONAL STATEMENT

Excerpt of Article 3 of the BFM (2000)	Article 2 of the TS (2012)
In the beginning man was innocent of sin and was endowed by his Creator with freedom of choice. By his free choice man sinned against God and brought sin into the human race. Through the temptation of Satan man transgressed the command of God, and fell from his original innocence whereby his posterity <u>inherit a nature and an environment inclined toward sin. Therefore, as soon as they are capable of moral action, they become transgressors and are under condemnation</u>. Only the grace of God can bring man into His holy fellowship and enable man to fulfill the creative purpose of God.	*We affirm* that, because of the fall of Adam, every person <u>inherits a nature and environment inclined toward sin</u> and that <u>every person who is capable of moral action will sin</u>. Each person's sin alone brings the wrath of a holy God, broken fellowship with him, ever-worsening selfishness and destructiveness, death, and condemnation to an eternity in hell. *We deny* that Adam's sin resulted in the incapacitation of any person's free will or <u>rendered any person guilty before he has personally sinned</u>. While no sinner is remotely capable of achieving salvation through his own effort, we deny that any sinner is saved apart from a free response to the Holy Spirit's drawing through the gospel.

This denial of inherited guilt is not intended to be a judgment that an affirmation of inherited guilt is outside of Christian orthodoxy or Baptist theology.[7] Christian history is replete with examples of noteworthy theologians who have affirmed the inherited guilt view, which is an attempt to explain the universal nature of humanity's sin. Some Baptist doctrinal statements have affirmed the inherited guilt view, as have other respected streams within the larger Christian tradition, such as Lutherans, Presbyterians, and Roman Catholics. Of course, groups can share one theological conviction (in this case inherited guilt) without sharing all theological convictions. One might wonder, however, if it is consistent to affirm Augustine's assumption of inherited guilt while rejecting his solution of infant baptism.

Although some Calvinistic Southern Baptists affirm the inherited guilt view, such a conclusion is unnecessary—even among Reformed theologians. Donald Macleod explains the seventeenth-century debate as follows,

---

7. For more on the two major interpretations of original sin among Baptists, inherited sinful nature only and inherited sinful nature and guilt, see Harwood, "Baptist (& baptistic) View."

The point at issue was the relation between imputed guilt and inherited corruption. According to the advocates of *immediate* imputation, the guilt of Adam's sin was imputed to his posterity on the basis that they *were* his posterity. Corruption of nature follows as the punishment of our guilt. According to the advocates of *mediate* imputation, on the other hand, guilt is mediated through our corruption: God holds us guilty not simply because, irrespective of any depravity, he sees us as guilty of Adam's sin, but because he sees in us the corruption derived from Adam. We are condemned not as Adam's posterity, but as wicked and corrupt.[8]

In other words, although some Reformed theologians argued that all people inherit Adam's guilt (immediate imputation), other Reformed theologians said all people inherit corruption then individuals later become guilty because of their own actions (mediate imputation).[9]

Is the Physical Death of Some Infants Evidence of Inherited Guilt?

The physical death of some infants is sometimes cited as evidence that all people inherit the guilt of Adam's sin. John Murray was a professor of Theology at Princeton Seminary and Westminster Seminary. In his work *The Imputation of Adam's Sin*, Murray makes a case for inherited guilt. He quotes Rom 6:23, which states the wages of sin is death, to argue that infants sometimes die because Adam's guilt is imputed to all people. Article 2 denies inherited guilt. What is the reply to John Murray's argument that infants sometimes die because of Adam's guilt? Romans 6:23 does not state that every physical death is the result of that person's guilt. Rather, physical death is not always the result of our own guilt.

Consider the tragic story of the first son of David and Bathsheba. Their infant son did not die because of his own guilt. The text of 2 Sam 12 is clear that the infant died as a result of David's sinful actions, which were ultimately a result of Adam's sin. Our view is not that infants are sinless; instead, they have inherited "a nature and environment inclined toward sin."[10]

---

8. Macleod, "Original Sin," 140.

9. For a full-length treatment of the doctrine of original sin by a Reformed theologian who rejects inherited guilt, or alien guilt, see Blocher, *Original Sin*. For the view of a Reformed theologian who affirms inherited guilt, see Murray, *Imputation*.

10. The phrase inherited death has been suggested. The argument for that phrase is that sin is *attached* to but not *fundamental* to the human nature; also, the phrase inherited death may better account for the dying of creation mentioned in Rom 8. Regardless,

Infants are *not guilty* before God because they have not yet knowingly acted in sinful ways. Why do they sometimes die? As was the case with David's first son, infants are sometimes impacted by the sweeping consequences of God's judgment against the sinful behavior of other people, such as the sinful actions of King David which resulted in the death of his infant son. But physical death as a result of another person's sin should not be equated with bearing the guilt of another person's sin. Because infants live in a body and world inclined toward sin, this sometimes results in the death of not-guilty infants. Consider also the murder of infant boys carried out by Pharaoh and by King Herod (Exod 1:22 and Matt 1:16). Does the Scripture indicate they died because of the guilt of Adam or because of the royal decree? The inherited sinful nature view affirmed in the TS is consistent with both the BFM and the Bible.

It is not necessary for all Southern Baptists to affirm the inherited sinful nature view. However, the inherited guilt view is not consistent with the language of Article 3 of the BFM.

In the following sections, evidence will be provided from the Bible, church history, and systematic theology in favor of the inherited sinful nature view, as expressed in Article 2 of the TS, over the inherited guilt view.

A DEFENSE FOR ARTICLE 2 FROM THE BIBLE

Southern Baptists who affirm the TS explicitly reject inherited guilt. The Bible teaches that Adam's sin had devastating consequences for humanity and no one escapes sinfulness. But we are held accountable by God for our own sin and guilt, not the sin and guilt of Adam.

Deuteronomy 1 & Numbers 14

Recall the story of the twelve spies. Two saw grapes; ten saw giants. Why did Israel wander in the desert for forty years? Because they voted with the ten spies, who failed to trust God. Deuteronomy 1 and Num 14 record God's judgment against them. Because the Israelites failed to trust God, the "evil generation" was prohibited from entering the Promised Land. With the exception of Joshua and Caleb, the older generation (defined in Num

---

the language of both the TS and the BFM claim that we now have both "a nature and environment inclined toward sin."

14:29 as twenty years and older) would not enter the Promised Land. Instead, they would wander around and die in the desert. After the last of that generation died, the younger generation of Israelites would enter the land. What was the single reason the younger generation was spared God's judgment? Their age.

This is not to suggest that twenty years is an age (or stage) of accountability for every person. But according to Deut 1:39, that younger generation had "no knowledge of good or evil." They lacked moral knowledge and were spared from God's judgment. In his commentary, Weinfeld writes that the phrase in Deut 1:39 refers to males "not yet of responsible age." In support of this view, he compares the phrase to Isa 7:15, cites the parallel passage in Num 14:31, and notes the age of twenty years as a time of accountability (Exod 30:14 and Num 1:3). Weinfeld adds, "According to rabbinic tradition, man is not accountable before the age of twenty."[11]

Although not held guilty for the sins of their fathers, the younger generation nevertheless experienced some of the negative consequences or wages of sin. They wandered in the desert, unable to inherit the Promised Land until the last person of the older generation died. In a similar way, infants today are not held responsible for the actions of previous generations, up to and including Adam. Like the younger generation in the Deuteronomy/Numbers account, infants experience the consequences of sin for which they are not counted guilty.

John MacArthur holds a similar interpretation of Deut 1:39 and links that with the spiritual condition of infants today. In his book *Safe in the Arms of God*, he writes, "The Israelite children of sinful parents were allowed to enter fully into the blessing God had for His people. They were in no way held accountable, responsible, or punishable for the sins of their parents. Why? Because they had no knowledge of good and evil, right or wrong." Then, MacArthur quotes Ezek 18:20 (ESV), which reads, "The soul who sins shall die. The son shall not suffer for the iniquity of the father, nor the father suffer for the iniquity of the son. The righteousness of the righteous shall be upon himself, and the wickedness of the wicked shall be upon himself."[12]

---

11. Weinfeld, *Deuteronomy*, 151.
12. MacArthur, *Safe*, 45.

Commentary on Article 2: The Sinfulness of Man

Psalm 51:5

After David's sin with Bathsheba and confrontation by Nathan, the king offers this confession in Ps 51:5, "Behold, I was brought forth in iniquity, And in sin my mother conceived me" (NASB). In what way should his statement be understood? David wrote that he was brought forth in "iniquity" (*'āwōn*) and conceived in "sin" (*ḥēṭ*). *A Concise Hebrew and Aramaic Lexicon of the Old Testament* (*CHALOT*) defines *'āwōn* as "activity that is crooked or wrong." Similarly it defines *ḥēṭ* as "fault (against men)" and "sin (against God)." In both instances, this standard lexicon defines the words in reference to wrongful actions. Did David regard the circumstances surrounding his conception to be sinful?

The following comments are made concerning Ps 51:5 in the United Bible Society's *A Translator's Handbook on The Book of Psalms*:

> In vivid language the psalmist confesses that he has been a sinner all his life. The literal language, "In iniquity I was given birth, and in sin my mother conceived me" (see 58.3), is hardly the basis for biological, anthropological, or theological pronouncements about the nature of the human being as sinner. Were the words to be taken literally, they would mean that the psalmist's mother sinned when she became pregnant (which implies either that sexual intercourse as such is sinful or that she was guilty of fornication or adultery), and that at the moment of his birth he was already a sinner. What the psalmist is saying is that he (and so, by implication, everyone) is a sinner; sin is ingrained in human nature and permeates all of human activity. In some languages it may be better to follow the example of TEV or of GECL: "Wrong and guilt have characterized my life ever since my mother gave birth to me."[13]

Other scholars who comment on the meaning of Ps 51:5 render a similar judgment. Franz Delitzsch explains that David's "parents were sinful human beings, and this sinful state (*habitus*) has operated upon his birth and even his conception, and from this point has passed over to him." Edward Dalglish observes that "the psalmist is relating his sinfulness to the very inception of life; he traces his development beyond birth (*chuwl*) to the genesis of his being in his mother's womb–even to the very hour of conception (*yacham*)." Bruce Waltke writes that it "supports the notion that at the

---

13. Bratcher and Reyburn, *Psalms*.

time of conception man is in a state of sin (. . .)." Mitchell Dahood concurs, "All men have a congenital tendency toward evil."[14]

Michael Goulder notes that "critics are almost unanimous in taking v. 5 to refer to the universality of human sin, transmitted from generation to generation." In his commentary, Hans-Joachim Kraus writes, "'Āwōn and ḥēṭ have from the hour of birth been the determining forces under whose signature life began. The petitioner wants to say that the primordial cause, the root cause of my existence, is interwoven with corruption."[15] None of these Old Testament scholars derive from Ps 51:5 that people are guilty of sin from birth. Instead, they affirm that sinfulness is present at the first moment of life.

Romans 5:12

Joseph Fitzmyer cautions readers of Rom 5 to distinguish between Paul's writings and the later teachings of the church. The Catholic scholar explains that the doctrine of original sin (the view that all people inherit both a sinful nature and guilt) is a later teaching of the church rather than an explicit teaching of Paul. The doctrine of original sin was developed from later Augustinian writings and solidified through the Sixteenth Council of Carthage, the Second Council of Orange, and the Tridentine Council.[16]

Romans 5:12 begins with the word "Therefore." What was Paul's previous argument? In Rom 5:1–2, Paul explains that we have been justified by faith and have peace with God through Christ. Also, through Christ we have access by faith to this grace. In vv. 3–5, those who have been given the Holy Spirit can hope in their suffering because of what God produces in them. Christ died for "the weak," "ungodly," people who were "still sinners" (vv. 6–8). Verse 9 begins in a way that is similar to v. 1 ("Since, therefore, we have been justified. . ."). Verse 1 mentions being justified by faith; verse 9 mentions being justified by his blood. Verses 9–11 provide assurance that we will be saved from God's wrath by the life provided by Jesus.

In verse 12, Paul states that "just as sin came into the world through one man, and death through sin, and so death spread to all men" (v. 12). Sin entered the world through one man, Adam. Death entered the world

---

14. Delitzsch, *Psalms*, 137; Dalglish, *Psalm Fifty-One*, 121; Waltke, "Reflections," 12; Dahood, *Psalms*, 4.

15. Goulder, *Prayers of David*, 53; Kraus, *Psalms*, 503.

16. Fitzmyer, *Romans*, 408–9.

through sin. Death spread to all men. Why? The answer is found in verse 12, "because all sinned." The text states neither "in whom all sinned" nor "because all sinned in Adam." Death spread because people sinned. Even worse, "death reigned from Adam to Moses" (v. 14). But Christ is anticipated, and Adam is described as "a type of the one to come" (v. 14).

The remark that "one trespass led to condemnation" (v. 18) is clarified in v. 19, "For as by the one man's disobedience the many were made sinners" (ESV). Do these verses teach that all people inherit the guilt and condemnation of Adam? If this is pressed as the meaning intended by Paul, then the parallel to all people inheriting guilt and condemnation is all people inheriting justification and life (v. 19). In order to affirm universal sinfulness but deny universal salvation, Millard Erickson posits a "conditional imputation" of Adam's guilt. People must ratify the work of Adam by personally and knowingly sinning just as they must ratify the work of Christ by personally and knowingly repenting of sin and confessing Christ as Savior and Lord.[17]

What does the text of Rom 5:12-21 not say? The text makes no mention of a covenant between God and Adam and it makes no mention of imputation of Adam's guilt. Can those concepts be found in various volumes of systematic theology? Yes. Can those concepts be found in this passage? No. In his monumental work *The Theology of Paul the Apostle*, James D. G. Dunn articulates his rejection of inherited guilt as follows: "Nevertheless, guilt only enters into the reckoning with the individual's own transgression. Human beings are not held responsible for the state into which they are born. That is the starting point of their personal responsibility, a starting point for which they are not liable."[18]

Perhaps other biblical texts support the doctrine of inherited guilt. Perhaps not. Either way, they are not discernible in Rom 5:12-21. Instead, we see that death spread to all of humanity because of the sin of one man, Adam. Thankfully, God answered the spread of death and condemnation through Adam with the hope of justification and life through Christ.

A DEFENSE FOR ARTICLE 2 FROM CHURCH HISTORY

Certain people question the denial of inherited guilt by citing historical statements affirming the view. We too have given careful study to the

17. Erickson, *Christian Theology*, 582.
18. Dunn, *Theology of Paul*, 97.

biblical text. And we are persuaded by the words of the Bible to reject inherited guilt in favor of inherited sinful nature. If it can be demonstrated from the words of the Bible that we have been wrong as a convention (failing to affirm inherited guilt since 1963), then we will revise Article 2. But we will not be persuaded by citations of systematic theology textbooks, even if some happen to have been written by Southern Baptists. Certain Southern Baptist theologians have been writing academic papers for several years attempting to argue that twisting a plain reading of the Bible to fit on a theological framework is precisely what has contributed to the present difficulties.[19] We prefer to deal in a conversation about the words of the Bible alone. The Reformation cry was *Sola Scriptura* (Scripture alone). We agree. Let the assertions and claims about this matter be drawn from an appeal to Scripture alone as we discuss this matter. To establish that this view is not a recent innovation within church history, examples will be provided from the following periods of church history: Patristic, Reformation, and Southern Baptist history.[20]

Known as "Golden Mouth" for his skills in oratory, John Chrysostom (374–407) is regarded as one of the most significant preachers in the first thousand years of Christian history. He wrote: "We do baptize infants, although *they are not guilty of any sins.*"[21]

Gregory of Nazianzus (ca. 330–390) preached, "For this is how the matter stands; at that time they begin to be responsible for their lives, when reason is matured, and they learn the mystery of life (*for of sins of ignorance owing to their tender years they have no account to give*), and it is far more profitable on all accounts to be fortified by the Font, because of the sudden assaults of danger that befall us, stronger than our helpers."[22] Gregory taught the following ideas in the passage above: First, people are not born with the responsibility of Adam's sin. Rather, they become morally responsible at the point in life at which their reason matures and "they learn the mystery of life." Second, they are not responsible for sins committed prior to this time of responsibility. Infancy is obviously included in the earliest period of life; Gregory called this period the "tender years," which is a time *prior* to people becoming "responsible for their lives." All sins committed

---

19. See Allen et al., "Neither Calvinists" and Hankins, "Beyond Calvinism."

20. More detail on these and other examples can be found in Harwood, *Spiritual Condition*, 81–152. Emphasis in the quotations is mine.

21. Chrysostom, *Infants*, 169.

22. Gregory of Nazianzus, *Oration* 40.28 (NPNF2 7:370).

Commentary on Article 2: The Sinfulness of Man

during these "tender years" are regarded by God as "sins of ignorance," for which the person will not have to give an account.

In *On Infants' Early Deaths*, Gregory of Nyssa (ca. 335–394) addressed the spiritual condition of infants. They were neither good nor bad; infants who died would be with God because their souls had never been corrupted by their own sinful actions.

Eastern theologians were not the only ones who rejected (or failed to advocate for) inherited guilt. Among the pre-Augustinian Western fathers, Tertullian (ca. 145–ca. 220) is often cited in support of the view that infants inherit sin and guilt. Although he mentioned that their souls are unclean in Adam, he also questioned why there was a rush to baptize infants, referred to their souls as innocent, and differentiated between infants and children based upon their capability to commit sin.[23]

Inherited guilt was rejected by one of the most important of the Magisterial Reformers, Ulrich Zwingli (1484–1531). Like Martin Luther, Zwingli rejected the Augustinian notion that baptism removed the guilt of original sin. However, he admitted to holding that view at one time. In 1525, he admitted that the controversy with Anabaptists "has shown us that it is not the pouring of water which washes away sin. And that was what we once believed, although without any authority in the word of God. We also believed that the water of baptism cleansed children from a sin that they never had, and that without it they would be damned. All these beliefs were erroneous, as we shall see later."[24] Zwingli still affirmed both Adam's seminal unity with humanity and sin's devastating effects upon humanity. But he stated the effects on infants in new ways.

Martin Luther attacked Zwingli's position as Pelagian because of his use of free will, so Zwingli offered a reply to Urbanus Rhegius in Augsburg. In defending his view of original sin, Zwingli asked this question: "For what could be said more briefly and plainly than that original sin is not sin but disease, and that the children of Christians are not condemned to eternal punishment on account of that disease?"[25] Zwingli defended his view by distinguishing between the words *disease* and *sin*. *Disease* refers to the "original contamination of man," "defect of humanity," or "the defect of a corrupted nature." Romans 5:14 reveals that Adam's fault brought

---

23. For a treatment of Tertullian's views in *A Treatise on the Soul, Against Marcion*, and *On Baptism*, see Harwood, *Spiritual Condition*, 96–101.

24. Zwingli, *Baptism*, 153.

25. Zwingli, *Original Sin*, 3.

this to every person. *Sin,* however, "implies guilt, and guilt comes from a transgression or a trespass on the part of one who designedly perpetrates a deed."

In his *Systematic Theology,* James Leo Garrett Jr. categorizes Zwingli's view as one of five "Theories Not Teaching the Imputation of Guilt" and labels it "Theory of Uncondemnable Depravity." Garrett identifies Zwingli with this view and explains, "This theory holds that human depravity always leads to sin but is not sin per se, and hence human beings are not condemned for their depravity but for the sins to which depravity has led."[26]

E. Y. Mullins (1860–1928) served as president of the Southern Baptist Convention, the Baptist World Alliance, and The Southern Baptist Theological Seminary (1899–1928). Mullins was the architect of the BFM. He rejected the doctrine of inherited guilt, as does the TS. Mullins argued that man is not guilty because of his nature. Also, according to Mullins, man is not guilty because he was represented by Adam in the garden or because we were seminally present in Adam. Rather, man "is guilty when he does wrong." For Mullins, Adam's guilt is not imputed to humanity. Mullins explained, "Men are not condemned therefore for hereditary or original sin. They are condemned only for their own sins."[27]

A DEFENSE FOR ARTICLE 2 FROM SYSTEMATIC THEOLOGY

The appeal to set aside the systematic theology textbooks, even those excellent volumes produced by Baptists, is not based upon the notion that our view cannot be supported. To the contrary, we find support for our view in a systematic treatment by a respected Baptist theologian who blazes a trail leading through the confusion and back to the Scriptures. Millard Erickson is a professor of theology whose book, *Christian Theology,* is commonly used in the classrooms of Southern Baptist colleges and seminaries. He is profiled among the statesmen and thinkers in a chapter of George and Dockery's book, *Baptist Theologians.* Erickson's many teaching posts have included both Southwestern and Southern seminaries.

26. Garrett, *Systematic Theology,* 1:489–91. Garrett also includes under "Theory of Uncondemnable Depravity" Charles G. Finney and New England Congregationalists Samuel Hopkins, Nathanael Emmons, Timothy Dwight, and Nathaniel W. Taylor.

27. Mullins, *Christian Religion,* 294, 302. For other examples of other Southern Baptists who have denied inherited guilt, see Harwood, *Born Guilty?,* 20–22.

Commentary on Article 2: The Sinfulness of Man

In *Christian Theology*, Erickson argues for a view known as conditional imputation. In this view, Adam's guilt is imputed to a person only *after* he knowingly sins. For this reason, infants are free from Adam's guilt and God's judgment. At the point that a person first knowingly sins, he becomes accountable to God. This is the justification for an age or stage of moral accountability. Pointing to Rom 5, Erickson explains that just as the work of Christ is not universally imputed but must be individually ratified (or received), so the work of Adam is not universally imputed but must be individually ratified (or received).[28]

Following the biblical intuition of Millard Erickson, the TS rejects imputed guilt. We understand the Bible to teach in Rom 5 and other biblical texts that Adam's sin had devastating consequences for humanity but we are held accountable by God only for our own sin and guilt.

CONCLUSION

While affirming the universal and inescapable sinfulness of all people, Article 2 makes two important denials, both of which conflict with particular doctrines of Calvinism. First, Article 2 denies that sinners are unable to respond to freely respond to God's gracious invitation to repent of sin and place their faith in Christ. Calvinists appeal to the doctrine of total depravity to claim that sinners are unable to repent and trust Christ apart from the monergistic work of regeneration. The TS differs. The universal appeals for people to repent and believe in Christ imply that any sinner can actually repent and believe in Christ. Second, Article 2 denies that people inherit the guilt of Adam's sin. Instead, the TS remains consistent with the BFM 1963 and 2000, which fail to mention inherited guilt and explicitly describe what people inherit from Adam. People inherit a nature and environment inclined toward sin. Eventually, people will become transgressors and be subject to condemnation. Neither the Bible nor the BFM requires an affirmation of inherited guilt. The TS, like many theologians throughout church history, simply goes one step further and denies inherited guilt.

---

28. Erickson, *Christian Theology*, 579–83.

BIBLIOGRAPHY

Allen, David L., et al. "Neither Calvinists nor Arminians but Baptists." White Paper 36. The Center for Theological Research (September 2010). http://www.baptisttheology.org/white-papers/neither-calvinists-nor-arminians-but-baptists/.

Blocher, Henri. *Original Sin: Illuminating the Riddle.* New Studies in Biblical Theology 5. Edited by D. A. Carson. Downers Grove: InterVarsity, 1997.

Bratcher, Robert G., and William D. Reyburn. *A Translator's Handbook on The Book of Psalms.* New York: United Bible Societies, 1991. In Translator's Workplace Version 5.0 software, Summer Institute of Linguistics and United Bible Society.

Chrysostom, John. *On Infants.* Edited and translated by Henry Bettenson. In *The Later Christian Fathers.* New York: Oxford University Press, 1970.

Dahood, Mitchell. *Psalms II: 51–100.* In vol. 17a of The Anchor Bible. Edited by William Foxwell Albright and David Noel Freedman. Garden City, NY: Doubleday, 1968.

Dalglish, Edward. *Psalm Fifty-One: In the Light of Ancient Near Eastern Patternism.* Leiden: Brill, 1962.

Delitzsch, Franz. *Biblical Commentary on the Psalms*, vol. 2. Translated by Francis Bolton. Grand Rapids: Eerdmans, 1949.

Dunn, James D. G. *The Theology of Paul the Apostle.* Grand Rapids: Eerdmans, 1998.

Eppling, Christopher J. "A Study of the Patristic Doctrine of Free Will." Unpublished ThM Thesis, Southeastern Baptist Theological Seminary, 2009.

Erickson, Millard J. *Christian Theology.* 3rd ed. Grand Rapids: Baker, 2013.

Fitzmyer, Joseph. *Romans: A New Translation with introduction and Commentary.* In vol. 33 of The Anchor Bible. Edited by William Foxwell Albright and David Noel Freedman. Garden City, NY: Doubleday, 1993.

Garrett, James Leo, Jr. *Systematic Theology: Biblical, Historical, & Evangelical.* 2 vols. Grand Rapids: Eerdmans, 1990, 1995.

Goulder, Michael. *The Prayers of David (Psalm 51–72): Studies in the Psalter, II.* Journal for the Study of the Old Testament Supplement Series 102. Edited by David J. A. Clines and Philip R. Davies. Sheffield, England: JSOT, 1990.

Gregory of Nazianzus. *Oration 40.* Translated by Charles Browne and James Swallow. In *Nicene and Post-Nicene Fathers*, second series, edited by Philip Schaff and Henry Wace, 7:360–78. 1894. Reprint, Peabody, MA: Hendrickson, 2004.

Hankins, Eric. "Beyond Calvinism and Arminianism: Toward a Baptist Soteriology." *Journal for Baptist Theology & Ministry* 8.1 (Spring 2011) 87–100. http://baptistcenter.net/journals/JBTM_8-1_Spring_2011.pdf.

Harwood, Adam. "The Baptist (& baptistic) View of Infants and Children in the Church." In *Five Views on Infants and Children in the Church*, edited by Adam Harwood and Kevin Lawson. Nashville: B&H Academic, forthcoming.

———. *Born Guilty? A Southern Baptist View of Original Sin.* Carrollton, GA: Free Church, 2013.

———. *The Spiritual Condition of Infants: A Biblical-Historical Survey and Systematic Proposal.* Eugene, OR: Wipf & Stock, 2011.

Kraus, Hans-Joachim. *Psalms 1–59: A Continental Commentary.* Translated by Hilton C. Oswald. Minneapolis: Fortress, 1993.

Lemke, Steve W. "A Biblical and Theological Critique of Irresistible Grace." In *Whosoever Will: A Biblical-Theological Critique of Five-Point Calvinism*, edited by David L. Allen and Steve W. Lemke, 109–62. Nashville: B&H Academic, 2010.

Commentary on Article 2: The Sinfulness of Man

MacArthur, John. *Safe in the Arms of God.* Nashville: Thomas Nelson, 2003.

Macleod, Donald. "Original Sin in Reformed Theology." In *Adam, The Fall, and Original Sin: Theological, Biblical, and Scientific Perspectives,* edited by Hans Maudeme and Michael Reeves, 129–46. Grand Rapids: Baker Academic, 2014.

Mullins, E. Y. *The Christian Religion in its Doctrinal Expression.* 1917. Reprint, Valley Forge: Judson, 1974.

Murray, John. *The Imputation of Adam's Sin.* 1959. Reprint, Phillipsburg, NJ: Presbyterian and Reformed, 1977.

Olson, Roger E. *Against Calvinism.* Grand Rapids: Zondervan, 2011.

Swinburne, Richard. *Providence and the Problem of Evil.* New York: Clarendon, 1998.

Waltke, Bruce. "Reflections from the Old Testament on Abortion." *Journal of the Evangelical Theological Society* 19.1 (March 1976) 1–13.

Weinfeld, Moshe. *Deuteronomy 1–11: A New Translation with Introduction and Commentary,* vol. 5 of The Anchor Bible. Edited by William Foxwell Albright and David Noel Freedman. New York: Doubleday, 1991.

Zwingli, Ulrich. *Of Baptism.* Translated by Geoffrey Bromiley. In The Library of Christian Classics, Vol. XXIV: Zwingli and Bullinger, 129–75. Philadelphia: Westminster, 1953.

———. *On Original Sin.* Translated by Samuel M. Jackson. In *On Providence and Other Essays,* 2–32. Durham, NC: Labyrinth, 1983.

Article 3: The Atonement of Christ

We affirm that the penal substitution of Christ is the only available and effective sacrifice for the sins of every person.

We deny that this atonement results in salvation without a person's free response of repentance and faith. We deny that God imposes or withholds this atonement without respect to an act of the person's free will. We deny that Christ died only for the sins of those who will be saved.

Psalm 22:1-31; Isaiah 53:1-12; John 12:32, 14:6; Acts 10:39-43; 16:30-32; Romans 3:21-26; 2 Corinthians 5:21; Galatians 3:10-14; Philippians 2:5-11; Colossians 1:13-20; 1 Timothy 2:5-6; Hebrews 9:12-15, 24-28; 10:1-18; 1 John 1:7; 2:2.

Commentary on
Article 3: The Atonement of Christ

David L. Allen

RECOVERING THE GOSPEL—WHY BELIEF IN AN UNLIMITED ATONEMENT MATTERS

ARTICLE 3 ADDRESSES THE atonement of Christ. It consists of one proposition in affirmation and three in denial. I expect there will be no disagreement on the affirmation regarding the penal substitution of Christ. The penal substitutionary atonement, though often attacked and vilified in modern theology, is the bedrock doctrine for explaining the work of Christ on the cross for the sins of the world. Sin can only be atoned by the shed blood of Christ on the cross as our substitute. The word "penal" connotes legal imagery. Jesus' death on the cross satisfied the justice and wrath of God against our sin. Apart from Christ, there is no salvation. Apart from his atonement, there is no salvation. Only the cross of Christ provides an available and effective sacrifice for the sins of every person.

The first proposition in the denial states: "We deny that this atonement results in salvation without a person's free response of repentance and faith." The operative word here is "free." The Scripture teaches that the atonement is only applied to those who meet the condition of repentance and faith. When it comes to the question of free will, all Calvinists affirm some form of divine determinism along with free will.[1] One key aspect of divine determinism is the doctrine of God's eternal decree which affirms that God predetermined from eternity who will be saved (the elect) and who will be damned.[2] Most affirm compatibilism, by which is meant all human actions are determined by God and yet humans are free and responsible for their actions. With respect to salvation, in a compatibilist framework, God changes the will of the individual by means of irresistible grace, such that having been regenerated, one genuinely and freely desires to trust Christ. According to compatibilism, the individual does not have the ability to choose any differently. Compatibilism is heavily dependent on Jonathan Edwards's concept that we always act according to our greatest desire.[3]

We do not believe that compatibilism comports with genuine freedom. The reason should be obvious. In this construct, God imposes regeneration, and the individual is "free" to exercise faith but he is not free to choose any differently. By any normal understanding of freedom, this is not freedom. In order to have freedom, there must be the opportunity for a genuine choice between at least two options, and there must be no coercion made with respect to the choice. Acts committed under compulsion are not truly free acts. Compatibilists maintain that their version of free choice is not "imposition" or "compulsion." We maintain that in essence, given the description of how one chooses to have faith in a compatibilist framework, such choices are not, in fact, genuinely free. Furthermore, Scripture (Rom 7) and human experience illustrate that we do not always act according to our desires. In fact, sometimes we act against our desires. This question of free will is a difficult issue in theology. The first proposition in the denial should be understood to mean that we deny compatibilism and affirm genuine (libertarian) freedom.[4] This is with the understanding that there is no such thing as absolute freedom, and that the freedom we do possess in no way conflicts with or ever overrides the sovereignty of God.

The second proposition in the denial states: "We deny that God imposes or withholds this atonement without respect to an act of the person's free will." This denial must be understood in light of the meaning of the

---

1. Westminster Confession, III, 1.

2. Westminster Confession, III, 3.

3. For a description of compatibilism from a Southern Baptist theologian, see Ware, *God's Greater Glory*.

4. On the problems with theological compatibilism, see Walls, "No Classical Theist."

first statement of denial and its explanation. While compatibilists argue that no one is saved apart from an exercise of their free will, we are simply saying that irresistible grace vitiates free will for reasons stated above. In the Calvinist system, the elect are regenerated by an act of God which it is impossible for them to resist or decline. It seems difficult to avoid the conclusion that God is indeed "imposing" salvation. However divine sovereignty and human responsibility interact, we must affirm both, for Scripture affirms both, and we must not go against Scripture nor should we go beyond Scripture.

The third proposition in the denial states: "We deny that Christ died only for the sins of those who will be saved." This is our denial of limited atonement. This third proposition addresses the question of the extent of the atonement. This is a far more intricate subject than most realize. I shall only be able to address the issue in summary fashion.[5]

When it comes to the atonement, it is crucial to keep three major concepts in mind: 1) intent, 2) extent, and 3) application. The "intent" of the atonement answers the question: "What was God's *purpose* in providing the atonement?" The "extent" of the atonement answers the question: "For whose sins did Christ die?" The "application" of the atonement answers the question: "When and to whom is the atonement applied?" Though these questions are interrelated, my comments below will be focused primarily on the question of "extent."

With respect to the question of the extent of the atonement, there are only two answers: 1) limited atonement—Christ died for the sins of the elect alone; 2) universal atonement—Christ died for the sins of all people. Calvinists who reject limited atonement believe Christ died equally for all with respect to extent, but has an unequal intent or will to save all through his death (their view of election makes this so along with their notion of God's two wills: revealed and decretal). But it is important to note that they do believe that Christ actually satisfied for the sins of all people. Most Baptists who are not Calvinists believe that Christ died equally for the sins of all people with equal intent to save all who believe. Thus, we agree with four-point Calvinists on the question of "extent," but not on the question of "intent." Five-point Calvinists believe that the "intent" and "extent" of the

---

5. For a more detailed presentation of the issues discussed in this response, consult Allen, "The Atonement," in *Whosoever Will*, along with chapters authored by Lemke on "Irresistible Grace" and Evans on "Reflections" in the same work.

atonement are identical: Christ died only for the sins of those he intends (wills) to save. These are important distinctions.

Historically, the first person to advocate limited atonement was Gottschalk of Orbais in the ninth century, and he was condemned by three French Councils.[6] Within the broad spectrum of the Reformation, none of the first generation reformers on the continent or in England affirmed limited atonement, including Calvin. In the generations to follow, many well-known Calvinists rejected limited atonement and argued against it explicitly or implicitly in their writings: Davenant (signer of Dort), Amyraut, Baxter, Bunyan, Preston, Howe, and Charnock, to name only a few. Also added to this list would be Jonathan Edwards, David Brainerd, Charles Hodge, Dabney, Shedd, and J. C. Ryle. Many others could be named, including Andrew Fuller who revised his famous work *The Gospel Worthy of All Acceptation*, where he totally rewrote his section on the extent of the atonement after coming to the conclusion that limited atonement was biblically incorrect.[7]

The key issue in the debate over the extent of the atonement has to do with the "sufficiency" of Christ's death. All Calvinists will affirm this sufficiency as "infinite" to save any and all. But, and this is crucial, what those who hold to limited atonement mean by this is that Christ's death *could have* paid for the sins of the whole world had God intended for it to do so, but he did not intend such and hence the death of Christ is limited to the sins of the elect. We believe, along with all Calvinists who reject limited atonement, that Christ's death is actually sufficient for the sins of all because it actually paid for the sins of all. This is called "infinite" or "universal" sufficiency.

Oftentimes one hears the famous statement, originally coined by Peter Lombard in the Middle Ages, the death of Christ was "sufficient for all but efficient only for the elect." This statement originally meant that Christ died for the sins of all, but the benefits of his atonement are only applied to those who believe (the elect). This is the biblical position. When you hear a Calvinist use this statement, you must ask "what does 'sufficient' mean?" That is the key question! The third proposition in the denial is meant to affirm

---

6. Thomas, *Extent of the Atonement*, 5.

7. See my discussion in Allen, "Preaching." See also Fuller, *Gospel Worthy*, which was first published in 1785. A second edition with his revisions was published in 1801. The second edition appears in *Fuller's Works*, 2:328–416. Consult also Morden, *Offering Christ to the World*, 69–76. Morden carefully demonstrates Fuller's shift on the subject of limited atonement.

an infinite, genuine, universal sufficiency in the death of Christ in that he died for the sins of all people.

But enough history. What does the Bible say? There are two kinds of texts in the New Testament that play a key role in the question of the extent of the atonement. There are those texts which use words like "all" and "world" with reference to the death of Christ. Then there are those texts which speak of Christ dying for his "sheep" or for the "church." Those who affirm limited atonement rightly understand these latter texts to be limited with reference to extent. This would not be surprising when the biblical speaker or author was specifically addressing those in the church. However, Calvinists then interpret the universal texts in a limited fashion, suggesting that in places like John 1:29, John 3:16 and 1 Tim 2:4–6, to mention three, "all" and "world" should be interpreted to mean "all without distinction," not "all without exception." Thus, the argument goes, "all" or "world" in these texts refers to: 1) all kinds of people; 2) Jews and Gentiles as a group; or 3) the elect only.

This is a linguistic/exegetical issue. Sometimes the Bible uses the words "all" and "world" in a sense that does not mean "all without exception." This point is not in dispute. The problem lies in the invalid hermeneutical/exegetical legerdemain that transmutes the words "all" or "world" into something less than all humanity in the New Testament passages where it is used in direct and indirect reference to the extent of the atonement. Passages like John 1:29, John 3:16, and 1 Tim 2:4–6 simply cannot be shackled with the limiting lexical chains which restrict the meaning of "world" and "all" to something less than all humanity. This is a huge linguistic mistake. D. A. Carson rightly pointed out, as have many Calvinists, that "world" in Scripture never means "the elect." Context usually makes it clear whether "all" or "world" means "all without exception" or "all without distinction." These three texts are clear, not to mention a dozen other New Testament texts. It is simply not exegetically possible to interpret "all" and "world" in the three texts listed above, and several others, in a limited fashion. I fear some of those who do are operating out of a pre-conceived theology which they bring to the text.

Calvinists often appeal to Paul's preaching in Acts to support the contention that the apostles never used such language as "Christ died for your sins." They conclude from this lacuna that Paul never employed such a phrase in evangelistic preaching or witnessing. But is such a conclusion valid? First, this is an argument from silence. It does not conclusively prove

Paul, Peter, or anyone else did not say it nor is it a valid argument that they did not believe it. Second, all of the sermons in Acts are condensations of the actual sermons given. Third, with respect to Peter's sermon in Acts 2, how else could he tell his hearers to repent and be baptized in the name of Jesus Christ for the forgiveness of their sins (Acts 2:38) if he did not somehow connect the death of Christ on the cross as accomplishing the means for their forgiveness and salvation? Are we to think that Peter's hearers did not understand that what Peter was saying in essence was that since Christ died for their sins, the door is opened for them to repent and believe? Furthermore, if Peter believed in limited atonement, how could he say, "God, having raised up his servant, sent him to you first, to bless you by turning every [*hekastos* in Greek, "each one, every one," BDAG, 298] one of you from your wickedness" (Acts 3:26)?[8] For any of the non-elect present in his audience, there was no atonement for them, so it would be impossible for them to be saved, even if they wanted to. It would also be disingenuous on Peter's part to give anyone such false hope.

There is direct, overt, evidence that Paul in his preaching did indeed tell unsaved people that Christ died for their sins and furthermore it was his consistent practice to do so. Such evidence comes from 1 Cor 15:3: "For I delivered to you as of first importance what I also received: that Christ died for our sins in accordance with the Scriptures . . . ." Here Paul is reminding the Corinthians of the message he preached to them when he first came to Corinth (Acts 18:1–18). He clearly affirms the content of the gospel he preached in Corinth included the fact that "Christ died for our sins." Notice carefully Paul is saying this is what he preached pre-conversion, not post conversion. Thus, the "our" in his statement cannot be taken to refer to all the elect or merely the believing elect, which is what the high-Calvinist is forced to argue. The entire pericope of 1 Cor 15:3–11 should be kept in mind. Notice how Paul comes back around to what he had said in verse 3 when he gets to verse 11: "Whether then it was I or they, so we preach and so you believed." The customary present tense in Greek used by Paul when he says "so we preach" along with the aorist tense in Greek for "believed" makes it clear Paul refers to a past point in time when they believed what it was his custom to preach. What did Paul preach to them in his evangelistic efforts to win all of the unsaved to Christ? He preached the gospel, which included "Christ died for our sins." And so they believed.

---

8. All Bible quotations in this chapter are from the English Standard Version.

Commentary on Article 3: The Atonement of Christ

The assertion that Paul did not preach a universal atonement is false based on 1 Cor 15:3–11. What do we mean when we preach to the unsaved, "Christ died for your sins"? Does it not intend to convey that God desires to save all and that God is prepared to save any and all since Christ's death is actually sufficient to save them? One wonders if a reluctance to say "Christ died for you" implicitly expresses a reluctance to tell unsaved people that God is willing to save them all and is prepared to do so as well if they will repent and believe.

Turning to theological issues, the key argument used by Calvinists for limited atonement is the double payment argument.[9] In essence, it argues that justice does not allow the same sin to be punished twice. There are at least four strong arguments against this: 1) it is never found in Scripture; 2) it confuses a commercial understanding of sin as debt with a penal satisfaction for sin (the latter is the biblical view); 3) even the elect are still under the wrath of God until they believe (Eph 2:1–3); and 4) it negates the principle of grace in the application of the atonement since nobody is owed the application.

The other theological argument used to support limited atonement is the "Triple Choice Argument." It is built on the double payment argument. Either Christ died for all the sins of all men, or all the sins of some men, or some of the sins of all men. If Christ died for the sins of all, then why are not all saved? The argument sounds good logically, but it is flawed. Scripture never says a person goes to hell because no atonement was provided for him. People are said in Scripture to perish because they do not believe. Even though Christ died for all, he does not apply salvation to all. Faith in Christ is the condition for salvation. Finally, the argument quantifies the imputation of sin to Christ, as if there is a ratio between all the sins of those Christ represents and the sufferings of Christ, an unnecessary move given the extrinsic sufficiency of Christ's death for the sins of the world.

Let's talk logic for a moment. Some read verses that say Christ died for his "sheep," "church," or "friends" and draw the conclusion that since these groups are limited, so the atonement must be limited. Not so fast! This line of argument is logically flawed because it invokes the "negative inference fallacy," which says the proof of a proposition does not disprove its converse. When Paul says Christ "gave himself for me" in Gal 2:20, we cannot infer that Christ died only for Paul. This is the logical mistake made

---

9. See Owen, *The Death of Death*, 296.

by all High Calvinists on this point. There is no statement in Scripture that says Jesus died only for the sins of the elect.

Some argue that if Jesus died for the sins of all people, then all people will be saved. This is a false conclusion for several reasons. First, the Scripture is clear that all will not be saved. Second, it confuses the extent of the atonement with the application of the atonement. No one is saved by the death of Christ on the cross *until they believe in Christ*. This point was made by Shedd, a Calvinist with impeccable credentials.[10] As stated above, Eph 2:1–3 makes clear that even the elect are under the wrath of God, "having no hope" (v. 12) until they believe. Third, as 2 Cor 5:18–21 makes clear, reconciliation has an objective and subjective aspect to it. The death of Christ objectively reconciles the world to God in the sense that his justice is satisfied, but the subjective side of reconciliation does not occur until the atonement is applied when the individual repents of sin and puts faith in Christ. Along these lines, notice Col 1:19–20 which speaks of Christ's universal reconciliation of all things. This of course does not mean "universalism," but it does mean that Christ's death on the cross is a crucial aspect of his lordship over all people and things (Phil 2:9–11). Every knee shall bow.

Finally, we believe there are some negative practical implications for ministry entailed by limited atonement with respect to preaching and evangelism.

1) God's universal saving will. First Timothy 2:4 and 2 Peter 3:9 affirm God desires the salvation of all people, not just the elect. It is difficult to sustain this clear teaching of Scripture from the platform of limited atonement.

2) The "well-meant gospel offer." Second Corinthians 5:19–20 states: "that is, in Christ God was reconciling the world to himself, not counting their trespasses against them, and entrusting to us the message of reconciliation. Therefore, we are ambassadors for Christ, God making his appeal through us. We implore you on behalf of Christ, be reconciled to God." Here we have God himself offering salvation to all. But how can he do this according to limited atonement since there is no provision for the salvation of the non-elect in the death of Christ? Furthermore, how can God make this offer with integrity? It seems difficult to suppose he can. Without belief in the universal saving will of God and a universal extent in Christ's sin-bearing, there can be no

---

10. Shedd, *Dogmatic Theology*, 2:477.

well-meant offer of salvation from God to the non-elect who hear the gospel call. It would be like being invited to the master's banquet table where no chair, table setting, and food has actually been provided. This implicates and impugns the character of God in the making of the offer of salvation to the non-elect because in fact there is no salvation to offer: Christ did not die for their sins.

3) The "bold proclamation." The bold proclamation of the gospel is an old term used to refer to telling people individually or corporately that "Christ died for *your* sins." Notice how some Calvinists use code language here. Those who believe in limited atonement will say "Christ died for sinners," which is code for "elect sinners." This is confusing at best and disingenuous at worst. Calvinists point out that they preach to all because they do not know who the elect are. Certainly true, but this misses the point. Belief in limited atonement puts the preacher in the difficult position of preaching to all people *as if* Christ's death is applicable to them even though they believe all are not capable of salvation. This creates a situation where preachers operate on the basis of something they know to be untrue. In addition, how will such a preacher respond to the following question from an unbeliever: "When you say Christ died for sinners, does that mean Christ died for me?" There is no way to answer that question with a firm "yes" from the platform of limited atonement. On the other hand, preachers who affirm universal atonement can boldly proclaim Christ died for their sins.

4) The BFM. Limited atonement is contrary to the Southern Baptist Convention's statement of faith. Article 3 of the BFM 2000 declares, "The sacredness of human personality is evident in that God created man in His own image, and in that Christ died for man; therefore, every person of every race possesses full dignity and is worthy of respect and Christian love." The use of the word "man" in context clearly indicates "mankind" as a whole. The BFM does not limit the death of Christ to the elect but to the same group which is made in his image, man.

Let me be clear. We all agree that doctrine matters. Doctrine informs praxis. This is not an issue of whether someone is committed to preaching and evangelism. This is not a question of whether one is passionate about preaching and evangelism. I take it for granted that Calvinists as well as Traditionalists desire to obey the Great Commission. That being said, and for the reasons stated above, I am arguing the case that a belief in limited atonement necessarily entails a hindrance to preaching and evangelism. Paul said the content of the gospel he preached included the fact that "Christ died for our sins" (1 Cor 15:3). Limited atonement denies and distorts a crucial aspect of the gospel: that Christ died for the sins of the world.

Thus, for biblical, theological, logical and practical reasons, we deny that Christ died only for the sins of those who will be saved. We believe that Christ died for the sins of all to provide a genuine offer of salvation to all, and that his death not only makes salvation possible for all, but actually secures the salvation of all who believe.

BIBLIOGRAPHY

Allen, David L. "The Atonement: Limited or Universal?" In *Whosoever Will: A Biblical-Theological Critique of Five-Point Calvinism*, edited by David L. Allen and Steve W. Lemke, 61–107. Nashville: B&H Academic, 2010.

———. "Preaching for a Great Commission Resurgence." In *The Great Commission Resurgence: Fulfilling God's Mandate in Our Time*, edited by Chuck Lawless and Adam W. Greenway, 281–98. Nashville: B&H Academic, 2010.

Evans, Jeremy A. "Reflections on Determinism and Human Freedom." In *Whosoever Will: A Biblical-Theological Critique of Five-Point Calvinism*, edited by David L. Allen and Steve W. Lemke, 253–74. Nashville: B&H Academic, 2010.

Fuller, Andrew. *The Gospel Worthy of All Acceptation, or the Duty of Sinners to Believe in Jesus Christ, with Corrections and Editions; to which is Added an Appendix, on the Necessity of a Holy Disposition in Order to Believing in Christ*. In *Fuller's Works*, rev. ed., edited by Joseph Belcher, 2:328–416. Philadelphia: American Baptist Publication Society, 1845.

Lemke, Steve W. "A Biblical and Theological Critique of Irresistible Grace." In *Whosoever Will: A Biblical-Theological Critique of Five-Point Calvinism*, edited by David L. Allen and Steve W. Lemke, 109–62. Nashville: B&H Academic, 2010.

Morden, Peter. *Offering Christ to the World: Andrew Fuller (1754–1815) and the Revival of Eighteenth Century Particular Baptist Life*. Studies in Baptist History and Thought 8. Waynesboro, GA: Paternoster, 2003.

Owen, John. *The Death of Death in the Death of Christ*. In volume 10 of *The Works of John Owen*, edited by W. H. Goold. New York: Robert Carter and Brothers, 1852.

Shedd, W. G. T. *Dogmatic Theology*. Nashville: Thomas Nelson, 1980.

Thomas, G. M. *The Extent of the Atonement: A Dilemma for Reformed Theology from Calvin to the Consensus (1536–1635)*. Carlisle: Paternoster, 1997.

Walls, Jerry. "Why No Classical Theist, Let Alone Orthodox Christian, Should Ever Be a Compatibilist." *Philosophia Christi* 13.1 (2011) 75–104.

Ware, Bruce. *God's Greater Glory: The Exalted God of Scripture and the Christian Faith*. Wheaton: Crossway, 2004.

Article 4: The Grace of God

We affirm that grace is God's generous decision to provide salvation for any person by taking all of the initiative in providing atonement, in freely offering the gospel in the power of the Holy Spirit, and in uniting the believer to Christ through the Holy Spirit by faith.

We deny that grace negates the necessity of a free response of faith or that it cannot be resisted. We deny that the response of faith is in any way a meritorious work that earns salvation.

Ezra 9:8; Proverbs 3:34; Zechariah 12:10; Matthew 19:16–30, 23:37; Luke 10:1–12; Acts 15:11; 20:24; Romans 3:24, 27–28; 5:6, 8, 15–21; Galatians 1:6; 2:21; 5; Ephesians 2:8–10; Philippians 3:2–9; Colossians 2:13–17; Hebrews 4:16; 9:28; 1 John 4:19.

Commentary on
Article 4: The Grace of God

Brad Reynolds

THE AFFIRMATIONS

The following assumptions are held regarding the affirmations: First, most Southern Baptists would agree with the affirmations in Article 4. Second, some who agree with the affirmations think they do not go far enough. Instead, they would add to them. Third, many who would deny them would do so on the basis of the phrase "any person." Thus, the affirmations concerning the grace of God are a minimal statement. Some of the supporting biblical passages will be considered below.

> "But we believe that we are saved through the grace of the Lord Jesus, in the same way as they also are." (Acts 15:11)[1]

John Polhill states regarding this passage, "God's acceptance of the Gentiles has drawn a basic lesson for the Jews as well. There is only one way of salvation—'through the grace of our Lord Jesus.'"[2] One could never earn one's way into heaven. Our greatest works are filthy rags to a holy God. Amazing grace is the sole vehicle God uses to offer life to man.

---

1. All biblical quotations in this chapter are from the New American Standard Bible.
2. Polhill, *Acts*, 327.

Commentary on Article 4: The Grace of God

"... being justified as a gift by His grace through the redemption which is in Christ Jesus." (Rom 3:24)

This verse connects to the "all" in verse 23. James D. G. Dunn comments,

> *The gospel is that God sets to rights man's relationship with himself by an act of sheer generosity which depends on no payment man can make*, which is without reference to whether any individual in particular is inside the law/covenant or outside, and which applies to all human beings without exception. It is this humbling recognition—that he has no grounds for appeal either in covenant status or in particular "works of the law," that he has to depend *entirely* from start to finish on God's gracious power, that he can receive acquittal only as a gift—which lies at the heart of faith for Paul. . . . For at this stage *everything*, the whole argument, the gospel itself, depends on the most fundamental insight of all: that man's dependency on God for *all* good (cf. 2:7, 10) is total, and that the indispensable starting point for any good that man does is his acceptance of God's embrace and his continual reliance on God's enabling to accomplish that good.[3]

Dunn correctly remarks that man being made right with God is an act of grace which man cannot earn but only receive as a gift.

"But God demonstrates His own love toward us, in that while we were yet sinners, Christ died for us." (Rom 5:8)

The amazing grace of God is inextricably linked to the amazing love of God. While we were yet sinners Christ took our place. He took on himself the judgment of God. He took on himself our sins. As our substitute, he paid our debt. Robert Mounce explains, "God did not wait until we had performed well enough to merit his love (which, of course, no one ever could) before he acted in love on our behalf. Christ died for us while we were still alienated from him and cared nothing for his attention or affection."[4] God does not demonstrate his love by prohibiting all evil from impacting our lives. He demonstrates his love by paying for the sin in our lives. The proof of God's amazing love is his Son. It is significant that God refers to himself as love (1 John 4:8). He does not refer to himself as hate. To claim God hates certain individuals without, in the same breath, claim-

---

3. Dunn, *Romans*, 179. Emphasis in the original.
4. Mounce, *Romans*, 136–37.

ing God loves his enemies and "God so loved the world" is to disregard a clear biblical teaching.[5] We should neither sacrifice the benevolence of God on the altar of theological systems nor avoid certain texts which assist in clarifying other biblical texts.

The affirmation above states that "grace is God's generous decision to provide salvation . . . ." Christ's birth, life, death, and resurrection are expressions of God's *grace*. The offer of the gospel is *grace*. The work of the Holy Spirit is *grace*. The salvation of any person is *grace*. All of these are examples of God's *grace*. The conviction of the Holy Spirit is a gracious act of God. The power of the gospel unto salvation (Rom 1:16) is a gracious act of God. Grace! Grace! Grace! God is the author and finisher of salvation. He provides *grace*.

How does God convict the sinner? By his Holy Spirit through the word of God. Where is the power of God for salvation? The power of God for salvation is found in the gospel, or the message of the cross (1 Cor 1:18). We share the good news of Jesus Christ because the gospel is the power of God for salvation for everyone who believes (Rom 1:16). Anabaptist leader Balthasar Hubmaier stated, "God by means of His sent Word gives power to all people to become His children."[6]

THE DENIALS

Since the points of disagreement center mostly around the denials in Article 4, more attention will be devoted to the denials. The first sentence denies the concept of irresistible grace. The second sentence denies the concept that faith is equivalent to works. Advocates of the TS reject the idea that when an individual, by his own free will, believes in Christ he has earned his way into heaven. The two sentences in the denials are connected and will be treated as such. This section will attempt to support the denials by addressing many of the biblical texts to which Article 4 appeals.

---

5. Romans 9:13, quoting Mal 1:2–3, quotes the Lord, "Jacob I loved, but Esau I hated." It is not necessary to insist that God made a decision prior to Esau's actions that he hated Esau any more than it is necessary to insist that a disciple of Jesus must hate one's family (Luke 14:26). In both instances, there are better ways to understand the teaching in context.

6. Hubmaier, *Freedom*, 450.

Commentary on Article 4: The Grace of God

> "Where then is boasting? It is excluded. By what kind of law? Of works? No, but by a law of faith. For we maintain that a man is justified by faith apart from works of the Law." (Rom 3:27-28)

The New Testament term for "faith" means "to rely on," "to trust," or "to believe."[7] To trust or not to trust seems to be one's personal decision. In this passage Paul juxtaposed faith and works. In other words, faith is never to be equated with works. To claim faith is a meritorious work is to make a claim contrary to the Scriptures. What is disputed is the origin of the faith in question. Is the faith owned by God and given to man as a gift (in the sense that God's grace is given to man as a gift) or is it an individual's faith? The next passage more clearly demonstrates the disagreement.

> "For by grace you have been saved through faith; and that not of yourselves, *it is* the gift of God; not as a result of works, so that no one may boast. For we are His workmanship, created in Christ Jesus for good works, which God prepared beforehand so that we would walk in them." (Eph 2:8-10)

It has been argued that the antecedent of *touto* ("that") in "that not of yourselves" is grace and faith. The problem is the text itself seems to deny such an interpretation. The Greek term for "that" is in the singular. This truth indicates that its antecedent is something (singular) and not some things (plural). Had God intended it to refer to both grace and faith, the plural feminine *tauta* ("these") was available for Paul's use. Paul could have easily stated "these are the gifts of God." But Paul did not use the plural. For these reasons, the forced application of the singular neuter pronoun "that" to refer to two feminine nouns would be inappropriate.

Thus, "that" functions as the antecedent to grace or to faith or to salvation. If one had to choose among the three, context points to salvation. If so, then this verse fails to provide biblical support for the idea that faith is a gift from God.

But an objection might be raised. "That" was not referring to grace or salvation but to faith. Although the neuter singular form of "that" *could* allow this interpretation, the feminine form would be clearer since faith is a feminine noun. Had God intended for "that" to refer to faith, the feminine singular form of "that" was available for use. But the literary context seems to prevent such an interpretation. Paul addresses salvation in verses 5-7 and verses 9-10. The rest of Paul's writings make it clear he is not worried about

---

7. Bultmann, "*pisteuō*," 203.

a misunderstanding that *faith* is by works but that *salvation* is by works. The Bible teaches that grace is God's grace given to man; it is never man's grace. And salvation is most certainly God's gift. But Scripture also seems to teach that faith or trust in God must be exercised by man, not passively received. Kenneth Keathley explains, "Faith is an action but not a work. Works are a subset of actions, so all works are actions. But the converse is not necessarily so; not all actions are works, and faith is an example of this. Exercising faith is something we do, but it is not a meritorious work."[8]

Paul affirms the faith of the believers in Ephesus (man's faith) a few verses earlier (1:13, 15). In the New Testament, faith is attributed to individuals rather than God thirty-nine times (Matt 9:2, 22, 29; 15:28; Mark 2:5; 5:34; 10:52; Luke 5:20; 7:50; 8:48; 17:19; 18:42; 22:32; Rom 1:8; 1 Cor 2:5; 15:14, 17; 2 Cor 1:24; 10:15; Eph 1:15; Phil 2:17; Col 1:4; 1 Thess 1:8; 3:2, 5, 6, 7, 10; 2 Thess 1:3; Phlm 6; Heb 10:23; 12:2; Jas 1:3; 2:18; 1 Pet 1:7, 9, 21; 2 Pet 1:5; 1 John 5:4). It is unwise to take a concept and force an interpretation upon a text because of a theological grid when such a concept is not found in the rest of Scripture. Calvin's comments on Eph 2 support the view of Article 4 that faith is not the gift Paul is referencing in this particular passage:

> (H)e arrives at this general conclusion, that they had obtained salvation by faith alone. First, he asserts, that the salvation of the Ephesians was entirely the work, the gracious work of God. But then they had obtained this grace by faith. On one side, we must look at God; and on the other, at man. God declares, that he owes us nothing; so that salvation is not a reward or recompense, but unmixed grace. The next question is, in what ways do men receive that salvation which is offered to them by the hand of God? The answer is, *by faith*; and hence he concludes that nothing connected with it is our own. If, on the part of God, it is grace alone, and if we bring nothing but faith, which strips us of all condemnation, it follows that salvation does not come from us. . . . Many persons restrict the word *gift* to faith alone. But Paul is only repeating in other words the former sentiment. His meaning is, not that faith is the gift of God, but that salvation is given to us by God, or, that we obtain it by the gift of God.[9]

Many Calvinistic Southern Baptists have already realized the implications of irresistible grace if faith is not considered a gift from God. Whether this

---

8. Keathley, "The Work of God," 578.
9. Calvin, *Commentaries*, 21:227–29. Italics in the original.

Commentary on Article 4: The Grace of God

was the impetus for many errant readings of this text is not known. What is known is that even John Calvin did not allow a theological conviction to alter the plain reading of the biblical text. Having closed the door on the concept of faith being a gift from God in this often-cited passage, three other passages will be considered which seem to teach that faith is a gift of God.

> "Jesus answered and said to them, 'This is the work of God, that you believe in Him whom He has sent.'" (John 6:29)

> "For to you it has been granted for Christ's sake, not only to believe in Him, but also to suffer for His sake." (Phil 1:29)

> "... who through Him are believers in God, who raised Him from the dead and gave Him glory, so that your faith and hope are in God." (1 Pet 1:21)

Is faith a gift from God or not? The English words "faith" and "believe" are translated in the New Testament from the same Greek word, *pistis*. When translated as a noun, it is "faith." When translated as a verb, it is "to believe." It is noteworthy that no Scripture attributes "faith" to God.[10] But three verses speak of one's believing as being from God. John 6:29 says God's work is that we believe in Jesus. Philippians 1:29 says God granted us to believe in Jesus. First Peter 1:21 states it is through Jesus we act in belief in God.

Even so, there are many more passages where one's "believing" is not attributed to God but is attributed to a person (Matt 21:32; 27:42; Mark 9:24, 42; John 3:12; Acts 15:11; 27:25; Rom 3:3, 22; 10:9, 14; 1 Cor 10:27; 1 Thess 4:14; 1 Tim 1:16; 4:10; esp. John 1:12; 1 Cor 1:21; 2 Tim 2:13). Of special note is 1 Cor 1:21, "For since in the wisdom of God the world through its wisdom did not *come to* know God, God was well-pleased through the foolishness of the message preached to save those who believe." In addition to these passages, individuals asked Jesus on two occasions to increase their faith (Luke 17:5; Mark 9:24).

How should faith and/or believing be understood? It is noteworthy that when God's word speaks of one's faith (noun), it is never attributed to God. But in three verses which speak of man believing (verb) in God we learn: 1) God grants them to believe, 2) it is through God they believe, and 3) it is his work. Is it the case that faith originates with man but believing

---

10. Jesus refers in Rev 2:13 to "my faith" but this is not in reference to saving trust. If it were, then it would imply that man could deny the saving faith of Jesus.

originates with God? No. The rest of the "believing" passages indicate that believing is also of man. We would be wise to tread lightly at this point. It seems that God created people with the ability to trust. That ability was not lost in the fall. But that ability was so twisted by the fall that we are now unable to trust in God without the grace of God. He gives this grace to all men but this grace can be resisted. Through him and his work we are granted to believe as we are drawn by the Holy Spirit and as we choose to repent and believe in him. In these passages we see an interplay between God's sovereignty and man's responsibility, neither of which can be denied. It would be imprudent to affirm any theological system which speculates beyond the clear teaching of Scripture.

> "Jerusalem, Jerusalem, who kills the prophets and stones those who are sent to her! How often I wanted to gather your children together, the way a hen gathers her chicks under her wings, and you were unwilling." (Matt 23:37)

Christ wept over Jerusalem and desired to gather them to himself, but they were unwilling. This text provides good reason to resist the concept of irresistible grace. God desired to bring man to himself, but man resisted. Note the words of Craig Blomberg, "Here Jesus wishes he could gather all the recalcitrant 'children' of Israel, to love, protect, and nurture them like a mother hen does with her baby chickens. Similar imagery recurs frequently in Jewish literature (e.g., Deut 32:4; Ps 36:7; Ruth 2:12; Isa 31:5). But God never imposes His love by overriding human will."[11]

> "You men who are stiff-necked and uncircumcised in heart and ears are always resisting the Holy Spirit; you are doing just as your fathers did." (Acts 7:51)

This is perhaps the clearest text in all of Scripture that God's grace is resistible. Nowhere does the Bible state that the Holy Spirit is irresistible. It was previously established that the conviction of the Holy Spirit is an expression of his grace. This text refers to people resisting the Holy Spirit. People can resist the conviction of the Holy Spirit drawing them to salvation. This text seems to rule out the possibility that God's grace is irresistible.

Were someone to ask me, "Don't you know your faith is a grace gift from God?" I hope I would respond, "Let's not limit God's grace only to his power given that people might believe. God's grace includes the giving of his only Son, the giving of the Holy Spirit, and the giving of the gospel to all

---

11. Blomberg, *Matthew*, 350.

the world that anyone may be saved—'Oh, the depth of the riches both of the wisdom and knowledge of God! How unsearchable are His judgments and unfathomable His ways!'" May we never limit the power or the scope of the grace of God.

CONFESSIONAL VOICES OF "TRADITIONAL" SOUTHERN BAPTISTS

Denying irresistible grace and affirming man's free will is consistent with the "Traditional" Southern Baptist understanding of the doctrine of salvation. Consider these quotations from the men who knew the theological contours of the Baptist Faith and Message perhaps as well as anyone, since each one served as the chairperson for his respective BFM committee in 1925, 1963, and 2000. Here, we appeal to E. Y. Mullins, Herschel Hobbs, and Adrian Rogers.

> "In his free act of accepting Christ and his salvation man is self-determined. He would not have made the choice if left to himself without the aid of God's grace. But when he chooses, it is his own free act."—E. Y. Mullins[12]

> "However, the Bible also teaches the free will of man as a person made in God's image. To violate man's free will would make him less than a person, only a puppet dangled on the string of fate. The Bible never teaches that. Man is free to choose, but is responsible to God for his choices. Otherwise God Himself is responsible for man's sin, which is unthinkable! The free will of man is seen in Ephesians 1:13: 'After that ye believed' or 'believing.' Exercising faith is an act of the human will. To say that only those chosen by God can believe is to ignore the plain teachings of the New Testament. If this be true, then Jesus' commissions to evangelize the world and the many pleas for lost people to believe in Him for salvation are meaningless."—Herschel Hobbs[13]

> "There are some who talk about 'irresistible grace,' the idea that you cannot say no to God. But the Bible tells of many people who resisted God's love. People have the dubious privilege of saying no

---

12. Mullins, *Christian Religion*, 344.
13. Hobbs, "God's Sovereignty."

to God without damaging His eternal attributes one bit."—Adrian Rogers[14]

CONCLUSION

As we leave this consideration of irresistible grace, man's free will, and faith, it is important to note the implication involved in Calvinism if God invites individuals to salvation knowing he has decreed they are incapable of being saved. This would imply God, at best, is insincere. But, one may ask, where has God invited universally? Among other texts, consider Isa 55 and Matt 11:28–30.

I conclude this chapter with sincere reverence. I fear the reality that I could be errant here. Nevertheless, I state boldly that I believe God gave his word to reveal truths, and thus it is my opinion that when the corpus of Scripture is considered there is strong evidence to confirm both the affirmations and denials of Article 4.

The sovereignty of God and the free will of man is an arena one should not enter with self-confidence. But I bristle at the suggestion that I have minimized or negated the sovereignty of God by affirming what God's word appears to teach, namely, that man has free will. It is no denial of God's sovereignty to say man has free will if God sovereignly gave man free will. Further, I would argue I have exalted God by affirming his ways are not easily understood. I find myself reflecting on what God said after he issued a universal invitation: "For as the heavens are higher than the earth so are My ways higher than your ways and My thoughts than your thoughts" (Isa 55:9).

I do not grasp all the intricacies involved in God's sovereignty and man's free will. No one does. Even now I wonder if I chose to write this chapter or if God ordained it (Prov 20:24). Even so, I affirm both rather than deny either one in order to grasp their relationship or affirm a theological system. I cringe when theological systems speculate beyond Scripture. Perhaps this is why so many people are saying, I am not an Arminian, and I am not a Calvinist; if you have to call me something, call me a Baptist. This does not mean that Arminians and Calvinists cannot claim to be Baptists. With no desire to be offensive, Baptists have always held tightly to the Bible

---

14. Rogers, *Passion of Christ*, 76.

and when we feel that any theological system speculates beyond Holy Writ we say: Keep your system; just give me the Bible, because I'm a Baptist.

BIBLIOGRAPHY

Blomberg, Craig. *Matthew*. New American Commentary 22. Nashville: Broadman and Holman, 1992.

Bultmann, Rudolph. "*pisteuō*." In *Theological Dictionary of the New Testament*, edited by Gerhard Kittel and Gerhard Friedrich. Translated by Geoffrey W. Bromiley, 6:174–228. Grand Rapids: Eerdmans, 1968.

Calvin, John. *Calvin's Commentaries*, vol. XXI. Translated by William Pringle. Grand Rapids: Baker, 1979.

Dunn, James D. G. *Romans 1–8*. Word Biblical Commentary 38A. Dallas: Word, 1988.

Hobbs, Herschel. "God's Sovereignty and Man's Free Will." *Oklahoma Baptist Messenger* (June 1, 1995).

Hubmaier, Balthasar. *Freedom of the Will, II*. In *Balthasar Hubmaier*. Translated and edited by H. Wayne Pipkin and John H Yoder. Scottdale, PA: Herald, 1989.

Keathley, Kenneth. "The Work of God: Salvation." In *A Theology for the Church*, rev. ed., edited by Daniel L. Akin, 543–600. Nashville: B&H Academic, 2014.

Mounce, Robert. *Romans*. New American Commentary 27. Nashville: Broadman and Holman, 1995.

Mullins, E. Y. *The Christian Religion in its Doctrinal Expression*. Valley Forge: Judson, 1917.

Polhill, John. *Acts*. New American Commentary 26. Nashville: Broadman and Holman, 2001.

Rogers, Adrian. *The Passion of Christ and the Purpose of Life*. Wheaton: Crossway, 2005.

Article 5: The Regeneration of the Sinner

We affirm that any person who responds to the gospel with repentance and faith is born again through the power of the Holy Spirit. He is a new creation in Christ and enters, at the moment he believes, into eternal life.

We deny that any person is regenerated prior to or apart from hearing and responding to the gospel.

Luke 15:24; John 3:3; 7:37–39; 10:10; 16:7–14; Acts 2:37–39; Romans 6:4–11; 10:14; 1 Corinthians 15:22; 2 Corinthians 5:17; Galatians 2:20; 6:15; Colossians 2:13.

Commentary on
Article 5: The Regeneration of the Sinner

Ronnie W. Rogers[1]

This chapter summarizes the "Traditional" Southern Baptist view of the relationship of faith and regeneration—being born again. Most Calvinists teach that regeneration precedes faith, which will result in a free but determined act of faith.[2] Non-Calvinists believe that faith precedes regeneration or that regeneration occurs, as stated in the Traditional Statement (TS), "at the moment he believes."[3] I will also point out how some of the harsh realities of Calvinism are contrary to the clear teachings of Scripture. I call these

---

1. This chapter draws from "Faith and Regeneration," published previously in my book *Reflections*, 76–83.

2. According to Calvinism, regeneration is something that God does monergistically against the sinful will of man. Then, after God has changed the nature of the elect person through this inviolable selective regeneration, man, whose nature has been so changed, will choose to exercise faith in Christ unto salvation. Calvinists regard the act of faith to be free, but the free act is determined by the new nature given by God. Thus, in Calvinism's soteriology, the idea of otherwise choice is non-existent.

3. I would label myself an *Extensivist*, which is one who believes that man was created in the image of God with libertarian free will (*otherwise choice*) and that God's salvation plan is comprehensive, involving an all-inclusive unconditional offer of salvation and eternal security of the believer; reception of which is conditioned upon *grace-enabled* faith rather than a narrow plan involving a limited *actually meaningful* offer of salvation restricted to the unconditionally elected, or any plan that, in any way, conditions salvation upon *merely* a humanly generated faith from fallen man.

disquieting realities. Although they are unsettling, one must accept them if he is going to be a consistent Calvinist.

The Scripture affirms that faith precedes and is the prerequisite for regeneration—being born again (John 1:12–13; 3:3, 15–16, 36; 5:24; 6:40; 7:37–39; 12:36; 16:7–14; 20:31; 1 Pet 1:23; 1 John 5:1, 4). These and other Scriptures show that spiritual life follows the sinner placing his faith in Jesus Christ. The Apostle John gave as his reason for writing his Gospel "so that you may believe that Jesus is the Christ, the Son of God; and that believing you may have life in His name" (John 20:31b).[4] It seems clear that "you" includes anyone who reads or hears John's Gospel. If salvation is monergistic and man is totally passive, then why would God inspire John to write his Gospel in order for people to read, believe, and be saved? According to Calvinism, God knows the non-elect cannot read and believe and the elect cannot believe prior to regeneration.

Calvinists posit that no one can read John's writings (or any Scripture) and believe unto salvation because salvation is monergistic—accomplished by God alone. According to Calvinism, a person must be regenerated first and then, and only then, can he read and believe; furthermore, not only *can* he then believe, he *must* believe. Consequently, this is to turn what John clearly says about reading and believing into an esoteric code for the Calvinist doctrine of regeneration prior to faith for only a select few rather than the clear teaching that God had John write this Gospel so that all people, by the grace of God, could see who Jesus really is and what he did for them, believe, and be saved.[5] Calvinism's belief that grace is only for a select few is a disquieting reality.

Jesus repeatedly called on people to believe so they would not die in their sins. For example, "Therefore I said to you that you will die in your sins; for unless you believe that I am *He*, you will die in your sins" (John 8:24, italics in the original). The inference is that Jesus truly desires that they believe and that they can believe and not die in their sins. This is contrary

---

4. All Bible quotations in this chapter are from the New American Standard Bible.

5. Jeremy A. Evans, seeking to soften the Calvinist order of things, writes, "This relationship is intended to be understood logically, not temporally. Temporally, the cause and effect relationship occurs simultaneously; logically, regeneration occurs before faith." See Evans, "Reflections," 259. Such distinctions fail to erase the temporal fact that according to Calvinism, regeneration (sometimes referred to as renovation or quickening) occasions faith rather than faith occasioning regeneration; to wit, regeneration is a *prerequisite in time* for the exercising of faith, and such faith is in fact temporally subsequent to regeneration. This is in absolute contrast to Scripture (John 1:12–13; 12:36) and Extensivism.

to the Calvinist secret.[6] The Calvinist secret is that while it is true that if one does not believe he will die in his sins, the other truth is that Jesus is telling them to do what he knows they cannot do unless they are one of the elect.[7] Therefore, Calvinism transmogrifies Christ's general, merciful plea into an esoteric, academic recitation. This is a disquieting reality indeed.

Calvinists frequently seek to analogize unconditional election with the reality that even in non-Calvinism not everyone gets the *same* opportunity to believe the gospel. However, these two realities are absolutely disanalogous. The non-Calvinist position is not that everyone receives the *same* opportunities because that is an impossibility, but that the Scripture portrays God's love providing everyone *an* opportunity to believe. Therefore, according to Calvinism, God's love withholds what he could have granted, whereas according to non-Calvinism, God's love provides everyone *an* opportunity, which is possible rather than the impossibility that everyone receives the *same* opportunity. Hence, it is urgent to recognize that today is the day of salvation (Luke 12:14–21; Acts 13:38–41; 17:30–31; Heb 13:7–19; Rev 22:20).[8]

---

6. Lewis Sperry Chafer is a Calvinist who emphasizes that unconditional election and selective regeneration (i.e. the non-elect really cannot be saved even though they hear "whosoever will may come") are not things to talk about with the unsaved. He writes in *Systematic Theology*, 3:172, "The entire theme concerns those only who are regenerated and should never be presented to, or even discussed in the presence of, the unsaved."

7. Jesus clearly warned them to repent, with every indication that they should and could. Jesus issued warnings repeatedly (Matt 4:17; 11:20–21; Luke 5:32; 15:7; 24:47) as did the apostles (Acts 2:38; 3:19; 8:22; 17:30; 20:21; 26:20). If Jesus knew some of them could not repent because they were not the elect, then his warnings seem disingenuous and misleading. Some Calvinists will say that Jesus was making a "good faith offer" (if there is such an idea) because as a man, he did not know who the elect were.

As an example of Jesus not knowing certain things in his humanity, they reference Jesus saying, "But of that day and hour no one knows, not even the angels of heaven, nor the Son, but the Father alone" (Matt 24:36). However, these are disanalogous. For the reference in Matthew to be relevant, it would have to include Jesus not knowing the date and then announcing a date for his return. There is a crucial difference between Jesus *not knowing* certain things due to his role as a servant and his *speaking forthrightly* things that are either misleading or not true—things that do not correspond fully to reality.

Jesus commanded them to repent because he was not willing that any would perish and that all would come to repentance (2 Pet 3:9), something that God has grace-enabled everyone who hears the truth to do.

8. It is impossible to offer the same opportunity for every person. Requiring that God do such is neither possible nor necessary to demonstrate God's love any more than to be offered a free gift requires everyone be offered the same number of times in exactly the same time frame and same way in order to have actually received the offer of a free gift. Also, when the Scriptures offered a chance and call for people to repent and believe,

The Scripture is replete, lucid, and compelling in teaching that faith precedes regeneration. Also, faith is *not* a gift given to some people in unconditional election or selective regeneration. Scripture is clear that God is working in order to give all men and women a *real* chance to trust him unto salvation (John 16:8–11). Salvation is offered as a free gift (Rom 3:24; 6:23) to all who are in need of forgiveness (Rom 3:23; 5:15, 18), and people are summoned to act upon the offer by accepting the gift by (grace-enabled) faith (John 1:12; Rom 3:22). As Norman Geisler states, "Never does the Bible say, 'Be saved in order to believe'; instead, repeatedly, it commands, 'Believe in order to be saved.'"[9]

Scripture affirms repeatedly that God supplies every man with the necessary grace in order for him to be able to exercise faith in Christ unto salvation and eternal life or to resist the genuine offer of salvation unto eternal damnation. The means of this grace enablement includes but is not limited to: conviction of the Holy Spirit (John 16:7–11), working of the Holy Spirit (Heb 6:1–6), and the power of the gospel (Rom 1:16). Additionally, Scripture affirms that man, because of these gracious provisions and workings of God, can choose to seek God, as did the Bereans, of whom it says because they studied the Scripture, "Therefore many of them believed" (Acts 17:12a). Moreover, it is clear from Scripture that no one can come to God without God drawing (John 6:44) and that God is drawing all men (John 12:32). The same Greek word for draw, *helkuō*, is used in both verses.[10] According to Lewis Sperry Chafer, "About 115 passages condition salvation on believing alone, and about 35 simply on faith."[11] Other grace enablements might include providential workings in and through other people, situations, and timing or circumstances that are a part of grace to provide the optimal opportunity for an individual to choose to follow Christ.[12]

Calvinists believe some are not actual opportunities to believe.

9. Geisler, *Systematic Theology*, 3:129.

10. This does not mean that all men will be saved. These verses only affirm that God draws all men to Christ and that all who come to Christ will have been drawn by God. Other biblical texts can be examined to establish the view that many of those people who are drawn by God to Christ will not repent and believe in him.

11. Chafer, *Systematic Theology*, 7:273–74.

12. These are grace enablements in at least three ways; first, they are provided by God's grace rather than deserved by mankind; second, the necessary components for *each and every* individual to have a *real* opportunity to believe unto salvation are provided and/or restored by God; third, they are provided by God without respect to whether

Commentary on Article 5: The Regeneration of the Sinner

Since the fall, man has been in such spiritual bondage that he cannot, nor will he have any desire to, come to God unless God offers "enabling grace." Enabling grace may be referred to at times as "calling," "conviction," "drawing," or "opening the heart" among other things, but all refer to God graciously granting sufficient grace for a person to hear and understand the good news, be able to choose to receive God's word of redemption, and by God-given grace exercise faith unto salvation or choose to remain in sin. A person can choose to do other than whatever he did in fact choose. There is nothing that a sinner can do to merit this *unconditional* enabling because it originates conceptually and manifests itself actually because of God's perfect love, mercy, compassion, and grace. Therefore, enabling grace exists and is granted because of what is in God rather than what is in man. Furthermore, this enabling through the work of the Holy Spirit (John 16:7–11) is coextensive with the preaching of the gospel and the work of the gospel in the heart of man (Acts 16:14; Rom 10:14; Heb 4:12).[13]

The Scripture teaches and demonstrates that the exercise of faith is a choice, meaning that one could do otherwise, and this is an inextricable part of man being made in the image of God. The fall so corrupted man that while man can still make many choices about many things or choose to act otherwise, he is now unlike Adam in that he is unable to exercise saving faith—choose God—on his own. However, God's enabling grace overcomes this inability. Consequently, the charge that rejecting Calvinism results in minimizing the damage of the fall, or that we are saying that man's free will is sufficient to choose to trust God on his own, are simply straw men. The question is not whether or not man is totally depraved, whether he needs God's grace to be able to come to God, or whether salvation is totally a work of God. Rather, it is this: Does the Scripture teach that God sovereignly chose to create man with the ability to exercise faith or not exercise faith, and does God restore that ability by means of grace

---

the individual will believe or reject, which response God knew in eternity past. The offer of the gospel is *unconditional,* but God sovereignly determined that the reception of the offer was conditioned upon grace enabled faith; thus, faith is the *means* to being regenerated, or saved, not the *reason* for being saved; finally, this truth of Scripture does not imply that God was held captive to the choice of man, but rather that God coextensively determined to create man and provide this genuine offer in eternity past; also, in order to fulfill this plan, God is not obligated to disseminate the gospel to people that he knows have rejected the light he has given them and will in fact reject the gospel that he enables the lost to believe or reject; although, he may still send the gospel to them.

13. See "Depravity of Man" in my book *Reflections,* 43–46.

enablements for everyone apart from unconditional election and selective regeneration in his salvation plan?

Calvinists refer to their beliefs as "the doctrines of grace," which is fine, but it actually does not tell us much. That is to say, the doctrines of any Biblicist are all "doctrines of grace." There simply are no other kinds in orthodoxy. It is similar to the Calvinist's continual reference to the sovereignty of God. It tells us nothing since all believers with any biblical fidelity and understanding of God believe in his sovereignty. Further, disavowal of the Calvinist's definition of the doctrines of grace and sovereignty is not a denial or undermining of the doctrines of grace and the sovereignty of God, but is simply a denial of Calvinism's definitions.

Non-Calvinists affirm that salvation is entirely a work of God because he has provided everything necessary by which sinners receive the salvation of the Lord. The offer of salvation is unconditional, whereas the experience of salvation by an individual is conditioned upon grace-enabled—not forced—repentance and faith (Luke 24:47; Acts 2:38). Many verses attest to the accuracy of this understanding of salvation. The call for people to repent and believe is seen in the book of Acts repeatedly, e.g. Acts 2:37–41; 3:19–26; 7:51; 8:6–14, 22–23, 36–37; 9:35, 42; 10:34–35, 43; 11:21; 13:8–13, 38–41, 46–47; 14:1; 15:19; 16:30–34; 17:2–4, 11–12, 17, 30–31; 18:4–8, 19, 27–28; 19:8–9, 18; 20:21; 22:18; 26:17–20; 28:23–24. The Epistles teach the same (Rom 5:1; Gal 3:26; Eph 2:8–9; Heb 11:6). In addition, God gave repentance as a grace gift (Acts 5:31; 11:18).

Accordingly, God works *substantively* through people. Regarding Paul's Damascus road experience, he said before King Agrippa that the Lord said to him,

> "But get up and stand on your feet; for this purpose I have appeared to you, to appoint you a minister and a witness not only to the things which you have seen, but also to the things in which I will appear to you; rescuing you from the Jewish people and from the Gentiles, to whom I am sending you, to open their eyes so that *they* may *turn* from darkness to light and from the dominion of Satan to God, *that* they may receive forgiveness of sins and an inheritance among those who have been sanctified *by faith in Me.*" (Acts 26:16–18, emphasis added; the word Jewish was italicized in the original)

By saying that God works through people and uses other things in bringing people to salvation, non-Calvinists do not mean the same thing

Commentary on Article 5: The Regeneration of the Sinner

as Calvinists who say that witnessing, praying, and tragedy are part of the process of bringing people to salvation. We mean that they are actually *substantive* and *integral* parts, while in Calvinism's soteriology nothing *actually substantively* matters except unconditional election. According to Calvinism, God unconditionally elected some to salvation, whom he monergistically brings to salvation through irresistible grace in selective regeneration—because man is totally passive until regenerated.[14]

One cannot ague logically or scripturally that man is *totally* passive and regeneration is *monergistic*—God working independent of the human will—on one hand while maintaining that what man does has a *substantive* role in the process. Man cannot both be active and passive at the same time in the same sense. A Calvinist may argue that man's actions are a part of the process, but he cannot argue that it is *substantively* or *inextricably* so, which in fact is the clear teaching and portrayal of Scripture. If one argues that man's actions do have a *substantive* and *integral* role, then it seems that Calvinism is positing that God either "foreknew" this or he predetermined it, which seems to mean that man is not totally passive and therefore regeneration is not monergistic.

The clear declaration of Scripture is that God genuinely desires for all to come to repentance (Luke 24:47; Acts 2:38; 2 Pet 3:9), gets no pleasure in the death of the wicked, and pleads with man to turn to him and be saved (Ezek 33:11). Moreover, the Scripture makes faith the unmistakable, undeniable responsibility of man, as enabled by grace, in order to receive salvation. The Scripture is lucid, as well as deliberately commanding and compelling, in presenting Christ as praying for the lost and pleading with man to repent and believe and scolding nonbelievers for their unbelief (Matt 11:20–24; 23:37; Luke 23:34; John 5:40–47; 11:42). Such pleading is

---

14. Man's passiveness is stated explicitly in the Westminster Confession, X, 2: "This effectual call [to salvation] is of God's free and special grace alone, not from anything at all foreseen in man, *who is altogether passive* therein, until, being quickened and renewed by the Holy Spirit, he is thereby enabled to answer this call, and to embrace the grace offered and conveyed by it" (italics added). I add to this the clarification that he is not only enabled, but according to Calvinism, he is enabled against his will, and not only enabled to believe but *made* to only be able to believe rather than choose between believing and not believing. I maintain that God indeed has foreknowledge, even of the future, contingent, free will choices of men and women, which is an indispensible part of his decrees and predestination. That is to say, contrary to Calvinism, he gave free will, paid everything necessary for the salvation of all, sent the call out to receive by faith, provided grace enablements and predestined to salvation those who would receive and respond to his grace by his grace.

disingenuous if God knows that man cannot do what he has pleaded with him to do (John 7:17), and such scolding for unbelief is heartless if man has no capacity for believing. It is important to note that in John 5:40–47, the Jews' disbelief is not because they have not been regenerated; rather, Christ attributes their unbelief to the fact that they do not love God, they receive glory from one another, and do not believe Moses, which clearly implies Christ thought they should and could believe.

Other examples of faith being man's responsibility and preceding regeneration can be seen in these words of John: "While you have the Light, *believe* in the Light, *so that you may become* sons of Light" (John 12:36, emphasis mine). Again John says, "But as many as *received Him*, to them He gave the right *to become children* of God, even to those who believe in His name, who were born, not of blood nor of the will of the flesh nor of the will of man, but of God" (John 1:12–13, emphasis mine). According to Paul, faith is both prior to regeneration and the condition that believers must meet in order to receive salvation. He writes, "For you are all sons of God *through* faith in Christ Jesus" (Gal 3:26, emphasis mine). Non-Calvinists deny the asseveration of Calvinism that obscures the clear and simple meaning of these verses with the interpretation that while this general call is for all, it can only be realized by the unconditionally elected because the secret will of God includes the inward efficacious call which is only for the unconditionally elected.

The unambiguous and ubiquitous claim of Calvinism is that faith is the evidence of the new birth. For example, John Piper avers, "Faith is the evidence of new birth, not the cause of it."[15] In like manner, R. C. Sproul declares, "We do not believe in order to be born again; we are born again in order that we may believe."[16] Further, Piper states, "Except for the continual exertion of saving grace, we will always use our freedom to resist God."[17]

Consequently, according to Piper, Sproul, and other Calvinists, given a choice, people will always choose to reject God and stay in their sin, and God causes *some* people to be born again, and only then will they believe. Hence, man is forced into a position of necessarily believing against his will. This is not to say that faith is forced against the person's will, but rather that regeneration was forced upon the person against his will. Again, Piper asserts, "The native hardness of our hearts makes us unwilling and unable

---

15. Piper, *Desiring God*, 63–64.
16. Sproul, *Chosen*, 73.
17. Piper, *Five Points*, 27.

to turn from sin and trust the Savior. Therefore conversion involves a miracle of new birth. This new birth precedes and enables faith and repentance. Nevertheless, faith and repentance are *our* acts. We are accountable to do them." Also, "God grants us the inclination we need."[18]

This is a clear example of what I call Calvinism's double-talk. By double-talk, I *specifically and only* mean thinking, praying, writing or speaking in such a way that obscures the disquieting realities of Calvinism. If a person accepts these realities, then he can be a knowledgeable and consistent Calvinist, but if one is unwilling to face them and accept them, he cannot be a consistent Calvinist. Additionally, I am not calling anyone a double-talker nor is my use of this term intended in any sense to be pejorative.[19]

In the Calvinist view, being born again is not a mere inclination, it is an inviolable determination made by God alone—monergistically. Piper clearly, as do other Calvinists, places regeneration prior to faith, which had to happen against the sinner's will, notwithstanding their statements which, at times, contradict or blur this reality. His statement that "faith and repentance are *our* acts" is a little misleading. While it is true, according to Calvinism, that the human does them after regeneration, faith and repentance are also the *unalterable* and *inevitable* acts of the once regenerated person. They are as determined as they are free.

Therefore, there *may be* some remote sense in which people are accountable, but one cannot glean any amount of uncertainty from a Calvinist understanding of accountability or responsibility; they redefine how Scripture commonly portrays these things and how they are understood in everyday life. While they are free to redefine an everyday usage—not Scripture's usage—they should be forthright about it so as not to obscure the truth of Calvinism. Furthermore, most, if not all, usages of accountability and responsibility in Scripture and everyday usage, at least, imply libertarian choice. That is what *most* people believe the Calvinist means, but it is emphatically not what they mean. This is a disquieting reality.

According to Calvinism, faith and repentance are responsibilities of the regenerated person that he is *not* free to resist. In other words, the bitter reality of Calvinism is that the predetermined elect are regenerated by God without regard to anything else, and that the one God chooses will be regenerated in absolute contradiction to the desires of his fallen nature. Then,

---

18. Piper, *Desiring God*, 62.

19. For more on this term, see my entry on "Double-talk" in "Glossary of Authorial Terms," in *Reflections*, 176–77.

the one who is regenerated will have no more option not to repent and have faith than he had not to be regenerated. Consequently, any implication or inference that the sinner, prior to regeneration, has a choice in being regenerated, exercising faith, or not being regenerated, and after regeneration has a choice of not exercising faith, is an illusion. This is a disquieting reality.

The lack of *real* choice to exercise faith or not is the chilling truth of Calvinism, and it is this truth that takes words like "responsibility," "accountability," and the normal teaching of Scripture's repeated pleas, injunctions, and warnings to new levels of obfuscation. I disagree with those who hold to such understandings, but I am even more profoundly troubled by unwillingness on the part of *many* Calvinists to speak regularly and forthrightly about these realities in such a way that people understand exactly what is involved in being a Calvinist. Some Calvinists fully understand this and do their best to communicate it. I applaud their forthrightness. But I am convinced that most people who embrace Calvinism do not fully understand or accept this truth of Calvinism, and/or they think it is not essential to Calvinism, when in fact it is. This is a disquieting reality.

Calvinism's endeavor to exalt God by emphasizing compatibilism, unconditional election and monergism actually diminishes God.[20] One simply cannot diminish the *work* of the Creator without diminishing its Creator, which Calvinism does by teaching that man was created to inevitably sin and be totally passive in regeneration. For example, what if one looked beneath the majestic mystique of the Mona Lisa only to find that Da Vinci actually painted by the numbers, or we learned that Beethoven's Fifth Symphony was actually composed by an alien being who could do nothing but produce such a masterpiece. Either discovery would tell us more about the creators of such works than the works themselves, and would in fact reduce our opinion of their creators. Calvinism's reduction of man's freedom to that of compatibilism tells us more about their, albeit possibly unwitting, diminished view of God—who apparently cannot be in sovereign control of truly free beings with choice to do otherwise—than it does about their view of man.

Calvinism teaches that the gospel is only, in any meaningful sense, offered to the unconditionally elected because God has chosen to grant only the elect his selective regeneration and withhold that same salvifically essential and determinative work from the non-elect, thereby inviolably

---

20. For more on compatiblism and free will, see the commentary on Article 8 of the TS in this volume.

prohibiting them from being enabled to receive the gospel unto forgiveness of sins and eternal life; hence, while a Calvinist *may* argue that he makes a good faith offer (if there is such a thing), it is incontrovertible that Jesus makes no such offer.

Calvinism's view that God withholds the essential element of regeneration, which leads to salvation, means that God does not in any sense desire the non-elect to be saved. Such a conclusion contradicts numerous biblical texts and the picture presented in Scripture of God's salvific love for all of the lost (Luke 24:47; John 8:24; Acts 2:38; 2 Pet 3:9; Rev 22:17).

Further, God's genuine offer of salvation to each and every lost person is based upon the attributes of God (perfect love, matchless mercy, indefatigable compassion and boundless grace) rather than the attributes of man. Thus, the non-Calvinist position is pedestalled upon a scripturally balanced exaltation of *all* of the attributes of God. Therefore, the non-Calvinist view of God and his *genuine* offer of salvation to all of the lost is not derived from an exaltation of man or by humanizing God, but rather by simply recognizing the exalted place Scripture affords God and his love.

"God so loved the world" (John 3:16) and genuinely *desires* for everyone to repent, believe, and be saved (2 Pet 3:9). God has provided everything that every fallen, undeserving and rebellious sinner needs in order to receive forgiveness in Christ (John 1:9–14; Acts 17:30–31; Rev 22:17). Consequently, any person can respond to the gospel with grace-enabled repentance and faith, and when he does, he is at that instant born again through the power of the Holy Spirit; he becomes a new creation in Christ with eternal life (John 10:10; Rom 6:4–11; 2 Cor 5:17; Gal 2:20; 6:15; Col 2:13).

BIBLIOGRAPHY

Chafer, Lewis Sperry. *Systematic Theology*, vol. 3: *Soteriology*. Dallas: Dallas Seminary Press, 1948.

———. *Systematic Theology*, vol. 7: *Doctrinal Summarization*. Dallas: Dallas Seminary Press, 1948.

Evans, Jeremy A. "Reflections on Determinism and Human Freedom." In *Whosoever Will: A Biblical-Theological Critique of Five-Point Calvinism*, edited by David L. Allen and Steve W. Lemke, 253–74. Nashville: B&H Academic, 2010.

Geisler, Norman. *Systematic Theology*, vol. 3: *Sin, Salvation*. Minneapolis: Bethany House, 2004.

Piper, John. *Desiring God: Meditations of a Christian Hedonist*. Sisters, OR: Multnomah, 1996.

———. *Five Points: Toward a Deeper Experience of God's Grace.* Ross-shire, Scotland: Christian Focus, 2013.

Rogers, Ronnie W. *Reflections of a Disenchanted Calvinist: The Disquieting Realities of Calvinism.* 2012. Reprint, Bloomington, IN: WestBow, 2016.

Sproul, R. C. *Chosen by God.* Wheaton: Tyndale, 1986.

Article 6: Election to Salvation

We affirm that, in reference to salvation, election speaks of God's eternal, gracious, and certain plan in Christ to have a people who are his by repentance and faith.

We deny that election means that, from eternity, God predestined certain people for salvation and others for condemnation.

Genesis 1:26-28; 12:1-3; Exodus 19:6; Jeremiah 31:31-33; Matthew 24:31; 25:34; John 6:70; 15:16; Romans 8:29-30, 33; 9:6-8; 11:7; 1 Corinthians 1:1-2; Ephesians 1:4-6; 2:11-22; 3:1-11; 4:4-13; 1 Timothy 2:3-4; 1 Peter 1:1-2; 2:9; 2 Peter 3:9; Revelation 7:9-10.

Commentary on
Article 6: Election to Salvation

Eric Hankins

INTRODUCTION

ARTICLE 6 RESTS ON the reality that election is clearly taught in the Scriptures and is an essential component of the doctrine of salvation. Election emphasizes the fact that salvation is accomplished through the Father's initiative, guaranteed by the person and work of Christ alone, and actualized in the lives of sinners through the power of the Holy Spirit. Election, therefore, communicates that salvation is completely gracious. It signifies the lavish generosity of God, who will save not just a few but an innumerable multitude. Election's announcement of God's sovereignty in salvation includes the role of the sinner's repentance and faith. God has chosen to bring into existence a people who belong to him by faith in a world where their decisions for or against Christ really matter. Rather than determining these choices himself, God has gloriously and sovereignly decided to accord to each sinner the responsibility of surrendering to the Holy Spirit's leading in the preaching of the gospel. Since gospel proclamation is the means by which God brings his elective purposes to bear, election cannot be understood apart from the plan of God to bring salvation to the world *through* his chosen people and their sharing of the gospel with the lost.

Commentary on Article 6: Election to Salvation

God desires the salvation of everyone (John 3:16; 1 Tim 2:3–4; 2 Pet 3:9). No one is excluded from his saving intentions. Article 6, therefore, denies that election language in the Bible refers to God's eternal and fixed choice of some individuals for salvation and not others without respect to their response to the gospel. If God desires the salvation of *all people*, it cannot be the case that he has actually determined to save only *some individuals*, while planning from eternity to consign the rest to everlasting punishment. When believers say, "God chose me," they cannot also mean, "and, from eternity, he did not choose others." To make such a statement is to dismiss the clear teaching of Scripture that God wants everyone to be saved. Therefore, when one says, "God chose me," he means, "God has done everything necessary to bring me to salvation in a world where people's decisions are a critical part of God's ultimate purposes." It is our belief, therefore, that the majority of Southern Baptists reject the idea that God predestines some people to hell.[1]

If God has decided in eternity past which individuals he will not save, then those individuals cannot be thought of either as being truly loved by God or as being the objects of his saving intentions. Calvinists protest that it is simply a mystery as to how God loves people he wills to condemn before they are ever born. Some assert that God has two wills, one "hidden" and one "revealed,"[2] or two kinds of love,[3] but most Southern Baptists view these answers as having neither a biblical nor logical basis. Moreover, Calvinists' affirmation of "single predestination" over against "double predestination" as a method for absolving God of the charge of actively causing the lost to spend eternity in hell is unconvincing. To say that God merely passes over the lost rather than actively causing their perdition is both a

---

1. Calvinists likely will object to the phrase "predestined to hell" as a mischaracterization of their position, insisting that God does not "predestine" some sinners to hell; rather, he "foreordains" it, or "permits" it by withholding the grace necessary for them to be saved. Such double-speak should be rejected as mere semantics in the service of hiding a truth of Calvinism most Southern Baptists find unbiblical and objectionable: there is no one in hell who ever had the opportunity to be anywhere else.
2. Piper, "Two Wills," 107–24; Grudem, *Systematic Theology*, 683–84.
3. MacArthur, "Does God love," par. 4–5.

distinction without a difference[4] and a flat refusal to own the implications of the Calvinist system.[5]

ARTICLE 6 AND THE BAPTIST FAITH AND MESSAGE

Article 6 is completely in keeping with the treatment of the doctrine of election in the Baptist Faith and Message (BFM), which has expressed Southern Baptist consensus on the matter for nearly a century and is based on a consensus that had emerged among Baptists in America nearly a century before that. Article 5 of the BFM states:

> Election is the gracious purpose of God, according to which He regenerates, justifies, sanctifies, and glorifies sinners. It is consistent with the free agency of man, and comprehends all the means in connection with the end. It is the glorious display of God's sovereign goodness, and is infinitely wise, holy, and unchangeable. It excludes boasting and promotes humility.

This definition of election stands in clear contrast to more Calvinistic Baptist confessions.[6] First, there is no mention of individuals who are not elect. The BFM does not affirm God's eternal and absolute rejection of certain individuals. Election is not God's plan to damn sinners; it is his plan to save sinners. Second, election is not configured in association with a deterministic view of divine action. The BFM makes no statement regarding God's decrees or his meticulous foreordination of all things including the supposedly "free" decisions of men. Instead, Article 2 emphasizes God's absolute foreknowledge of the free decisions of his creatures.

Older Calvinistic Baptist confessions deal with election before treating the doctrines of Christ, man, and salvation, making God's choice of some individuals but not others the lens through which these other doctrines should be understood. The BFM places election after these doctrines.

---

4. If I have the ability and opportunity to rescue someone who is drowning, then I have an obligation to render aid. If I simply stand aside and let them die, then I am morally culpable. Calvinist objections that the sinner is already dead will not suffice. If I have the ability and opportunity to regenerate a spiritually dead person but do not, then my culpability is the same.

5. Keathley, *Salvation and Sovereignty*, 148–49.

6. See, i.e., The Second London Baptist Confession of Faith (1689), The Philadelphia Confession of Faith (1742), The Baptist Catechism (Charleston Association, 1813), and the Abstract of Principles (1858).

Commentary on Article 6: Election to Salvation

In doing so, election *serves* God's glorious desire to save all rather than *constraining* it. The framers and revisers of the BFM had these much more Calvinistic Baptist confessions available to them, confessions which are much more consistent with the Westminster Confession's vision of election. Southern Baptists, however, have always been more comfortable with an understanding of election that was simpler, less speculative, and fully compatible with God's desire for the salvation of all people.

ELECTION AND SOUTHERN BAPTIST "NON-CALVINISM"

Most Southern Baptists categorically deny that certain individuals are selected for hell before creation. They know what election *does not* mean. What is needed in Southern Baptist life is a clear statement of what election *does* mean. Southern Baptists affirm that election is taught in the Bible, that God is sovereign in salvation, and that he has a very specific plan for each life but a plan that includes their free choices. A strategy that many Southern Baptists adopt to deal with election is to employ what they think is "compatibilism," their idea that God's sovereign choice of some individuals is compatible with man's free response to the gospel. Strictly speaking, however, "compatibilism" is a technical philosophical term asserting that *determinism* and free will are compatible.[7] Compatibilism is actually the Calvinistic view of divine action which sees every event as foreordained by God such that no human has the freedom of choice. Instead, "freedom" is the ability to do what one desires most. However, since people are not able to choose what they desire, those desires must be determined by God. This view of the relationship between divine action and human willing is simply unacceptable to most Southern Baptists who believe that the clear sense of Scripture is that people have real choices for which they are morally responsible.[8]

A POSITIVE CONSTRUCTION OF ELECTION

A truly Southern Baptist understanding of election, one that is faithful to God's desire to save all and to the necessity of a real response to the gospel must incorporate the totality of the biblical witness concerning this

---

7. *Stanford Encyclopedia of Philosophy*, s.v. "Compatibilism."
8. Hammett, "Human Nature," 316–17.

doctrine. Election language in Scripture emphasizes the nature of God's ultimate plan to bring about the salvation of myriads of people without negating the real response of individual sinners to his offer of covenant relationship. It must be constantly kept in mind that the Bible does not unfold as systematic theology, but salvation-history. The Scriptures reveal what God is doing in history, especially the history of Israel, and make clear what God's actions demonstrate about his character and purposes. The question of God's ultimate plan for history through Israel is a controlling exegetical and theological question of both the Old and New Testaments. God's choice of Israel, therefore, is fundamental to the meaning of election in the Bible. Several crucial features emerge from the Scriptures' treatment of Israel's election. First, the distinction between Israel and everyone else is comprehensively and maximally *salvific*. God does not choose Israel and damn the nations.[9] He chooses Israel to be a light of salvation to the nations. Second, this world-wide scope of election is based upon God's covenantal promises to bring his creation to completion in relationship with humankind. Third, election promises are typically mediated to and through one man, from whom these promises go out to all the earth (i.e. Adam, Noah, Abraham, Moses, David, the Messiah). Fourth, these covenant promises, which are made to the whole covenant community and, through them, to the whole world, consequently must be ratified by faith in order to be realized by individuals. Fifth, these election promises are antecedent to any individual response, and they will be fulfilled because God alone has categorically committed himself to bringing about their fulfillment.[10]

These five main trajectories of the election of Israel in the Old Testament govern the meaning of election language as it flows out into various applications in the New Testament. These trajectories cover the *why, where, how, who, when,* and *what* of election.

Covenantal

First, election is *covenantal*. This addresses the *why*, the purpose, of election. God has promised to redeem, and election speaks of God's intention and plan to keep that promise. Election functions within God's sovereign

---

9. Trimm, "Did YHWH Condemn," 536.

10. See Keathley, *Salvation and Sovereignty*, 58–62, for a helpful discussion of the concepts of "antecedent" and "consequent" with respect to sovereignty and freedom in God's desire to save.

commitment to bring about his ultimate purposes for all things, and it is hardwired to his desire for everyone to come to repentance and faith. This desire for maximum salvation is expressed fully in God's covenant purposes for creation from the very beginning (Gen 1:26–28): God has always desired to be in real relationship with the crown of his creation, through whom the whole cosmos would be brought to completion.[11] Election, therefore, is not an end to itself. Rather, it is a crucial part of God's covenant plan for the redemption of the created order. Yet, within God's sovereign desire for maximum salvation, covenant also demands a real response.[12]

The core reference point for covenant and election is God's choice of Abraham. The ultimate purpose of that choice was that through Abraham all the nations of the earth would be blessed (Gen 12:1–3; cf. Gal 3:8), and Abraham's response to that covenant offer really mattered. God did not choose Abraham in distinction to the nations but on behalf of the nations. Israel was chosen to be a kingdom of priests, the ones through whom all the peoples of the earth would come to worship the one true God. The salvation-historical script from which the writers of the New Testament are always working is that God's elective covenantal purposes through Israel have come to fruition in the person and work of Christ breaking forth in a church that is world-wide, composed of believing Jews *and* Gentiles, the sign that the covenant with Abraham to redeem the world is being fulfilled.[13] Election is covenantal.

Christocentric

Second, election is *Christocentric*. This speaks to the *where* (and *how*), the location (and means), of election. Where does election take place? *In Christ.* How? *Through Christ.* God's ultimate purposes for creation are grounded

---

11. Merrill, *Everlasting Dominion*, 17; Dumbrell, *Creation and Covenant*, 27.

12. See, i.e., Deut 29:14–21. Israel is reaffirming the covenant promised to the patriarchs and to future generations. However, if there is an individual man or woman who boasts, "I have peace with God though I walk in the stubbornness of my heart," the Lord will "single him out" from the people for destruction (vv. 18–21). Although the covenant is for the whole community, the individual must respond in faith in order to benefit from those corporate covenant promises.

13. Dumbrell, "Abraham," 19, 29. Paul asserts this connection between Abraham, election, the gospel, and the nations in Gal 3:8: "The Scripture, foreseeing that God would justify the Gentiles by faith, preached the gospel beforehand to Abraham, saying, 'All the nations of the earth will be blessed in you.'" Cf. Rom 4:13–25.

in the life, death, and resurrection of the Son. All that was promised to, in, and through Israel has been fulfilled in Christ. In Christ, the universal need for the salvation of humankind by God was met in the particular appearing and ministry of the God-Man. Paul speaks of believers being chosen and predestined "in him" (Eph 1:4, 11) and predestined to be adopted "through Jesus Christ" (v. 5). Paul tells the Romans that they are "predestined to be conformed to the image of His Son so that He would be the firstborn among many brethren" (8:29, NKJV). Christ is the Elect One (Luke 9:35; 23:35; and 1 Pet 1:20; 2:4, 6). Through this One Man, through the universal and unlimited nature of his atonement, all people are now under the aegis of God's electing love.

God's desire to have a people for himself is secured by what has been accomplished in Christ. Those individuals who are united with Christ by faith are the elect, not by virtue of what they have done, but by virtue of what Christ has done. Through Christ, God's covenant offer to Israel is now an offer he makes to the whole world, but, as it was with individual Israelites, so it must be with individual sinners—they must respond in faith (Deut 29:19–21). Moreover, as the people of God, the body of Christ, and the temple of the Holy Spirit, the elect are now the gracious means through which the gospel of Christ, the power of salvation, goes out to the whole world. The church, in becoming ever more like Christ, puts the glory of God on display before the nations so that *all* might come to repentance and faith.

Categorical

Third, election is *categorical*. This addresses the *who*, the subject, of election: God alone. In sovereign freedom alone, the Father has chosen the Son, and, in sovereign freedom alone, the Son has submitted himself to the Father (John 5:18–30). In and through the Son by the power of the Holy Spirit, the Father elected to have a people for himself in whom and through whom he will fulfill his covenant to redeem the world. Like his decision to create, his decision to elect is non-contingent and unconditional. God initiates and superintends election, and his decision to have a people for himself cannot be stopped. He will accomplish what he has determined to accomplish, because he is God. Election is of grace. God's choice of Israel was not based on her present or future worthiness, but on God's free decision alone. Indeed, God fulfills that commitment perfectly and completely in Christ. God's choice to have an eschatological people in Christ mirrors his election of Israel. God does not elect this people because he foresees that they will behave righteously. He elects them through categorical freedom, grace, and love. Because God's electing purposes are based on his gracious decision alone, he can provide this salvation for anyone.

Concurrent

Fourth, election is *concurrent*, which relates to the *when* of election, addressing the issues of time and eternity and the movements of sovereignty and free will. While Calvinists speak of election as unconditional and happening from eternity and Arminians see it as conditional and happening in time, the Scriptures affirm elements of both views. God's total sovereignty and people's real responsibility in salvation are "simultaneously true."[14] To diminish God's sovereignty in salvation (or anything else) leaves the outcome of human destiny subject to doubt and beyond God's control. To diminish human responsibility is to concede causal determinism, reducing human decision-making to a farce. Yet, Kenneth Keathley notes, "The Bible so congruently interweaves divine and human actions that it is a mystery where one ends and the other begins (cf. John 6)."[15] Concurrence in election means that God's sovereignty in election extends ultimately to the individual believer in such a way that, without God's electing, initiating, and superintending, no individual has the hope of salvation. It, however, also means that the free response of humans to God's electing activity is real and essential to salvation.[16]

Corporate

Finally, election is *corporate*, speaking to the *what*, the object of election.[17] Election is the outworking of God's desire to save all. It is expressed in his

---

14. Keathley, "The Work of God," 559. "Some advocates of the concurrent election position appeal to God's timelessness; others base their arguments on his ability to know even hypothetical situations (this ability is called *middle knowledge*), while still others argue that, since the Bible clearly teaches concurrence but does not provide an explanation about how concurrence works, then the matter should simply be left as a mystery."
15. Keathley, "The Work of God," 567.
16. This is essentially Millard Erickson's view in *Christian Theology*, 327–35.
17. Klein, *New Chosen People*, 21.

desire to have a *people* for himself. When the choice of individuals is raised in the Scriptures, it always refers to God's activity through that individual to bring about his purposes for maximum salvation. The concept of election is not focused on the question, "How does God save individuals?" The Bible answers that question clearly, but with a different concept: faith. Individuals are saved by grace through faith in Christ. This is not to say that the election of a people and the salvation of individuals are unrelated. Because Christ is the Elect One, the people of God are elect in and through him.

Because Christ is the Savior of each individual by faith, a proper theological implication is that union with Christ makes an individual a member of the elect. Since the Son is freely chosen to bring about the existence of the elect, the Son himself is the first member, the image for those who are predestined to conform to it, making Christ the firstborn among many brothers (Rom 8:29). Therefore, the corporate entity is no "empty class."[18] Because maximum salvation was always the purpose of election, the fact that multitudes have come to faith and multitudes are yet to come is simply the intended outcome of God's sovereign activity in election.

ELECTION IN ROMANS 9–11

This five-fold matrix of election in Scripture structures the following soteriological claim: election is God's sovereign, unstoppable, promised plan to save a multitudinous people for himself through faith in Christ alone. While this plan is sufficient to save every sinner, those who are excluded from it are excluded only by their own decisions within the collective rebellion and brokenness of humankind, an outcome that functions fully within God's sovereign purposes to bring maximum salvation by faith.

This matrix reveals that the texts most often cited as *proof* that election means God's fixed choice of some and not others are actually making the *opposite* point. Romans 9–11 is arguably the "pillar passage" for the Calvinist view of election, but it actually fits beautifully into this matrix and reveals that God's saving intentions are for all, not just a select few. There is no question that the election of Israel forms the basis for these chapters. Whatever election means here it must be collated with what God was doing in his choice of Israel. Paul's point in the letter from beginning to end is that, as the Jewish apostle to the Gentiles, he is proclaiming that God's commitment to bring salvation to the world through Israel has been

---

18. Klein, "Is Corporate Election," 9.

fulfilled in Israel's Messiah and through the Messiah's people. In Rom 9–11, *covenant* is the driving force. The question of 9:6 (Has God's covenant with Israel failed?) is answered in 11:25–26 (Israel's present resistance to the gospel is temporary, purposed by God for maximum salvation among the Gentiles, which will result in *all* Israel being saved.). The conclusion of this plan is exclaimed in verse 32: "that He might have mercy on *all*" (emphasis mine). Who benefits from these covenant promises? *Anyone* who *believes* (Rom 10:9–13). *Concurrence* is in view in the ease with which Paul speaks of God's absolute sovereignty in the plan of salvation (Rom 9:6–29) and then turns in the next verse to find Israel's own unbelief as the precipitating cause of God's current rejection of them, the remedy for which is faith in Christ alone for anyone who will confess and believe (9:30–10:16).

Christocentrism is on display in the core of this passage in Rom 10:5–17. Christ is the fulfillment of the new covenant promised to Israel in Deut 30:12–14 (Rom 10:6–8). Belief in the lordship of the living Christ alone results in salvation for *all people*. The *categorical* nature of this sovereign plan to save all is on display especially in chapter 9. God, indeed, can save whomever he wants however he wants, but the question is, "Who does God want to save?" Does he want to save certain ones and not others? That hardly seems to be the point of a passage that ends with the proclamation that there will be mercy for all. The point of Rom 9 is that nothing can stop God's plan for maximum salvation, not even Israel's unfaithfulness. In fact, her unfaithfulness is actually a part of the plan to bring salvation to the whole world (9:17–18; 11:11–15). God is hardening Israel for a little while, not according to some hidden will to save some and not others, but according to his revealed will to save anyone and everyone who believes.

Corporate

Finally, election in Rom 9–11 is *corporate*. Paul is talking about God's dealings with two groups, Jews and Gentiles, who are being made into one group (Rom 11:16–24). God's choice of Israel (and his sovereign administration of Israel's unbelief) has resulted in his choice of *all* who believe. Again, not everyone will hear the good news (10:14b, "how shall they believe in Him of whom they have not heard?") and not everyone will believe (10:21, "But to Israel he says: 'All day long I have stretched out My hands To a disobedient and contrary people.'"). Paul's point about election in Rom 9–11 is clear: God never gives up on people. No one is outside of his reach or his mercy.

Anyone can be saved. His electing purposes for maximum salvation are unstoppable, yet they fully include the real responses of people to the gospel.

CONCLUSION

It is inaccurate to say that God elects some individuals and not others to salvation on the basis of his inscrutable decrees. Calvinism's reading evacuates the biblical concept of faith, which requires real freedom as necessary for salvation. God saves individuals by providing salvation through Christ in the announcement of the gospel in the power of the Holy Spirit. The individual who responds to the offer of the gospel with repentance and faith is saved. By virtue of an individual's being saved by faith in the Elect One, he is now a member of the elect. The phrase "God chose me" can only mean that God has always planned to bring salvation to sinners in a way that takes seriously both their radical sinfulness and their responsibility to respond in faith. It cannot mean that God chooses some and not others without respect to their response of faith to the gospel.

Biblical election, therefore, is part of the answer to the question, "How does God fulfill his sovereign, loving desire to save sinners?" The answer is that despite the universal and ubiquitous rebellion of all men, God decided, in Christ, to choose a people to whom salvation would come and through whom salvation would go out to all people, no matter what. Therefore, the burden of election language in the Bible is not the demonstration of how it is that God wants to save *anyone*. That is an Augustinian concern. Election in Scripture stands with the announcement that God wants to save *everyone*. God is not looking out over the mass of the damned, pinching his nose and picking out a few. He is looking at the world he loved so much that he made a way for whoever believes in him to have life, and he has guaranteed that he will have such a people in Christ through whom the gospel will go out to the whole world.

What does this view of election mean for Southern Baptists? It means that we can say that God moved heaven and earth to bring the gospel to sinners like us. He did so through Christ and through the long chain of the faithfulness and obedience of his people. We are the beneficiaries of his electing purposes when we respond in faith to that gospel preached to us, and, when we take that good news to others, we put the electing purposes of God on display. Election means that we did not save ourselves. Until the gospel was preached to us, until the Spirit of God moved in that preaching,

Commentary on Article 6: Election to Salvation

we were hopeless and helpless, undeserving of and uninterested in a relationship with God. Yet, God refused to stop. He has chosen to pursue his rebellious creatures to the uttermost. The end will reveal his elective purposes were not designed for a great exclusion but a maximum salvation.

BIBLIOGRAPHY

Dumbrell, William J. "Abraham and the Abrahamic Covenant in Galatians 3:1–14." In *The Gospel to the Nations: Perspectives on Paul's Mission*, edited by Peter Bolt and Mark Thompson, 19–31. Downers Grove: InterVarsity, 2000.

———. *Creation and Covenant: A Theology of Old Testament Covenants*. Eugene, OR: Wipf & Stock, 1984.

Erickson, Millard J. *Christian Theology*. 3rd ed. Grand Rapids: Baker, 2013.

Grudem, Wayne. *Systematic Theology: An Introduction to Biblical Doctrine*. Grand Rapids: Zondervan, 1994.

Hammett, John S. "Human Nature." In *A Theology for the Church*, rev. ed., edited by Daniel L. Akin, 285–336. Nashville: B&H Academic, 2014.

Keathley, Kenneth. *Salvation and Sovereignty: A Molinist Approach*. Nashville: B&H Academic, 2010.

———. "The Work of God: Salvation." In *A Theology for the Church*, rev. ed., edited by Daniel L. Akin, 543–600. Nashville: B&H Academic, 2014.

Klein, William. *The New Chosen People: A Corporate View of Election*. Eugene, OR: Wipf & Stock, 2001.

———. "Is Corporate Election Merely Virtual Election? A Case Study in Contextualization." Unpublished, undated paper at http://evangelicalarminians.org/files/Klein.%20Is%20Corporate%20Election%20Merely%20Virtual%20Election.pdf.

MacArthur, John. "Does God love the elect and hate the non-elect?" http://www.gty.org/resources/questions/QA184/does-god-love-the-elect-and-hate-the-nonelect.

Merrill, Eugene H. *Everlasting Dominion: A Theology of the Old Testament*. Nashville: B&H Academic, 2006.

Piper, John. "Are There Two Wills in God? Divine Election and God's Desire for All to Be Saved." In *The Grace of God and the Bondage of the Will*, edited by Thomas R. Schreiner and Bruce A. Ware, 107–24. Grand Rapids: Baker, 1995.

Trimm, Charlie. "Did YHWH Condemn the Nations When He Elected Israel? YHWH's Disposition Toward the Non-Israelites in the Torah." *Journal of the Evangelical Theological Society* 55.3 (2012) 521–36.

Article 7: The Sovereignty of God

We affirm God's eternal knowledge of and sovereignty over every person's salvation or condemnation.

We deny that God's sovereignty and knowledge require him to cause a person's acceptance or rejection of faith in Christ.

Genesis 1:1; 6:5–8; 18:16–33; 22; 2 Samuel 24:13–14; 1 Chronicles 29:10–20; 2 Chronicles 7:14; Psalm 23; 51:4; 139:1–6; Proverbs 15:3; Joel 2:32; John 6:44; Romans 11:3; Titus 3:3–7; Hebrews 11:6; 12:28; James 1:13–15; 1 Peter 1:17.

Commentary on
Article 7: The Sovereignty of God

Steve W. Lemke

GOD'S OMNISCIENCE AND EXHAUSTIVE FOREKNOWLEDGE

THE FIRST AFFIRMATION IN Article 7 is of "God's eternal knowledge"—an affirmation of God being all-knowing (omniscient), and of the fact that God knows all things from eternity, and thus from a human perspective of time he foreknows of all things (see Ps 139:1–10; Rom 8:29–30; 11:2; 16:27). The Baptist Faith and Message (BFM) 2000 strongly affirms God's omniscience. The affirmation of God's omniscience is strengthened in each of the succeeding versions of the BFM. Interestingly, the term "all knowing" does not appear at all in the BFM 1925. The descriptor of "all wise" was added to the BFM in 1963.[1] In the BFM 2000, however, multiple claims of God's perfect knowledge are affirmed. Article 2 of the BFM 2000 twice describes God as "all powerful" and "all knowing," and adds that "His perfect knowledge extends to all things, past, present, and future, including the future decisions of His free creatures." It also repeats the description of God as "all wise" from the 1963 statement, and the affirmation that God is

---

1. BFM 1963, Article 2a ("God the Father").

"infinite in holiness and all other perfections," a phrase repeated in all three versions of the confession.[2]

Why does the BFM 2000 add the double reference to God being all knowing, and the statement that God's "perfect knowledge extends to all things past, present, and future, including the future decisions of His free creatures"? Baptists and other evangelicals in 2000 were dealing with the movement known as Freewill Theism, or Openness of God theology. In this view, God does not have perfect foreknowledge. Although he knows all that is available to be known, it is impossible for him to know "the future decisions of His free creatures."

Traditionalists and most conservative evangelicals, however, reject the Openness of God view and hold a high view of God's perfect knowledge and foreknowledge. God has perfect knowledge, including the "future decisions of His free creatures."[3] However, Traditionalists also reject the interpretation by many Reformed thinkers that foreknowledge actually means "foreloved"—that is, that God (fore)loved (only) those whom he elected. The election of these "foreloved" people was not premised upon any response on their part. It was an unconditional election imposed on them by means of irresistible grace. However, "foreloved" is clearly not what Scripture means when it speaks of those whom he "foreknew" (Rom 8:29). In any standard lexicon, the Greek word for foreknew (*proegnō*) simply means knowing something before it happens.[4]

Let us further examine several important implications of this statement in the BFM 2000 that God foreknows the "future decisions of His free creatures."

> (a) *Human choices are "free," not forced by deterministic decrees*. If persons did only what was decreed by God from before the beginning of time, humans would not be "His free creatures," but would be under compulsion. One who has no choices is not free. The denial in Article 7 that God's perfect knowledge of future human choices *causes* "a person's acceptance or rejection of faith in Christ" is supportive of this concept of freedom.[5]

2. BFM 2000, Article 2 ("God") and 2a ("God the Father").

3. For more about how the BFM 2000 is responding to Openness of God theology, see Blount, "Article II," 14–17.

4. See, for example, *Theological Dictionary of the New Testament*, s.v. "proginōskō, prognōsis."

5. For more on the problem of reconciling determinism with human freedom, see

(b) *God can foreknow the future free choices of individuals.* This point is denied by Openness of God theologians, but is affirmed overwhelmingly by Baptists and other conservative evangelicals. God's knowledge is not limited to past and present events, but extends into the future (Acts 2:23; Rom 8:29; 11:2; 1 Pet 1:2). God's perfect knowledge and omniscience is a characteristic we would expect of anyone worthy of the name "God." A god without omniscience and foreknowledge would simply not be God.

(c) *God can foreknow the future free choices of individuals without overriding their freedom.* Many Reformed theologians profess that God's foreknowledge of the future essentially overrides any meaningful human freedom. They argue that if God foreknows what a person will decide, and God's foreknowledge is perfect, then the person cannot decide differently than God believes they will choose. This logic is flawed in at least three ways.

(1) Saying that God's foreknowledge takes away any real human choices *fundamentally misunderstands God's relation to time.* God is not bound by time; he exists in eternity. It is impossible for time-bound humans to understand fully what it means to live in eternity. There is mystery here. However, one can be sure that God's relationship to time is different than it is for humans. Whereas from a human perspective the distinction between the past, present, and future have immense significance, God lives in the "eternal now" in which everything is the present.[6] So, although his *fore*knowledge is before the present in *human* time, God experiences it in something like our experience of the present. Because God is outside of human time, his knowledge is not subject to the normal limitations of time.

(2) Saying that God's foreknowledge takes away any real human choices *fundamentally confuses the difference between knowledge and causation.* Two plus two is four, but not because I know it; rather, it is true because it is true in reality. In fact, two plus two equals four whether I believe it or not. Knowing something does not cause it to happen. Again, the misconception that God's foreknowledge of future human

---

Evans, "Reflections," 253–74.

6. For a fuller discussion of God existing in the "eternal now," and its implications for conditional election and salvation, see Land, "Congruent Election," 45–59.

choices *causes* "a person's acceptance or rejection of faith in Christ" is denied in Article 7 of the TS.

(3) Saying that God's foreknowledge takes away any real human choices *fundamentally confuses necessity* (what *must* happen) and *certainty* (what *will* happen). There is an immense difference between necessity and certainty. Since God's knowledge does not *cause* future events, his (fore)knowledge does not make these events *necessary*. Future events are contingent on the "future decisions of His free creatures."[7]

Human analogies break down here, because we are bound by time and imperfect knowledge, while God is not bound by these limitations. However, ponder this analogy. Imagine that John has listened to the end of a football game in which his team makes a remarkable comeback at the end of the game to win the contest. He is watching a replay of the game with his friend Bill who does *not* know the outcome of the game (or that John knows its outcome). As their team is behind throughout most of the game, Bill laments that their team is going to lose the game, but John keeps telling Bill that he believes they can come back and win. John encourages Bill to have faith in their team. Sure enough, as John knew they would, the football team comes back and wins a dramatic victory at the end of the game. Bill is amazed that John had such confidence that their team would come back and win the game. In truth, of course, John did not really have "faith"—he had knowledge of what would actually happen that was inaccessible to Bill. The main point is this—John's knowledge of what would happen at the end of the game had exactly *nothing* to do with his team winning the game. His knowledge did not predetermine the blocking of the line, the throws of the quarterback, or the catches of the receiver. John knew the result with *certainty*, but not of *logical necessity*. He simply knew ahead of time what would actually happen without causing what happened. Likewise, God knows our future choices with certainty without making them logically necessary.

Applied to salvation, Traditionalists believe that God elects and predestines those whom he foreknows will respond to the proclamation of the gospel through the conviction of the Holy Spirit with repentance and faith

---

7. For more on the confusion of contingency and necessity, see Keathley, *Salvation and Sovereignty*, 8–9, 31–38; and Picirilli, *Grace, Faith, Free Will*, 36–63.

in Christ as Savior and Lord. This pattern is stated nowhere more clearly than in Rom 8:29–30, which serves as a prologue to Rom 9–11:

> For those whom He foreknew, He also predestined to become conformed to the image of His Son, so that He would be the firstborn among many brethren; and these whom He predestined, He also called; and these whom He called, He also justified; and these whom He justified, He also glorified. (Rom 8:29–30)[8]

Note that predestination, calling, and justification are conditional upon God's foreknowledge of those who would be led by the Holy Spirit to respond to the gospel with repentance and faith. God does not first decree or predestine those who are elect and then foreknow those who would be saved based upon his decree. Rather, God's foreknowledge of human responses comes first, with God's election, calling, and justification flowing from his foreknowledge. Romans 11:1–2 likewise affirms this pattern of divine foreknowledge of foreseen faith preceding election and justification:

> I say then, God has not rejected His people, has He? May it never be! For I too am an Israelite, a descendant of Abraham, of the tribe of Benjamin. God has not rejected His people whom He foreknew. (Rom 11:1–2a)

Just who are these people whom God foreknew? Scholars debate whether Paul is referring here to: a) the election of Israel to salvation; or b) to their election as a people as God's instrument, or vehicle, for salvation to all peoples. Assuming that the apostle is addressing the salvation of Israel, he makes it clear that it is not merely physical Israel to whom he is referring:

> But it is not as though the word of God has failed. For they are not all Israel who are descended from Israel; nor are they all children because they are Abraham's descendants, but: "through Isaac your descendants will be named." That is, it is not the children of the flesh who are children of God, but the children of the promise are regarded as descendants. (Rom 9:6–8)

So who is Israel, if not physical Israel in the lineage of Abraham, Isaac, and Jacob? The apostle makes it very clear in Rom 9–11 that anyone who has ears to hear can understand. True Israel whom God will save consists of whosoever will come to him by faith, as the following verses make clear:

---

8. Unless otherwise noted, all Bible quotations in this chapter are from the New American Standard Bible.

> What shall we say then? That Gentiles, who did not pursue righteousness, attained righteousness, even the righteousness which is by faith; but Israel, pursuing a law of righteousness, did not arrive at that law. Why? Because they did not pursue it by faith, but as though it were by works. They stumbled over the stumbling stone, just as it is written, "Behold, I lay in Zion a stone of stumbling and a rock of offense, And he who believes in Him will not be disappointed." (Rom 9:30–33)

> But what does it say? "The word is near you, in your mouth and in your heart"—that is, the word of faith which we are preaching, that if you confess with your mouth Jesus as Lord, and believe in your heart that God raised Him from the dead, you will be saved; for with the heart a person believes, resulting in righteousness, and with the mouth he confesses, resulting in salvation. For the Scripture says, "Whoever believes in Him will not be disappointed." For there is no distinction between Jew and Greek; for the same Lord is Lord of all, abounding in riches for all who call on Him; for "Whoever will call on the name of the Lord will be saved." (Rom 10:8–13)

To summarize, then, Traditionalists believe the Bible teaches that God is omniscient with exhaustive foreknowledge of the future, including not only all future events but also all possible events. Salvation (including election and predestination) is based upon God's foreknowledge of the repentance and faith of believers in response to the impulse of the Holy Spirit. God's foreknowledge secures rather than denies genuine human freedom. God's election is based on him foreseeing "the future decisions of His free creatures" to respond in repentance and faith to the proclamation of the gospel.

GOD'S OMNIPOTENCE AND SOVEREIGNTY

The second affirmation in Article 7 voices an exalted view of God's sovereignty. The sovereignty of God is one of the most basic truths of Scripture, affirmed in multiple texts in the Bible. God revealed himself to Abraham, Isaac, and Jacob as *El Shaddai*, or "God Almighty" (Gen 17:1; 35:11; Exod 6:3).[9] The Greek word often used to describe God's omnipotence is *pantokratōr*. This is a compound word combining *kratos* (power) with *pas*

---

9. Harris et al., *Theological Wordbook*, 2:907.

(all), so its meaning is all powerful or almighty.[10] It is often translated as the "Lord Almighty" (2 Cor 6:18; Rev 1:8; 4:8; 11:17; 15:3; 16:7, 14; 19:6, 15; 21:22). In the *King James Version*, Rev 19:6 reads "the Lord God omnipotent reigneth," a phrase made popularized even more by its repetition in the "Hallelujah Chorus" of Handel's *Messiah*. God's sovereignty is also affirmed by the repeated use of the motif of God (and Jesus) as King who reigns over the kingdom of God (especially in the Gospel of Matthew).

Somewhat surprisingly, the BFM 2000 does not use the words "sovereign" or "sovereignty" either in the article on God or the article on God the Father. However, these words do appear in two other places. In Article 5 on "God's Purpose of Grace," God's gracious election is described as a "glorious display of God's sovereign goodness," and in Article 9 on "The Kingdom," which affirms that "The Kingdom of God includes both His general sovereignty over the universe and His particular kingship over men who willfully acknowledge Him as King." Furthermore, the notion of God's kingly rule is affirmed in the BFM. Article 2 describes God as the "Ruler of the Universe," and that "God the Father reigns with providential care over His universe." The Baptist Faith and Message does, then, affirm a high view of divine sovereignty.

Theologians sometimes quibble over the definition of God's omnipotence, dealing with hypothetical issues that bring little (if any) light to this doctrine. Some ancient philosophers asked, for example, if God could create a rock so heavy that he could not lift it, or if he could create such a rock but could not lift it (and thus, again, that he is not fully omnipotent). The seeming paradox is that if he could not create such an unliftable rock then he cannot do everything (and thus is not fully omnipotent) or, if he could create such a rock but could not lift it (again suggesting that he is not fully omnipotent). Another such mental puzzle is whether God could create a square triangle. Again, the point of these illustrations is to suggest that there are some things that are conceptually impossible, that even God cannot do. The problem with such definitions is equating omnipotence with God having the power to do everything and anything, even things that are conceptually impossible. God's "inability" to create an unliftable rock is a pseudo-inability; there is no finite object such as a rock which is above his ability to move, because he is omnipotent. The question posed by this puzzle is a false dilemma. Likewise, making square triangles is impossible

---

10. *Theological Dictionary*, 3:914–15.

not because God lacks some ability, but because it is conceptually impossible. A square triangle simply no longer fits the definition of a triangle.

However, because (like most Traditionalists) I have such a high view of the sovereignty of God, for me personally, I am extremely reluctant to say that there is anything that God cannot do. There are things that God will not do because they are not consistent with his character or his will, but this does not indicate any inability or deficiency on his point. He simply has no interest in doing such things. Jesus asserted that things that seen impossible to humans are possible for God (Matt 17:20; 19:26; Mark 10:27). The angel speaking to Mary (discussing the miraculous nature of the virgin birth) stated that "nothing will be impossible with God" (Luke 1:37, NASB). Likewise, Jesus affirmed (discussing the miraculous nature of salvation) that all things are possible with God (Matt 19:26a; Mark 10:27b). So I am reluctant to say even that God could not change the laws of our universe or create a new universe in which triangles could be squares, but I doubt that he will because doing so merely to prove his ability would be out of character for God. Jesus resisted the temptations of Satan to exert his powers by turning stones into bread, or having angels catch him after he jumped off the pinnacle of the temple (Matt 4:1–11; Luke 4:1–13). God exerts his remarkable powers for his own redemptive purposes, not to impress humans.

The fact that God *can* do anything, thus, does not demand that he *must* do anything and everything to be God. In fact, because God is truly sovereign, he cannot be forced to do anything he does not will to do. To be sovereign means to be in control, not to be under the control of others. The most important issue, then, is not what might God *possibly* could do, or what *we think he should do*; it is what he *has done, is doing*, and *will do*. Reformed theologians and Traditionalists, then, do not differ essentially in affirming the sovereignty of God. They both affirm a high view of divine sovereignty and omnipotence. The difference between them is not *that* God is sovereign, but *how* he exercises his sovereignty.

God's General Sovereignty

God's sovereignty may be discussed in at least two ways. First of all, there is God's *general sovereignty* over his creation. God is the Creator and Sustainer of the world through his providential care. As the BFM 2000 affirms, one way that God reigns in his kingdom is "His general sovereignty over the universe."[11] How does our omnipotent God exercise his sovereignty over creation?

It is important to distinguish between God's *omnipotence* and *sovereignty*. God's omnipotence concerns what he *could* do; God's sovereignty concerns what he *wills* to do. That God *can* do anything does not demand that he *must* do anything. God is free in his sovereignty to act as he sees fit. Note that Article 7 defends God's freedom and sovereignty by denying that he is *required* to act in a particular way.

Many Reformed theologians believe in what they call God's "*meticulous providence*." Meticulous providence is the belief that God controls and causes every detail in the universe. John Calvin taught that "not one drop of rain falls without God's sure command,"[12] and that "God by His secret bridle so holds and governs (persons) that they cannot move even one of their fingers without accomplishing the work of God much more than their own."[13] In essence, every detail in human life is caused directly by God. For example, Paul Helm claims that "God controls all persons and events equally" because "God could hardly exercise care over them without having control over it."[14] The Westminster Confession of Faith asserts that God in his providence "doth uphold, direct, dispose, and govern all creatures, actions, and things, from the greatest even to the least."[15] Paul Kjoss Helseth describes God's role in providence as "omnicausality"—he literally causes all things.[16] B. B. Warfield makes this claim even more explicit: "There is nothing that is, and nothing that comes to pass, that [God] has not first decreed and then brought to pass by His creation or providence."[17] Meticulous providence, then, reduces to *theological determinism*—the view that God predetermines all events from the beginning of time, and thus human actions are only playing out an inviolable script which God wrote before time began.

---

11. BFM 2000, Article 9 ("The Kingdom").

12. Calvin, *Institutes*, 1:204. Calvin similarly asserts God's meticulous providence in matters such as which mothers have milk and others do not (*Institutes*, 1:201).

13. Calvin, *Secret Providence*, 238.

14. Helm, *Providence*, 20–21; see also Feinberg, "God Ordains," 17–60; Helseth, "God Causes," 25–77.

15. Westminster Confession, V, 1.

16. Helseth, "God Causes," 37–43.

17. Warfield, "Predestination," 2:21.

Calvinistic thinkers suggest that if God does not have this level of control, then he is not really sovereign. This belief places the Reformed thinker in an unhappy dilemma. On the one hand, if God causes all things then that obviously makes God the author of evil. Although many Reformed thinkers try to avoid this consequence, it is unavoidable. If God controls and causes every single detail, then evil is the result of his actions. It is contradictory to say that God causes everything and yet does not cause some (evil) things. However, if, on the other hand, Reformed thinkers deny that God causes evil, they cannot then affirm that he controls all things. They cannot have it both ways.[18]

In trying to avoid this obvious dilemma, at times some leading Calvinists seem to be using words in confusing, misleading, or disingenuous ways. For example, some Reformed thinkers use language such as "concurrence" or divine "permission," such that human agents take the blame for evil rather than God. Most evangelicals would agree with this apparently more moderate way of describing God's providence—a way that seems open to God allowing human participation in decisions through his divine "permission," and for human "concurrence" in bringing about events. However, more careful investigation reveals that Calvinists do not mean by these words what they appear to mean. For example, regarding divine permission, John Frame insists that God does not permit anything passively, but instead his permission is "an *efficacious* permission"[19]—that is, God causes everything and the "permission" is essentially an illusion. In a similar discussion, although Francis Turretin acknowledges that Calvinist theologians utilize the word "permission," he insists that this word is not intended "in the Pelagian sense of otiose 'permission' which takes away his own right and sets up the idol of free will in its place."[20] Likewise, while "concurrence" seems to suggest human participation in determining events, this is not what Calvinists appear to mean by this label. Herman Bavinck asserts that "the primary (cause) works through the secondary (causes)," such that "the secondary causes can be compared to instruments."[21] There is no genuine concurrence, then, between God and humans; humans are merely tools whom God uses. Similarly, Wayne Grudem understands "concurrence" to

---

18. For more on problem of evil in regard to Reformed theology, see Little, "Evil," 275–98.
19. Frame, *Doctrine of God*, 178.
20. Turretin, *Institutes*, 1:516–17.
21. Bavinck, *Reformed Dogmatics*, 2:614–15.

Commentary on Article 7: The Sovereignty of God

mean that God compels humans "to cause them to act as they do."[22] Despite these somewhat misleading terms such as divine "permission" and his "concurrence" with humans, in fact only God causes and directs all things. Humans are not free to change or adjust even a single detail in the universe, since God alone is the "free determiner of all that comes to pass in the world."[23]

Traditionalists believe that God is completely sovereign over all creation, but we differ with how he *exercises* that sovereignty. We believe that nothing in the universe is ever beyond his control. He can intervene in the course of history and in our personal lives whenever he desires. However, God often chooses to allow human decisions to be meaningful and for the natural consequences of actions to happen. He normally allows the world to run according to the laws of nature. Whenever we say that God "ordains all things,"[24] "causes all things,"[25] or "controls all things,"[26] the logical consequence is that God is portrayed as the author of evil, because evil things are a significant part of "all things."[27] Perhaps saying that God "directs all things," God "knows all things,"[28] or that "nothing is outside of God's ultimate control" are more fruitful and precise ways of describing how God exercises his general sovereignty. God "directing all things" affirms that he is over the entire universe and nothing is outside his control, but it does not portray him as a micromanaging God who must directly ordain or cause every detail of human life, including human choices. However, allowing human freedom to be meaningful in no way can frustrate God's will. God's will shall be done and his kingdom shall come regardless of human decisions or mistakes (Matt 6:10). God is moving history toward its consummation in the return of Christ, ushering in the victorious kingdom of God.

God's Sovereignty in Salvation

A second aspect of God's sovereignty regards the salvation of persons. This soteriological aspect of divine sovereignty is the primary focus of Article 7,

22. Grudem, *Bible Doctrine*, 142.
23. Warfield, "Predestination," 8.
24. Feinberg, "God Ordains," 17–60.
25. Helseth, "God Causes," 25–77.
26. Ososami, *Majesty of God*, 120–21.
27. Craig, "God Directs," 79–139.
28. Geisler, "God Knows," 61–98.

for it affirms God's "sovereignty over every person's salvation or condemnation." The denial made in Article 7 is that "God's sovereignty and knowledge require him to cause a person's acceptance or rejection of faith in Christ."

Traditionalists affirm a high view of divine sovereignty in salvation. *No one* is saved *apart from* or *contrary to* God's sovereignty. The BFM 2000 affirms that divine election, reflected through regeneration, justification, sanctification, and glorification, demonstrates a "glorious display of God's sovereign goodness."[29] Again, the question is not *whether* God is sovereign over salvation, but *how* he exercises his sovereignty over salvation. God can sovereignly determine whatever requirements for salvation he demands of humans.

What conditions *does* God in fact place on humans for salvation? As already seen in the discussion of Rom 9–11, the elect are not simply a select group of people chosen by God arbitrarily. In fact, election is reserved for those who come to God through *faith*, such that whosoever will may come to salvation (Rom 9:30–33; 10:8–13). Many other Scriptures identify faith as a necessary condition for salvation. For example, in the prologue to the Gospel of John: "He came to His own, and those who were His own did not receive Him. But as many as received Him, to them He gave the right to become children of God, *even to those who believe in His name*" (John 1:11–12, emphasis mine). Indeed, neither election nor predestination is mentioned a single time in Scripture when someone asks how to be saved. Instead, consistently in Scripture, persons who ask how to be saved are told to repent of sin and believe in Christ (Acts 2:37–40; 8:27–39; 16:30–31).

The BFM underscores this requirement that God sovereignly places on individuals for salvation. The kingdom of God involves "His particular kingship over men who *willfully acknowledge* Him as King. Particularly the Kingdom is the realm of salvation into which *men enter by trustful, childlike commitment* to Jesus Christ."[30] Divine election is "consistent with the *free agency* of man,"[31] and salvation is "*offered freely to all who accept* Jesus Christ as Savior and Lord"[32] Clearly, then, God has determined that election is not truly unconditional, but is conditional on persons responding to the conviction of the Holy Spirit with repentance and faith in Jesus Christ as Savior and Lord.

---

29. BFM 2000, Article 5 ("God's Purpose of Grace").
30. BFM 2000, Article 9 ("The Kingdom"). Emphasis mine.
31. BFM 2000, Article 5 ("God's Purpose of Grace"). Emphasis mine.
32. BFM 2000, Article 4 ("Salvation"). Emphasis mine.

Commentary on Article 7: The Sovereignty of God

Reformed theologians may not agree with the denial in Article 7 that "God's sovereignty and knowledge require him to cause a person's acceptance or rejection of faith in Christ." They view salvation as *monergistic*—that is, a work done entirely by God. Traditionalists agree with monergism to some degree—that only God can save us, and we cannot save ourselves (Eph 2:8–10). There is nothing we could possibly do that would earn or deserve salvation. But Traditionalists disagree with Reformed thinkers about how God has sovereignly chosen to actualize salvation. Calvinistic thinkers believe all people are characterized by *total depravity*, understood as the *total inability* of anyone to respond to God. We are spiritually dead, and therefore unable to seek or respond to God. However, for his own secret reasons, God chose and predestined a small group of people to be his elect from before the foundation of the world. This group is predestined by God's *unconditional election*—it is absolutely unconditional on anything that we do. God compels the elect to believe by imposing *irresistible grace* on them to regenerate them.[33] The order of salvation is reversed such that believers are regenerated and then believe, rather than believe and then experience being born again.

Article 7 in the statement on salvation rejects the notion that "God's sovereignty and knowledge require him to *cause* a person's acceptance or rejection of faith in Christ," and thus rejects unconditional election and irresistible grace. The Bible clearly and repeatedly states that persons can resist salvation and God's will for their lives (for example, see Matt 27:37; Luke 7:30; 13:34; Acts 7:51; 26:14). Traditionalists also disagree with the claim that salvation is given us without any response required from us. God has sovereignly established the criteria that are essential for salvation. What necessary requirements has God sovereignly established for salvation? The Bible makes it abundantly clear that God requires *repentance and faith* for salvation. Every formulaic statement of what is required for salvation makes the necessity of repentance and faith for salvation crystal clear (Matt 10:32–33; Mark 16:15–16; John 3:14–17; 6:40; 11:26; 12:46; Acts 2:21, 27–30; 10:43; 16:30–31; Rom 9:33; 10:9–11; 1 John 5:1). Again, the question is not what God *could* or *might* have done, but what he *has* done. Therefore, *if we truly believe in the sovereignty of God*, we must be obedient to the criteria he has established for salvation. God does foreknow, elect, and predestine a particular type of person from before the foundation of the world—and

---

33. For a more thorough critique of irresistible grace, see Lemke, "Irresistible Grace," 109–62.

that is *believers*! Based upon his foreknowledge of those who will (under the conviction of the Holy Spirit) repent of their sins and trust Christ as their personal Lord and Savior, God elects, predestines, justifies, and glorifies (Rom 8:29–30).

God desires the salvation of not just a chosen few, but of anyone and everyone in the world who responds to him in faith (Matt 10:32–33; 18:14; John 1:7; 3:16–17; Acts 2:21; Rom 10:13; 1 Tim 2:4; 2 Pet 3:9; 1 John 2:2; Rev 22:17). He sovereignly and graciously elects and predestines all those who believe. Of course, our seeking, desiring, or responding to God's invitation of salvation does absolutely nothing to earn or deserve our salvation, any more than Naaman washing himself in the Jordan River seven times healed his leprosy (2 Kgs 5:1–14). Naaman's washing himself in the river just made him wet; it had no curative qualities. It was entirely God who healed him. But had Naaman not been obedient to meet God's conditions by washing himself, God undoubtedly would not have healed Naaman. Likewise, there is nothing we could do to earn or merit our salvation. Only God can save us from our sin. However, God will not save an unrepentant sinner, and he will not save one who refuses to trust Christ as Savior and Lord. Unless we meet God's conditions of repentance and faith, God will not save us.

Salvation is of God. He could have placed any conditions he wanted on salvation. He could have chosen to elect people without their assent. He could have required that they sell all their possessions and submit to torture as a condition for salvation. The question is not what God *could have* done, but what he *has* done—the actual criteria he has established for salvation. The Bible affirms and Article 7 of the TS asserts that God has sovereignly chosen to require repentance for sin and faith in Christ of any who would be saved, through the power of the Spirit of God. So we must teach, and so we must believe.

BIBLIOGRAPHY

Bavinck, Herman. *Reformed Dogmatics*. 4 vols. Translated by John Vriend. Grand Rapids: Baker Academic, 2003–8.

Blount, Douglas K. "Article II: God." In *Baptist Faith and Message 2000: Critical Issues in America's Largest Protestant Denomination*, edited by Douglas K. Blount and Joseph D. Wooddell, 13–24. Lanham: Rowman and Littlefield, 2007.

Calvin, John. *A Defence of the Secret Providence of God, by Which He Executes His Eternal Decrees*. Translated by Henry Cole. 1856. Reprint in *Calvin's Calvinism*. London: Sovereign Grace Union, 1927.

Commentary on Article 7: The Sovereignty of God

———. *Institutes of the Christian Religion*. Edited by John T. McNeill. Translated by Ford Lewis Battles. In The Library of Christian Classics. 2 vols. Philadelphia: Westminster, 1960.

Craig, William Lane. "God Directs All Things." In *Four Views on Divine Providence*, edited by Dennis W. Jowers, 79–139. Counterpoints: Bible & Theology. Edited by Stanley N. Gundry. Grand Rapids: Zondervan, 2011.

Evans, Jeremy A. "Reflections on Determinism and Human Freedom." In *Whosoever Will: A Biblical-Theological Critique of Five-Point Calvinism*, edited by David L. Allen and Steve W. Lemke, 253–74. Nashville: B&H Academic, 2010.

Feinberg, John. "God Ordains All Things." In *Predestination & Free Will: Four Views of Divine Sovereignty & Human Freedom*, edited by David Basinger & Randall Basinger, 17–60. Downers Grove: IVP Academic, 1986.

Frame, John. *The Doctrine of God: A Theology of Lordship*. Phillipsburg: P&R, 2002.

Geisler, Norman. "God Knows All Things." In *Predestination & Free Will: Four Views of Divine Sovereignty & Human Freedom*, edited by David Basinger & Randall Basinger, 61–98. Downers Grove: IVP Academic, 1986.

Grudem, Wayne. *Bible Doctrine: Essential Teachings of the Christian Faith*. Grand Rapids: Zondervan, 1999.

Harris, R. Laird, et al. *Theological Wordbook of the Old Testament*. 2 vols. Chicago: Moody, 1980.

Helm, Paul. *The Providence of God*. Contours of Christian Theology. Edited by Gerald Bray. Downers Grove: InterVarsity, 1994.

Helseth, Paul Kjoss. "God Causes All Things." In *Four Views on Divine Providence*, edited by Dennis W. Jowers, 25–77. Counterpoints: Bible & Theology. Edited by Stanley N. Gundry. Grand Rapids: Zondervan, 2011.

Keathley, Kenneth. *Salvation and Sovereignty: A Molinist Approach*. Nashville: B&H Academic, 2010.

Land, Richard. "Congruent Election: Understanding Salvation from an 'Eternal Now' Perspective." In *Whosoever Will: A Biblical-Theological Critique of Five-Point Calvinism*, edited by David L. Allen and Steve W. Lemke, 45–59. Nashville: B&H Academic, 2010.

Lemke, Steve W. "A Biblical and Theological Critique of Irresistible Grace." In *Whosoever Will: A Biblical-Theological Critique of Five-Point Calvinism*, edited by David L. Allen and Steve W. Lemke, 109–62. Nashville: B&H Academic, 2010.

Little, Bruce A. "Evil & God's Sovereignty." In *Whosoever Will: A Biblical-Theological Critique of Five-Point Calvinism*, edited by David L. Allen and Steve W. Lemke, 275–98. Nashville: B&H Academic, 2010.

Ososami, Bode. *The Majesty of God*. Central Milton Keynes: AuthorHouse, 2010.

Picirilli, Robert E. *Grace, Faith, Free Will: Contrasting Views of Salvation: Calvinism and Arminianism*. Nashville: Randall House, 2002.

Theological Dictionary of the New Testament. 10 vols. Edited by Gerhard Kittel and Gerhard Friedrich. Translated by Geoffrey W. Bromiley. Grand Rapids: Eerdmans, 1964–76.

Turretin, Francis. *Institutes of Elenctic Theology*. 3 vols. Edited by James T. Dennison Jr. Translated by George M. Giger. Phillipsburg: P&R, 1992–97.

Warfield, B. B. "Predestination." In *The Works of Benjamin B. Warfield*, vol. 2: *Biblical Doctrines*. Grand Rapids: Baker, 1991.

Article 8: The Free Will of Man

We affirm that God, as an expression of his sovereignty, endows each person with actual free will (the ability to choose between two options), which must be exercised in accepting or rejecting God's gracious call to salvation by the Holy Spirit through the gospel.

We deny that the decision of faith is an act of God rather than a response of the person. We deny that there is an "effectual call" for certain people that is different from a "general call" to any person who hears and understands the gospel.

Genesis 1:26–28; Numbers 21:8–9; Deuteronomy 30:19; Joshua 24:15; 1 Samuel 8:1–22; 2 Samuel 24:13–14; Esther 3:12–14; Matthew 7:13–14; 11:20–24; Mark 10:17–22; Luke 9:23–24; 13:34; 15:17–20; Romans 10:9–10; Titus 2:12; Revelation 22:17.

Commentary on
Article 8: The Free Will of Man

Braxton Hunter

INTRODUCTION

ARTICLE 8 FOCUSES ON what the TS means by the term "free will" because one's view of free will determines one's view of soteriology. Since Traditionalists believe that anyone can be saved, then anyone must be able to respond freely for or against the offer of the gospel. It is common for laymen and theologians alike to misunderstand the terminology and philosophical implications of free will. This chapter will attempt to bring some simplicity and clarity to this issue. Affirming the reality of a robust view of free will in no way jeopardizes an equally robust view of God's sovereignty. As Article 8 notes, a view of free will that accords to human beings the ability to accept or reject the gospel is actually an expression of God's sovereign purposes for his creation. The charge that Traditionalists deny, limit, or reduce the sovereignty of God has been answered in previous chapters. Indeed, if the intention of Article 8's affirmation is properly understood, the charge will be completely laid to rest.

Anyone Can Be Saved

THE CALVINIST AND TRADITIONALIST UNDERSTANDINGS OF FREE WILL

Chapters on previous articles have briefly addressed the question of what is meant by the term free will. Here, we will flesh it out in greater detail. Typically, Calvinists hold to what philosophers refer to as compatibilism. On the compatibilist view, man is free to do whatever he wants, but not free to want whatever he wants. That is to say, man has freedom to exercise his will in accordance with his desires, but he has no control over those desires. Since man cannot manipulate those desires, and man is not naturally inclined toward God, the compatibilist maintains that man will never freely respond to God. If he responds to God, it will be because his desires have been acted upon by God such that his "decisions" will follow from those desires. So long as a man's actual decisions are not directly determined (only his desires are determined) he is said to be free. In response to Article 8 of the TS, Tom Ascol explains,

> This is exactly what we do in evangelism. We call spiritually dead people to come to life. We call on those who do not have spiritual ability to repent and trust Christ. As we preach the gospel, we know that the Word of the Lord must be accompanied by the power of the Lord or no one will be saved. When God graciously does this saving work, it is not a vitiation of man's will. It is a gift of resurrection.[1]

Without a careful eye, one is likely to miss Ascol's point. God coerces man's desires so that man's will is now inclined toward God.

What is troubling for Traditionalists is that there is no appreciable difference between compatibilism and determinism. On determinism, most common among philosophical naturalists, free will is illusory. One may experience the various events and actions of his life as though they represent genuine choices; however, this is a byproduct of living in a closed system of cause-and-effect. No choice of any kind actually exists. Reconsidering compatibilism with this in mind, we must conclude that to say man is free to do what he wants, but not free to want what he wants, is to say that man is not genuinely free to make undetermined choices. It is for precisely this reason that compatibilism is often referred to as soft-determinism. On these grounds, William Lane Craig asserts,

---

1. Ascol, "Response," par. 12.

Commentary on Article 8: The Free Will of Man

> Determinists reconcile universal, divine, causal determinism with human freedom by re-interpreting freedom in compatibilist terms. Compatibilism entails determinism, so there's no mystery here. The problem is that adopting compatibilism achieves reconciliation only at the expense of denying what various scriptural texts seem clearly to affirm: genuine indeterminacy and contingency.[2]

Scripture so frequently gives the impression that man is not only free but also responsible, which seems to support some version of libertarian freedom. If this were not the case, then a number of biblical passages (such as those documented in the TS) become awkward. If man is bound by his will to only choose according to his sinful desires, then he simply cannot choose godliness. Worse still, he is punished for choosing A rather than C when, in fact, only A, B, and D were available to him. Such a proposal seems absurd. One might retort that this is precisely the beauty of Calvinism. God breaks in and draws the lost individual out of the bondage of his will and into a grace that is, quite literally, irresistible. This does not resolve the problem. Realizing such an existential transformation would be, indeed, a cause for exuberance for the most appreciative new believer. Grace would render him undeniably grateful. Nevertheless, placing the emphasis on the glorious salvation of the convert does not answer, but sidesteps the conundrum. When one considers the future citizen of hell, the difficulty emerges. On such a view, God is found punishing, and in some cases angry with, individuals for choosing wrongly among a set of all wrong options. This is one of several reasons most Southern Baptists find compatibilism to be an unsatisfactory theological explanation.

Traditionalists typically hold to some form of libertarian free will. According to this model, man has, as a special gift from God, the ability to transcend cause and effect and actually make real decisions. These decisions may be influenced by outside factors, but not to the point of coercion.[3] Libertarian free will is consistent with the language of Article 8 in the phrase "actual free will (the ability to choose between two options)." However, it is not our position that man can freely ascend to God without the offer and work of "the Holy Spirit through the gospel." The view that man can freely act without the in-working of God or can make the

---

2. Craig, *Reasonable Response*, 176.

3. This definition of libertarian free will is Christian-specific. By this I mean that a secular philosopher might not refer to God in a similar definition. In defining the libertarian position, I have focused the context on the issue at hand.

first move toward God can be understood as hard libertarianism. This is the view of the will accepted by Pelagianism and semi-Pelagianism but is explicitly rejected by the TS. Rather, the offer of the gospel and work of the Holy Spirit is available to anyone and is necessary for salvation. The denial "that the decision of faith is an act of God rather than a response of the person," means that, although God is responsible for the salvific work and offer, man is responsible for receiving or rejecting the gift. This view is known as soft libertarianism.

Soft libertarianism is not only consistent with Scripture but seems to be suggested by it directly. In his article, "When a Christian Sins," Paul Himes argues that in 1 Cor 10:13 only a soft-libertarian free will comes into view. In this passage, the Apostle Paul explains, "No temptation has overtaken you except such as is common to man; but God is faithful, who will not allow you to be tempted beyond what you are able, but with the temptation will also make the way of escape, that you may be able to bear it."[4] After making a powerful case on several fronts, Himes claims,

> Under the compatibilist view, then, at situation (x), faced with temptation (y), agent (w) cannot *desire* to choose not to sin, for his desire is already determined by his value scale, which is already determined by factors out of his control. If (w) cannot *desire* to choose not to sin, then he is not able to choose not to sin, hence he is unable to endure temptation. Thus, for the compatibilist, "in situation (x), faced with temptation (y), (w) cannot endure" (and "could not have endured"). Thus compatibilism has not adequately explained 1 Cor 10:13. . . .[5]

While Himes is careful to note that this case for libertarian free will centers on human sin rather than salvation, it is difficult to see why one would make a distinction between the two settings once libertarian free will has been established. It is the very nature of libertarian free will that is often objectionable to compatibilists. Thus, 1 Cor 10:13 counts in favor of the libertarian view of biblical freedom.

---

4. All Bible quotations in this chapter are from the New King James Version.
5. Himes, "When a Christian Sins," 342.

Commentary on Article 8: The Free Will of Man

THE PROBLEMS WITH COMPATIBILISM

The Questionable Status of Scriptural Support

Indeed, the proof texts typically offered as evidence of compatibilism hardly suffice upon close examination. Ephesians 1:11 states, "In Him also we have obtained an inheritance, being predestined according to the purpose of Him who works all things according to the counsel of His will." Traditionalists certainly agree that God "works all things according to the counsel of His will." What the passage does not say is precisely how this predestination occurs. Is it with respect to conformity to the image of God's Son? Is it those who God knows will be saved? Is it with respect to the church in general, in other words, corporate election? Is this predestination as the Molinist understands it? Each of these is a possible understanding of predestination held by Southern Baptists. As Malcom Yarnell points out, "Southern Baptists affirm diverse understandings of divine election."[6] The goal of the TS is not to speak authoritatively for all Traditionalists on all texts. The point is that there is no good textual reason to favor a compatibilist view of this passage. Thus, this verse makes a poor proof-text in that it hardly necessitates compatibilism.[7]

John 8:34 declares, "Jesus answered them, 'Most assuredly, I say to you, whoever commits sin is a slave of sin.'" Much has been made of this imagery. However, the man in prison shackles may still see the authorities through the bars and beg for mercy. All people experience the addicting power of sin in this world. Yet, to say that humans cannot cry out in repentance without the *irresistible* enabling of God is going beyond the text and into eisegesis. In context, Jesus spoke these words in response to the Jews who were claiming that they were not enslaved by any other earthly authority. Jesus was demonstrating that we are still plagued with sin, because our unsanctified, not-yet-glorified flesh is inclined toward it. Understood in this way, without all the theological baggage, the passage merely affirms the impact sin has on humanity. Therefore, our Lord utters a propositional truth claim which should be uncontroversial to Calvinists and Traditionalists.

---

6. Yarnell, "TULIP of Calvinism," par. 6.

7. In order to serve as a fitting proof text for compatibilism, the compatibilist interpretation would need to have greater plausibility. By plausibility I mean that it would need to be more likely the case than not. Yet, there is no *prima facia* reason to assign greater plausibility to such an interpretation.

In John 6:44, Jesus explains, "No one can come to Me unless the Father who sent Me draws him; and I will raise him up at the last day." This verse raises the ongoing debates regarding limited atonement and irresistible grace. Traditionalists maintain that everyone who hears the gospel can be saved. Salvation is not limited to a chosen few. Moreover, it might be the case that when Jesus says in the next verse, "Therefore everyone who has heard and learned from the Father comes to Me," that he is referring to the God-fearing Jews who were open to God's message through Jesus and became some of his earthly disciples. Unfortunately, viewed through Calvinistic lenses, this passage is understood to teach that the Father manipulates the desires of man and draws him to the point of salvation. Emboldened by this concept, sympathetic scholars often argue that on the basis of the original language, the term translated "draws" should be understood in a more robust way. God drags the sinner, as if in a net from which he cannot escape, and literally coerces the sinner's natural desire and instantiates Christian belief.[8]

Briefly, three difficulties materialize which warrant consideration. First, whatever the proper interpretation may be, it would seem to be at odds with the typical Calvinist view of irresistible grace. The same word is used in John 12:32 as Jesus assures, "And I, if I am lifted up from the earth, will draw all peoples to Myself." If the Calvinist is consistent in his interpretation, universalism would seem to be implicated by this passage. Second, however the term translated "draw" is understood in texts dealing with physical objects (material items), that the context of human will, mind or heart (non-material items) is in view already alters the way it is being used. Finally, despite the misconception regarding Traditionalists held by certain Calvinists, we have clearly affirmed that man cannot redemptively come to God without the work of the "Holy Spirit through the gospel." Thus, the passage in question does not strike against the TS position and fails to serve as a declaration of compatibilism.

The Logical and Moral Problems

Not only is the biblical basis for compatibilism suspect, it cannot avoid the logically problematic situation of the sinner being punished for choosing

---

8. Sproul, *Chosen By God*, 52. While making the case for this interpretation, Sproul quotes *Kittel's Theological Dictionary*, explaining that the passage means to "compel by irresistible superiority."

Commentary on Article 8: The Free Will of Man

one of his only sinful options, A. In Luke 12:4 and Mark 9:42–49, for example, Jesus warns individuals of what will happen if they remain at enmity with God. He stresses the nature and reality of hell to serve as a clear motivation and clarion call to redemption. In Matt 23:37–39, Jesus explains that peace could have been had on the part of those unbelievers he references if only they would have come to God, but he says of them, "you were not willing." While many Calvinists are quick to point out that salvation may not have been in view here, the call to make a libertarian choice in submission to the Father surely is. If compatibilism is true, then there is no way that these stiff-necked people could have chosen C; thus, the passionate declaration of Christ would have been misdirected.

The Problem of General and Effectual Calling

The problems of compatibilism are further compounded by the questionable separation of the "general" and "effectual" calls of God. Article 8 denies this distinction. The only logical purpose of the general call is to attempt to obviate the moral and logical problems stated above. If the effectual call goes out to only the elect, and only the elect can respond to it, then what of the general call? Two possible reasons for the general call come into view. It could be that the general call is merely the byproduct of the preaching of the word for the elect. In attempting to spread the gospel so that the elect might respond, the message spills over to the non-elect. They hear, but cannot respond to the message. After all, Calvinists agree that they should evangelize every person because of their ignorance of who is and is not elect. Still, on this view, the general call does not even actually go out to every man. It goes out to the elect and is heard by others. Perhaps the general call exists so that the guilt of those who do not respond to it is made even more apparent. However, if this is the case, we must loop back to the problem previously mentioned. They are still being punished for choosing A rather than C, when C was not available to them. Either way, what is the purpose of the general call? It seems to be a strange byproduct of a compatibilistic view of biblical freedom. Such a division between a general and effectual call is not necessary for those who see biblical freedom as libertarian, and thus it is denied in the statement. Common proof texts related to the division of the effectual and general calls such as Rom 8:29–30 do not require readers to fall into a framework which is fraught with the philosophical problems mentioned. Is the Calvinistic explanation of such texts the only possible understanding? Does it represent a position that can be demonstrated with overwhelming certainty? No.

Compatibilism's Vulnerability to Atheistic Arguments

Compatibilism also is vulnerable to the strongest arguments for God's non-existence offered by atheists. The incoherence arguments known as "arguments from evil," seek to demonstrate that either God's existence is not possible (a logical argument from evil), or God's existence is improbable (an evidential argument from evil) because of the amount of suffering, pain, or evil that exists in the world. A loving God, it is claimed, would not create a world in which such evil exists. When Christian apologists respond to such charges, they offer theodicies in defense of God. The theodicies that fit best with compatibilism are the "greater good" and "character building" theodicies. Greater good theodicies make the case that God created a world with evil for the purpose of establishing some greater good via the presence of those evils. Character building theodicies usually make a similar move with respect to the development of human moral character. Nevertheless, each of these theodicies leaves us with a God who is the ultimate causal agent behind all evil that exists.

Jerry Walls has argued that on such compatibilistic views, God is ultimately to blame in that a person who commits an evil act against his neighbor was ordained to commit that evil act because he was bound by those desires which bring the greater good—God's glory. Walls summarizes and responds to this view,

> [If] God must display justice by punishing evil in order fully to manifest his glory, then sin and evil must occur for God's full glory to be demonstrated. The disconcerting consequence here is that God needs evil or depends on it fully to manifest his glory. This consequence undermines not only God's goodness, but his sovereignty as well.[9]

Free will theodicy fits best with soft libertarianism and avoids the implication that God is the causal agent behind evil actions by placing individual volition into the hands of mankind. Evil occurs because man was given libertarian free will by God. If man is given the ability to make free choices, it is inevitable that he will ultimately choose to commit some evil.

---

9. Walls, "Classical Theist," 75.

Even natural disasters can be explained if a free will theodicy is brought to bear on the story of the fall.

One might argue that even theodicies based on the concept of free will do not justify God's allowance of evil. Why would he not create men with libertarian free will, yet work as a preventative force so that evil does not occur? Again, two problems would be introduced in such a world. One is philosophical and the second, practical. First, a rephrasing of this question would be, "Why doesn't God force man to freely do no evil?" Hopefully, the incoherence of the idea is obvious. Forcing someone to freely do something is a flat contradiction. Second, if God were to allow for evil free actions but miraculously work to prevent harm, certain natural laws could not be trusted. A world in which God is constantly preventing evil when it is about to happen is a world in which the laws of science would be constantly suspended such that, in one setting, fire burns, but in a potentially dangerous setting, fire cannot be produced. For obvious reasons, a world in which the laws of science vary would be a difficult world in which to live. Moreover, a free will theodicy can bring out the benefits that other theodicies seek to highlight.

Admittedly, character building and greater good theodicies recognize the powerful and transformative vehicle for change that tragedy often reveals itself to be. The problem, as stated above, is that God is understood to be the causal agent behind those evil events. Yet, advocates of free will theodicies hold that while the evil itself is the work of man, character development and greater goods often result. This means free will theodicies also recognize the positive benefits of having endured evil, yet do not make the major theological mistakes of the competing views.

On this view, created beings are the causal agents behind the evil that exists in the world. Such a charge cannot be made against the Father. While some might demand that God's foreknowledge of evil events should have dissuaded him from creating the world at all, most will likely see that the existence of the created order is an intrinsic good which outstretches the inevitability of evil and suffering. Of all people, those who believe in Christian eschatology should recognize this. As for the current state of affairs, we are to blame for evil, but God is to be praised for good. The existence of evil, then, is best explained by the existence of human libertarian freedom. Any view which denies libertarian creaturely freedom necessarily holds God to be the causal agent behind all evil.

Anyone Can Be Saved

A SOFT LIBERTARIAN MODEL OF SOTERIOLOGY

If a position resembling the Traditional view is to be adopted, then it seems needful that a libertarian soteriological explanation be given. Nevertheless, what follows is but one explanation that might be accepted by Traditionalists. As previously mentioned, Southern Baptists who have in the past been described as "non-Calvinists" have understood salvation in a few varying ways which neither violate orthodoxy nor depart from soft libertarianism. With this disclaimer in mind, I will begin with a consideration of the sovereignty of God.

God's sovereignty necessitates his power, ability and freedom to act authoritatively with respect to the created order. It does not mean that he is incapable of creating free agents in that created order. Indeed, his glory shines all the more evidently in that, via his omniscience, he is able to instantiate a universe of free agents while ensuring that ultimate victory is certain. The Creator would only lack sovereignty if it were the case that he found himself unable to superintend or affect his creation. God, however, is both aware of all temporal events and able to affect them. Neither open theism nor lack of sovereignty holds. Furthermore, this sovereignty implies that the salvation of the believer is in no way meritorious.

Despite man's soft-libertarian free will, he is in no way deserving of praise for accepting the gift of grace. Even if one rebuts that the acceptance of the gift of salvation itself is, in some way, an intrinsically admirable work on the part of the new believer, Traditionalists are prepared to offer a response that seems philosophically favorable.

Because Scripture teaches that grace is of God (Eph 2:8) and that God is not responsible for human sin (Luke 17:1–2), a model is necessary that would satisfy both of these propositions. Typically, Calvinists are criticized for implicating God as the source of evil, while non-Calvinists are accused of teaching that man merits his own salvation. Thus, a soteriological view must be located that would plausibly handle these matters.

In *Salvation and Sovereignty*, Kenneth Keathley argues for an "ambulatory model of overcoming grace."[10] Keathley writes, "If you believe, it is because (and only because) the Holy Spirit brought you to faith. If you do not believe, it is only because you resisted. The only thing you are able to 'do'

---

10. Though Keathley's work represents a definitively Molinist position, the ambulatory model does not necessitate a Molinist view.

is negative."[11] In other words, man is not able to achieve a work of grace for himself, however, he is free to resist God's grace. The explanatory power of the model should be apparent. On this view, man cannot be praised, since he did not bring about the grace he has experienced, but he is at fault if he denies the grace of God by exercising his freedom to that end. This view represents soft libertarianism in the truest sense. These two propositions make for an understanding of divine sovereignty and creaturely freedom wherein God alone is glorified in salvation, and man alone is responsible in condemnation. The case is made even more apparent if one accepts that God's grace is so great that he chose to create a world in which those who freely receive this gift would be saved.

SOFT LIBERTARIANISM AND THE BAPTIST FAITH AND MESSAGE

The Baptist Faith and Message (BFM) contains two articles that come to bear directly on the matter under discussion. Article 3 (which explains the Southern Baptist view of the doctrine of man) asserts, "Man is the special creation of God, made in His own image." Naturally, this is uncontroversial. However, it is vital for understanding the will of man. That man is created in the image of God is consistent with soft libertarianism in that the latter would require that freedom is a gift from God and a similarity that individuals share with him. The article goes on to explain,

> In the beginning man was innocent of sin and was endowed by his Creator with freedom of choice. By his free choice man sinned against God and brought sin into the human race. Through the temptation of Satan man transgressed the command of God, and fell from his original innocence whereby his posterity inherit a nature and an environment inclined toward sin.

Again, no conflict exists. It certainly counts in favor of soft-libertarianism that the BFM states that Adam had the attribute of freedom. By this we may assume some form of libertarianism, since man was not yet affected by sin. The point of dispute among Southern Baptists is this phrase: "his posterity inherit a nature and an environment inclined toward sin." Believers who advocate a soft-libertarian position find no difficulty with this statement. We agree that man is influenced by his sinful environment and

---

11. Keathley, *Salvation and Sovereignty*, 104.

nature. The caveat, which is not ruled out by the article, is that this results in a hindered will, but not a will of only determined desires. Therefore, Traditionalists can gladly affirm Article 3.

The same is true for Article 5 of the BFM, which speaks to "God's Purpose of Grace." Article 5 begins with the claim, "Election is the gracious purpose of God, according to which He regenerates, justifies, sanctifies, and glorifies sinners." Naturally, Calvinists and Traditionalists are in disagreement regarding how, when and for whom these events become a reality. The statement, however, in no way excludes a libertarian perspective. Indeed, the following phrase avers, "It is consistent with the free agency of man . . . " Even if some ambiguity surrounds what is meant by "free" in this passage, when interpreted according to its use in Article 3, libertarianism emerges. Either way, a libertarian position is no doubt consistent with the article. Lastly, since Traditionalist soft-libertarians affirm God's sovereignty and the concept of the eternal security of the believer, the rest of the article appropriately articulates a view that we celebrate.

CONCLUSION

All of the evidence above serves to support the view represented by Article 8 of the TS. Scripture clearly implies the existence of human libertarian free will, both directly and indirectly. The separation of the general and effectual calls, held by Calvinists, is an awkward byproduct of a compatibilist theological view that ultimately fails to salvage its unacceptable implications. The idea that God would hold man accountable for following the desires over which he has no control undercuts any legitimate understanding of human responsibility. Man is only responsible if he exercises volition. Compatibilism leaves believers with little or nothing to say concerning the problem of evil. If God is the causal agent behind the evil of the world, then it would seem that some atheistic arguments from evil may be valid. This, of course, cannot be true. Therefore, it is more plausible that man is responsible for the evil of the world because of his libertarian freedom. Ultimately, God is sovereign over man in that God is in control of the world he chose to create, and he could have acted otherwise. As the affirmation clarifies, man has libertarian free will because it was endowed to him by God, "as an expression of His sovereignty." This gift of libertarian free will to every person, though damaged by sin so thoroughly that it could never empower the sinner to choose Christ on his own, must still be exercised in response to the enabling power of the Holy Spirit in the proclamation of the gospel.

BIBLIOGRAPHY

Ascol, Tom. "Response to A Statement of the Traditional Southern Baptist Understanding of God's Plan of Salvation, Part 11." http://tomascol.com/response-to-a-statement-of-the-traditional-southern-baptist-understanding-of-gods-plan-of-salvation-part-11/.

Craig, William Lane, with Joseph Gorra. *A Reasonable Response: Answers to Tough Questions on God, Christianity and the Bible.* Chicago: Moody, 2013.

Himes, Paul A. "When a Christian Sins: 1 Corinthians 10:13 and the Power of Contrary Choice, in Relation to the Compatibilist-Libertarian Debate." *Journal of the Evangelical Theological Society* 54.2 (June 2011) 329–44.

Keathley, Kenneth. *Salvation and Sovereignty: A Molinist Approach.* Nashville: B&H Academic, 2010.

Sproul, R. C. *Chosen By God.* Carol Stream, IL: Tyndale, 1994.

Walls, Jerry. "Why No Classical Theist, Let Alone Orthodox Christian, Should Ever Be a Compatibilist." *Philosophia Christi* 13.1 (2011) 75–104.

Yarnell, Malcolm. "The TULIP of Calvinism in Light of History and the Baptist Faith and Message." http://www.sbclife.net/Articles/2006/04/sla8.

Article 9: The Security of the Believer

We affirm that when a person responds in faith to the gospel, God promises to complete the process of salvation in the believer into eternity. This process begins with justification, whereby the sinner is immediately acquitted of all sin and granted peace with God; continues in sanctification, whereby the saved are progressively conformed to the image of Christ by the indwelling Holy Spirit; and concludes in glorification, whereby the saint enjoys life with Christ in heaven forever.

We deny that this Holy Spirit-sealed relationship can ever be broken. We deny even the possibility of apostasy.

John 10:28–29; 14:1–4; Romans 3:21–26; 8:29–30, 35–39; 2 Corinthians 4:17; Ephesians 1:13–14; Philippians 1:6; 3:12; Colossians 1:21–22; 2 Timothy 1:12; Hebrews 13:5; James 1:12; 1 John 2:19; 3:2; 5:13–15; Jude 24–25.

COMMENTARY ON
Article 9: The Security of the Believer

Steve Horn

INTRODUCTION

ONE AFTERNOON A FEW years ago, a couple who lived down the street from the church came to see me. The woman pulled out a copy of Charles Stanley's *Eternal Security: Can You Be Sure?*[1] and asked, "Do you believe what's in this book?" I confessed that I had not read it but was reasonably sure that I believed what was in it. The couple went on to tell me that they had bought the book simply because of the title. The woman had read the whole thing in one evening, and her husband had read enough of it the next morning to get the essential idea. Seeing on the book jacket that Stanley was a Baptist, they decided to go to the nearest Baptist church to get more details. Coming from a religious tradition that had taught them that it was impossible, even perhaps sinful and certainly arrogant, to claim assurance of salvation,[2] this couple was eager to know the peace and joy that accompanies eternal security.

---

1. Stanley, *Eternal Security*. Stanley tells the story of how he came to reject the erroneous view of apostasy that he had learned in a Pentecostal Holiness church.

2. See as an example the Roman Catholic View as presented in Keathley, "Perseverance," 168.

The doctrine of the eternal security of the believer is of great significance for Southern Baptists and is central to the way we do the work of evangelism and discipleship. One might suppose that all Southern Baptists agree on this matter and that, therefore, this is not one of the contested doctrines in the current Calvinist debate.[3] Indeed, the idea of eternal security is stated unequivocally in Article 5 of the Baptist Faith and Message (BFM),

> All true believers endure to the end. Those whom God has accepted in Christ, and sanctified by His Spirit, will never fall away from the state of grace, but shall persevere to the end. Believers may fall into sin through neglect and temptation, whereby they grieve the Spirit, impair their graces and comforts, and bring reproach on the cause of Christ and temporal judgments on themselves; yet they shall be kept by the power of God through faith unto salvation.

The language of Article 12 of the Abstract of Principles is quite similar. The issues of greatest concern in both of these documents are the genuineness of conversion, the impossibility of apostasy, and the inevitability of some continued sin in the life of the genuine believer.[4] Any Southern Baptist confession seeking to aver salvation by faith through grace alone must also have this kind of strong statement concerning eternal security. Millard Erickson gets to the crux of this issue. On one hand, a theology that does not affirm eternal security leads to anxiety about one's spiritual condition. On the other, a view of eternal security that does not point to genuine conversion leads to "indifference to the moral and spiritual demand of the gospel."[5]

Calvinists and Traditionalists agree about the reality of eternal security, but this does not mean that there are no serious issues to unravel in the discussion. First, what is the basis of assurance? Second, can one affirm perseverance without necessarily committing himself to all of the other "doctrines of grace"? Third, how does each perspective deal with the difficult passages which seem to hold to some form of apostasy? Fourth, can the wrong view of assurance lead to "false conversions"?

---

3. For example, the 2013 document "Truth, Trust, and Testimony in a Time of Tension: A Statement from the Calvinism Advisory Committee" does not include in the list of tensions any reference to the doctrine of eternal security.

4. Noticeably absent from both the BFM and the Abstract of Principles is the language of the Westminster Confession, XVII, 2, which states, "This perseverance of the saints depends not upon their own free will, but upon the immutability of the decree of election."

5. Erickson, *Christian Theology*, 914.

Commentary on Article 9: The Security of the Believer

WHAT IS THE BASIS OF ASSURANCE?

Even though the differences between the Abstract of Principles, which is more Calvinistic, and the BFM appear to be slight, they illustrate a challenging dynamic even within this supposedly uncontested doctrine. The BFM begins with the declaration, "All true believers endure to the end," which inserts the language of the New Hampshire Confession's article on perseverance before the first sentence of the Abstract. The BFM, therefore, begins the discussion of perseverance with an emphasis on *belief*, which is muted in the Abstract. The clear implication is that the BFM seeks to make clear that *believing* is the basis for security. Additionally, the BFM makes specific that it is "believers" who are the subject of God's preserving power. The direction of Southern Baptist soteriology as it moved into the twentieth century was toward an emphasis on the centrality of belief as the basis for assurance, buttressed by the reality of sanctification.

While most Southern Baptists tend to use "perseverance of the saints" and "eternal security" interchangeably, nuances in the terminology also reveal the differences in the bases of assurance. The Calvinist view of "perseverance of the saints" places the emphasis of assurance on the evidence of the believer's activity rather than the believer's faith in the provision of Christ. The danger, of course, is that such thinking can slide inadvertently into a works-oriented basis for security. Consider this example from the popular and prolific John Piper: "It's true that Paul believed in the eternal security of the elect ('Those whom [God] justified he also glorified' [Rom 8:30]). But the only people who are eternally secure are those who 'make their calling and election sure' by fighting the good fight of faith and laying hold on eternal life."[6] Such reasoning complicates the issue of eternal security and potentially leads to more doubt than assurance by making the works of obedience the basis of eternal security rather than promises of Christ that belong to the believer by faith. There is, to be sure, a tension in Scripture due to its exhortative nature.

Kenneth Keathley, however, manages the tension between faith and works in this way: "Good works and the evidences of God's grace do not provide assurance. They provide warrant to assurance but not assurance itself."[7] Therefore, to avoid confusion about what is meant about our view of assurance, it may be better to speak of "security of the believer" rather

---

6. Piper, *Let the Nations*, 46.
7. Keathley, "Perseverance," 186.

than "perseverance of the saints." Security of the believer emphasizes a present state-of-being based on faith that persists into the future rather than the continual manifestation of certain actions in the future. Eternal security is the companion of salvation by grace. One of the reasons that Baptists have overwhelmingly believed in a doctrine of eternal security is the strong belief in salvation by grace. Belief in the work of Christ for salvation results in the assurance of salvation. As Keathley notes, "Assurance of salvation must be based on Jesus Christ and His work for us—nothing more and nothing less."[8]

CAN SOMEONE AFFIRM ETERNAL SECURITY WITHOUT AFFIRMING ALL FIVE POINTS OF THE TULIP?

Eternal security revolves around two significant questions. First, can one know with certainty that he is saved? Second, can the one who knows with certainty today that he is saved trust that he will never fall away permanently?[9] Southern Baptists of all stripes want to answer with a resounding "yes" to both questions. Either individuals have the promise of eternal security or they do not. The discussion is often framed as if there are only two options—the Calvinist position that says "yes" and the Arminian position that says "no."[10]

If Calvinism is the only option for a strong view of eternal security, then the real possibilities for dialogue among Southern Baptists will be at impasse. In this arrangement, it is supposed that the non-Calvinist cannot affirm assurance of salvation because agnosticism on the issue of assurance is fundamental to Arminianism. Though he certainly cannot speak for every Calvinist, the language of Erwin Lutzer is the sort of tone that creates potential for heated and unhelpful debate. Lutzer says, "Whether or not you believe in eternal security depends on where you stand on the free-will

---

8. Ibid., 171.

9. For a succinct presentation of the issues at hand, see Keathley, "The Work of God," 597. See also Keathley, "Perseverance," 163–87.

10. Erickson, *Christian Theology*, 914–17. This criticism notwithstanding, Erickson does a superb job of succinctly describing the two opposing views, supplying the important Scriptural texts that support each view and drawing the conclusion that the majority of Southern Baptists will affirm the certainty of eternal security.

controversy." Also, "The free will that accepts Christ is the same free will that can reject him."[11]

Tom Ascol follows Lutzer at this point. In a blog post criticizing the Traditional Statement, Ascol writes:

> If the nature of fallen man's will is such that he has the power of contrary choice either to trust Christ or reject Christ, how and why is this power lost once such a man becomes a Christian? Why must a Christian always remain a Christian? How can God keep him in the faith without "vitiating" his free will? It seems like this scheme leaves Christians with less of an "actual free will" (as Article Eight designates it) after conversion than before. These questions are sincere and I hope that the promoters and defenders of this document will address them. The hermeneutic that rejects unconditional election and effectual calling of believers cannot sustain, with consistency, their eternal security.[12]

Ascol's view of assurance rests on a compatibilist view of freedom that has been shown elsewhere in these essays to be quite problematic. Since God cannot be the cause of evil, since faith requires a genuine response that includes the ability to do otherwise, and since humans are not robots, the Calvinistic understanding of freedom must be rejected. Ascol's view actually drives a wedge between the reality of perseverance and the possibility of assurance. If salvation is based utterly on God's unconditioned choice of some and not others based on his hidden counsels, then how does one know that he is one of the elect? Should assurance of salvation be grounded in one's "feelings" or "sense" that he belongs to Christ? Such feelings can be false. What about the evidence of good works? The lost are capable of doing good things. It appears that the only sure foundation for assurance is the Traditionalist view that assurance is based on the accomplishments of Christ and his promises to anyone who believes by faith. How does one know he is saved? He believes that Jesus is who he says he is and that he will do what he says he will do. Feelings can certainly support such assurance, but there will be days when such feelings are not present. Works support such assurance but there will be days when such works are not present. If the inner sense of the Spirit's presence and the outward working of the Spirit are never on display, then soul-searching as to one's salvation

---

11. Lutzer, *Doctrines that Divide*, 225.

12. Ascol, "Response," par. 8–9. In the original, the last sentence begins a new paragraph.

is indeed necessary, but the basis of the search is still the same. The question is not, "Do my affections substantiate my election?" or "Have I done enough?" but "Have I trusted in Christ alone for salvation?" Assurance is not rooted in the doctrine of election or the doctrine of sanctification. It must be rooted in the doctrine of justification, or perseverance becomes a cause of doubt not a source of assurance. Calvinism tends to include inner witness and outward works as part of the basis for assurance because of the demands of determinism. The Traditional view, because it has a different view of freedom, allows assurance to rest on the only suitable cornerstone: justification by faith.

To answer Ascol's question about the nature of freedom after conversion, a question must first be asked of him: On the Calvinist view, why do the regenerate continue to sin? If inability to respond to God has been exchanged with the ability to respond to him, why does the redeemed person sin? If the answer is that he chooses to do so, then Calvinism is no different than the non-Calvinist view. All that is left is that God withholds the grace necessary for the believer to always do right, which, once again, opens a Pandora's Box concerning God's morality. On the Traditionalist view, the true convert has willingly surrendered himself to the sealing, transformational power of the gospel. He has said yes to God's commitment to unending fellowship. There is no going back; the freedom to walk away has been surrendered. However, as the Word says, such slavery is the truest kind of freedom (Rom 6:15–26).

WHAT ABOUT THE SO-CALLED APOSTASY PASSAGES?

Ascol's question raises the issue of the so-called apostasy passages of the New Testament, which Arminians use to support their position. If faith is a critical feature of assurance, and if faith requires a free response, then does it not stand to reason that one could "unfaith" at some later point and lose his salvation? Are there not indeed some Scriptures that support such a view? Though apostasy is not a serious debate among Southern Baptists, some degree of thought should be given to passages that others use as proof texts to cast doubt on eternal security. Ascol's point seems to be that the Traditional view, because of its particular view of freedom, does not permit such passages to be interpreted any other way than affirming apostasy.

The passages normally in question are from Hebrews: 2:1–4; 3:7–19; 4:11–16; 6:4–12; and 10:19–39. Those who affirm eternal security have approached these passages in one of two ways. Some have indicated that these passages are hypothetical in nature, dealing with what *might* happen if someone *could* renounce his faith in Christ. The other approach is that the addressees were simply not true believers. Primarily because of the language of actual experience of salvation in 6:4–12, it seems clear that genuine believers are in the writer's mind. The hypothetical argument is not plausible either. The details in these passages lend themselves to real, not hypothetical, issues.

The question of apostasy in these passages can best be answered by the context—the call to endure.[13] When my wife delivered our son, I was instructed by the nurses to "coach" my wife. Obviously, our child would have been born with or without my "coaching." Saying "You can do it" did not imply that I thought there was the possibility that she might not give birth. Anyone going through pain of labor greatly needs encouragement. The writer of Hebrews was simply encouraging his fellow believers to persevere in keeping with the "already/not yet" eschatological import of the New Testament. He had every confidence that they were going to persevere. However, to the recipients, the exhortation, no doubt, was much needed in the midst of very difficult circumstances.

WHAT ABOUT FALSE CONVERSIONS?

A view of eternal security like the one here presented raises a pastoral and practical implication. One of the issues often raised by Calvinists is the fear of false conversions. This fear is expressed by Wayne Grudem:

> But here we see why the phrase *eternal security* can be quite misleading. In some evangelical churches, instead of teaching the full and balanced presentation of the doctrine of the perseverance of the saints, pastors have sometimes taught a watered-down version, which in effect tells people that all who have once made a profession of faith and been baptized are "eternally secure." The result is that some people who are not genuinely converted at all may "come forward" at the end of an evangelistic sermon to profess faith in Christ, and may be baptized shortly after that, but then they leave the fellowship of the church and live a life no different from the one they lived before they gained this "eternal security." In this way people are given false assurance and are being cruelly

---

13. Guthrie, *Hebrews*, 224, states, "We must keep in mind that the genre of this passage is exhortation."

deceived into thinking they are going to heaven when in fact they are not.[14]

Certainly, there is some validity to Grudem's concern, and there are some who, by their carelessness, water down the gospel and preach "cheap grace." A gospel that does not call people to surrender by faith to the absolute lordship of Christ is no gospel at all; such a message cannot save. Sadly, there are people who have responded emotionally to a truncated version of the gospel and have wrongly believed themselves to have been saved; they placed their hope in an insufficient reality.

The Calvinist response to this situation, however, solves nothing. First, if God has already decided who is elect, then what does it matter whether the gospel is preached correctly or not (or preached at all for that matter)? The protestation that God elects the ends as well as the means simply begs the question. Second, as has already been argued, if election is unconditional, then what is the basis, outside of the hidden counsels of God, for assurance? What often happens is that the affirmation of certain doctrines become the proof upon which confidence rests, creating a false sense of security based on puffed-up knowledge. Third, did not Christ and Paul themselves have "false converts"? After sitting under such preaching and teaching, both Judas and Demas walked away. Was there some deficiency in what they had been taught? Was it because God secretly withheld saving grace while permitting their false belief for his own glory? Or, is the best and biblical explanation that Judas and Demas had shrunk the gospel down to fit their own selfish ends and never surrendered fully to the true message of salvation? In the end, we must go back to a balanced view of Scripture that all who believe in him will be saved and that genuine belief will result itself in good works. The true solution to false conversions is the biblical solution: preach the whole gospel, passionately call people to repentance and faith, strengthen believers in the body of Christ, and trust the Lord to keep his promises.

Consider the confidence with which the apostles spoke of their assurance. Paul says, "I know whom I have believed, and I am convinced that he is able to guard until that Day what has been entrusted to me" (2 Tim 1:12b, ESV). An effective communicator of the gospel must speak with this kind of assurance in order to offer assurance to his hearers. He cannot say, "I think I will have eternal life" or "I hope I am of the elect." With confidence, the bold witness must be able to communicate that he has believed in the

---

14. Grudem, *Systematic Theology*, 806, italics his.

grace of God unto salvation. The one without that assurance will always be timid in sharing his faith. Perhaps no greater word of assurance has ever been expressed than John's words: "I have written these things to you who believe in the name of the Son of God, so that you may know that you have eternal life" (1 John 5:13, HCSB). The one who doubts will forever be paralyzed into silence, at worst, or at least, be timid because of doubt. True assurance is based upon a strong belief in grace, the work of Christ upon the cross, and the word of God. May that firm assurance be held in the heart of every believer so that we might have the courage to share that assurance so that all who believe in Jesus for eternal life will have confidence in every circumstance. May we say with great assurance and conviction that all are savable, and those who repent of their sin and believe in Jesus are saved forever.

BIBLIOGRAPHY

Ascol, Tom. "Response to A Statement of the Traditional Southern Baptist Understanding of God's Plan of Salvation, Part 12." http://tomascol.com/response-to-a-statement-of-the-traditional-southern-baptist-understanding-of-gods-plan-of-salvation-part-12/.

Calvinism Advisory Committee. "Truth, Trust, and Testimony in a Time of Tension." http://www.sbclife.org/Articles/2013/06/sla5.asp.

Erickson, Millard J. *Christian Theology*, 3rd ed. Grand Rapids: Baker, 2013.

Grudem, Wayne. *Systematic Theology: An Introduction to Biblical Doctrine*. Grand Rapids: Zondervan, 1994.

Guthrie, George. *Hebrews*. The NIV Application Commentary. Grand Rapids: Zondervan, 1998.

Keathley, Kenneth. "Perseverance and Assurance of the Saints." In *Whosoever Will: A Biblical-Theological Critique of Five-Point Calvinism*, edited by David L. Allen and Steve W. Lemke, 163–87. Nashville: B&H Academic, 2010.

———. "The Work of God: Salvation." In *A Theology for the Church*, rev. ed., edited by Daniel L. Akin, 543–600. Nashville: B&H Academic, 2014.

Lutzer, Erwin. *The Doctrines that Divide: A Fresh Look at the Historic Doctrines that Separate Christians*. Grand Rapids: Kregel, 1998.

Piper, John. *Let the Nations Be Glad: The Supremacy of God in Missions*. 2nd ed. Grand Rapids: Baker, 2003.

Stanley, Charles. *Eternal Security: Can You Be Sure?* Nashville: Thomas Nelson, 1990.

Article 10: The Great Commission

We affirm that the Lord Jesus Christ commissioned his church to preach the good news of salvation to all people to the ends of the earth. We affirm that the proclamation of the gospel is God's means of bringing any person to salvation.

We deny that salvation is possible outside of a faith response to the gospel of Jesus Christ.

Psalm 51:13; Proverbs 11:30; Isaiah 52:7; Matthew 28:19–20; John 14:6; Acts 1:8; 4:12; 10:42–43; Romans 1:16, 10:13–15; 1 Corinthians 1:17–21; Ephesians 3:7–9; 6:19–20; Philippians 1:12–14; 1 Thessalonians 1:8; 1 Timothy 2:5; 2 Timothy 4:1–5.

COMMENTARY ON
Article 10: The Great Commission

Preston Nix

NOT ONLY DID GOD provide the means whereby lost humanity can be saved, but also God ordained the method whereby the message of salvation is to be communicated to the lost world. Of all the methods that the Lord could have employed to communicate the gospel to a lost and dying world, God in his sovereignty chose to use the method of human instrumentality to accomplish that task. Jesus commissioned the church to communicate his saving grace to all peoples in all the nations of the world throughout all time. This call in Scripture to join the Lord in reaching the world with the message of salvation is known as the Great Commission. The term itself indicates that followers of Jesus Christ are expected to partner with the Lord in his mission of reaching the world with his message of salvation, hence the word "Commission," indicating a joint mission effort between God and man.

The Great Commission has been a subject of discussion before Southern Baptists in recent years. At the Southern Baptist Convention meeting in Phoenix in 2011, the convention voted on a controversial proposal under the title the Great Commission Resurgence (GCR). Apart from disagreement over the political, fiscal, and organizational aspects of the GCR report and adopted proposal, all Southern Baptist leaders are agreed that since approximately three-fourths of SBC churches are plateaued or declining, coupled with the fact that one-fourth of the churches consistently report no baptisms annually, a true resurgence in the practice of the Great

Commission among the churches in the denomination is of absolute necessity for the future of the SBC. In addition, a special committee was appointed by the SBC President to study the viability of a name change for the Southern Baptist Convention. The end result was that a name change was not proposed but a new descriptor was recommended for churches to utilize that feel that the name Southern Baptist is a hindrance to their outreach efforts in their contexts. The adopted informal name was Great Commission Baptists indicating the evident value and the focused thrust of the churches which make up the membership of the denomination. Southern Baptists from their inception have been a people committed to fulfilling the Great Commission in order that the world may be won to faith in Jesus Christ.

Surprising to many Southern Baptists is the fact that the term "Great Commission" does not appear anywhere in the Bible. Although the term itself is not found in Scripture, the concept of commission is certainly evident. No doubt the Lord Jesus called for his disciples during his earthly ministry then as well as his followers now and throughout history to partner with him in his mission from the Father to communicate God's offer of forgiveness and eternal life to all who would repent of their sin and place their faith in him. Although the focus is usually on what is called the Great Commission from the passage found in Matthew 28, the Bible records at least five Great Commission passages, one at the end of each of the four Gospel accounts and another at the beginning of the book of Acts.[1] In these five different passages the Lord Jesus extended the crystal clear call for his followers to join him in his mission of communicating the gospel to the world. These five Great Commission passages together constitute the missions imperative of the New Testament church.[2]

Because each of these Great Commission passages contains a particular focus of the Lord's call to join him in communicating the gospel, it should prove to be beneficial to examine all of the passages in order to gain a comprehensive perspective of this clarion call to the church. The particular focus of each of the passages will be incorporated in the discussion in order to assess the full intent of the Lord Jesus for the faithful involvement of the church in his mission to communicate his message of salvation to

---

1. The five Great Commission passages are: Matt 28:18–20; Mark 16:15; Luke 24:46–48; John 20:21; and Acts 1:8.

2. Banks, *Great Commission*, 13. See Boice, *Foundations*, 651, and Hobbs, *Baptist Faith and Message*, 108.

the world.³ The greater focus will be given to the most recognized Great Commission passage because Matt 28:18–20 provides the fullest account of Christ's commission to his church.⁴

THE MOTIVATION FOR THE GREAT COMMISSION

Before Jesus actually delivered the Great Commission to his disciples, he established his divine prerogative to issue it.⁵ He prefaced the Great Commission with these words, "All authority has been given to Me in heaven and on earth" (Matt 28:18b).⁶ To possess authority means to have the right and ability to command others to respond. Jesus declared that he possessed all authority in the universe.⁷ He did not state that he possessed a little authority or even a large amount of authority. He did not say he possessed some authority or even most authority. Jesus declared without equivocation that he possessed absolute authority, both universal and unlimited in its scope. With that statement he revealed himself as sovereign Lord and King of the universe.⁸ He then commanded his disciples to "go, make disciples."⁹ If someone with all power and all authority tells someone else to do something, the only logical and sane response is for the person to act in total obedience. Herein is revealed the major motivation for fulfilling the Great Commission: the command of Christ which necessitates the obedience of every believer.

---

3. Arias and Johnson, *Great Commission*, 11–14.

4. As Hobbs, *Baptist Faith and Message*, 108, states, "An analysis of Matthew 28:18–20 is most revealing."

5. As Coleman, *Great Commission Lifestyle*, 31, aptly observes, "All too easily we rush into the action mandate without pausing to consider what Jesus says first."

6. All Scripture references are from the New American Standard Bible.

7. Donald McGavran indicated that the part of the Great Commission that believers are most prone to forget is Christ's declaration of authority, which provides the foundation as well as the motivation for fulfilling the Great Commission. Glasser, "Last Conversation," 59.

8. Robert Coleman declared, "Jesus is Lord, able to do whatever He wills, and before Him every knee must bow." He went on to say, "He has absolute sovereignty; His authority reaches across the vast expanse of the planet and unto the farthest star." Quotations from Coleman, *Great Commission Lifestyle*, 19, 31.

9. "Before challenging us with the imperative, Jesus reassures us with an indicative. Before He commands He asserts, and what He asserts is His unmitigated sovereignty." See Ascol, "Great Commission Tension," 151.

Although other valid motivations for fulfilling the Great Commission are evident in Scripture, including the compassion of believers for Christ that compels them to witness for him, the condition of lost sinners and the concern of the saved for their souls, as well as the coming of Christ, the final judgment, and the terrors of hell, the primary motivation for sharing the gospel is the command of Christ which every believer should obey. That fact was impressed strongly upon the mind of a young pastor who related the following incident which occurred early in his ministry:

> A few weeks after my eighteenth birthday I became pastor of a small rural church. Soon after, I was asked to preach on a Sunday afternoon at the Associational Church Training Meeting. I preached on why the church and the individual believer should be evangelistic. Some of the reasons I gave were that people are lost without Christ, sinful, on the way to hell, and in need of a new birth. All of these reasons seemed convincing to me. At the conclusion of my message, our Director of Missions walked slowly toward the pulpit and in a deliberate manner said: "Brethren, it seems to me that we ought to be witnesses because Jesus told us to."
>
> The Director of Missions was exactly right, and I have never forgotten the lesson that I learned that day. While all the reasons that I had mentioned are valid, we should seek to reach people for Christ just because Jesus told us to do it. That is reason enough, and it should be motivation enough. If Jesus' command will not prompt us to share our faith, nothing will.[10]

The Lord Jesus demands and expects that his followers evangelize their world. He allows no exceptions and refuses all excuses from those who claim to be his disciples. Obedience to the commission of Christ results in the salvation of souls. Disobedience to the commission of Christ impedes the progress of the gospel. Whether or not Christians share their faith does make a difference in the expansion of the Kingdom of God. Roland Q. Leavell writes,

> Evangelism has its compelling urge within an obedient, loving heart. . . . Christians need to take seriously the commission of Christ. Evangelistic results will never come until disciples obey the command of Christ to go to the nations and make disciples. Great

---

10. Bailey, *As You Go*, 6–7.

evangelistic harvests have and will come when disciples obey the orders of the King.[11]

THE MANDATE OF THE GREAT COMMISSION

Following his unmistakable assertion of his absolute authority, the Lord Jesus then handed down the clear mandate of the Great Commission. Jesus' authoritative command to his followers was "make disciples of all nations." The imperative verb in Matt 28:19 is: "make disciples," which is accompanied by three participles: going, baptizing, and teaching. As a result, four actions are required in order to fulfill the biblical mandate of the Great Commission. These actions flow in a logical and chronological order.[12]

Move to Potential Disciples

The first action in verse 19 that believers must take in order to fulfill the mandate of the Great Commission is to move from where they are to where lost people are in order to see them come to faith in Jesus Christ. That action is expressed in the word "go." The verb is a participle which can be translated literally "as you are going." Although most interpret this participle as an assumption on the part of Christ that his followers would be going about sharing the gospel, the verb also can be seen as a direct admonition from Jesus for his followers to go share the gospel. A participle in the Greek language can have imperatival force, and because the verb is in the emphatic position (at the very beginning of the sentence) that would add credence to viewing the verb "go" as it is translated traditionally in most versions of the Bible as a simple imperative.[13] In other Scriptures the Lord Jesus clearly commanded his followers to go and take the message of salvation to the lost world. In the Great Commission passage in Mark 16:15, Jesus commanded, "Go into all the world and preach the good news to all creation." At the close of one of his parables Jesus related the words of the master of the household, "Go out into the highways and along the hedges and compel them to come in, so that my house may be filled" (Luke 14:23). To the former Gadarene demoniac who became a disciple of Christ and

---

11. Leavell, *Evangelism*, 16.
12. Johnston, "Unleashing the Power," 11.
13. Leavell, *Evangelism*, 15.

wanted to accompany Jesus, the Lord said, "Go home to your people and report to them what great things the Lord has done for you, and how He had mercy on you" (Mark 5:19). The Lord Jesus Christ clearly commanded his followers to go to those who did not know him and communicate the good news of how sinful mankind can be made right with the holy God of the universe. Contemporary followers of Christ are commanded to do the same: go and share the gospel with others. Christians must move to where lost people are in order that the unsaved can hear the message of salvation. Unless someone goes and tells them how to be saved, they cannot hear and respond to the gospel message (Rom 10:13–17).

Make Disciples

The second action, according to Matt 28:19, which believers must take in order to fulfill the mandate of the Great Commission is to make disciples of all nations. In fact, that is the primary action and focus of the passage since "make disciples" is the only imperative in the Matthean commission. To make disciples means, very simply, to lead persons to place their faith in Christ. A disciple is a follower of Christ, but more specifically, from the very meaning of the word itself, a disciple is a disciplined learner of the Lord Jesus Christ. The popular cry of many concerning Christ's mandate of the Great Commission is that believers are commanded to make disciples for Christ, not simply to get decisions for Christ. The reality is that this imperative of the mandate means to win the lost to faith in Christ by proclaiming to them the gospel. Probably a better rendering of the single word in the Greek language popularly translated "make disciples" is "win disciples." The rationale for that translation is sound grammatically, linguistically, contextually, biblically, historically, and logically. Considering the other Great Commission passages, in order to make a disciple, first, the gospel of repentance and forgiveness must be declared to the potential disciple. That person must be won to faith in Christ in order to become a disciple or follower of Jesus. The word *mathēteuō* in Matt 28:19 does not refer to the ongoing process of discipleship or sanctification in the life of the new believer but to the initiation of salvation or conversion. The command to disciple new converts is found in the participle "teaching them to observe" later in the passage. No distinction exists between a convert and a disciple in this passage as is taught popularly by many today.[14] The

---

14. Johnston, "Unleashing the Power," 5–6. For an insightful discussion of the biblical

mandate of the commission is to proclaim the gospel to the lost and to seek to lead them to become faithful followers of the Lord Jesus Christ.

Mark Disciples

The third action necessary to fulfill the mandate of the Great Commission is to mark disciples by "baptizing them in the name of the Father, and of the Son, and of the Holy Spirit." When the newly reached convert is baptized by immersion in water he identifies with the Lord Jesus Christ through that symbolic act depicting the death, burial, and resurrection of Jesus Christ. Simultaneously, the new disciple identifies with the church into which he is baptized. The new convert also gives testimony of death to his former life, the cleansing of sin, and the new life he has received from Christ. Through baptism the church marks the new convert as a disciple of Jesus Christ and a member of the body of Christ.

Mature Disciples

The fourth action necessary to fulfill the mandate of the Great Commission is to mature disciples; that is, to help the new converts to become fully functional, faithful, fruitful followers of the Lord Jesus Christ. This action is revealed in Jesus' words "teaching them to observe all things I commanded you" (Matt 28:20a). The admonition to mature disciples refers to the process of discipleship through which new believers should be guided. This teaching aspect of the Great Commission is what many mistakenly refer to as "make disciples," which as revealed previously is winning individuals to faith in Jesus Christ. At this time in the life of the new convert he or she is to be equipped by other believers to walk with the Lord, worship the Lord, and witness for the Lord. Specifically, the new disciple is to be taught to obey the Lord and observe all his commandments. He is not simply to be given instruction in all things that the Lord commanded, but to be admonished to obey the Lord in all things.

Traditionally, the initial stage of discipling a new convert has been called "immediate follow-up" and the ongoing process of discipleship for a new believer has been referred to as "long-term follow-up," or discipleship

---

and practical rationale for translating *mathēteuō* as "win disciples" rather than "make disciples," see pp. 1–13. See also Johnston, *Evangelizology*, 1:501–5.

training. The teaching, mentoring, or equipping process of a new disciple can be done through a one-on-one relationship with a believer more mature in the faith discipling a new follower of Christ. This traditionally has been called a "Paul and Timothy" relationship, reflecting the role the Apostle Paul played in helping the younger Timothy mature in his faith and service to the Lord. The discipling process can be done in an informal group setting or in a more formal discipleship class for new believers led by a more mature believer in the faith.

THE MEANS OF THE GREAT COMMISSION

The means, or the agency, by which the Great Commission is accomplished is indicated in the promise Jesus gave to his followers at the conclusion of his commission on the designated mountain in Galilee as recorded in Matthew's Gospel. He declared, "I am with you always, even to the end of the age" (Matt 28:20b). He promised the disciples that his presence would accompany them as they attempted to fulfill the mandate of the Great Commission. This is the empowering presence of the Holy Spirit, Who is the presence of Jesus with believers now. Through the Lord's power the Great Commission can and will be accomplished.

This truth is borne out in other Great Commission passages in the Gospel accounts of both Luke and John, as well as the book of Acts. Following Jesus' admonition that the disciples were to proclaim in his name to all the nations repentance for the forgiveness of sins, because they had been witnesses of his death and resurrection (Luke 24:46–47), he told them to remain in Jerusalem until they received the Father's promise of the Holy Spirit and "were clothed with power from on high" (Luke 24:49). The Holy Spirit came upon them on the day of Pentecost, evidenced by the sound of a rushing wind, tongues like flames of fire on their heads, and their ability to witness for the Lord in other languages (Acts 2:1–13). Jesus previously had told the disciples that as the Father had sent him on mission to the earth he was sending them on mission, and symbolically portrayed how they would receive the gift of the Holy Spirit by breathing on them (John 20:21–22). Immediately prior to his ascension in his parting words of commissioning to his disciples, Jesus declared, "(Y)ou will receive power when the Holy Spirit has come upon you; and you shall be My witnesses both in Jerusalem, and in all Judea and Samaria, and even to the remotest part of the earth" (Acts 1:8). Clearly from these passages of Scripture (Acts 2:1–13) the means or agency by which the Great Commission is performed is the empowering presence of the Holy Spirit through the life of the obedient witnessing believer. Only the power of God's Holy Spirit can change people's lives. The Spirit, through the witness of the believer, convicts the lost of their sin against God, convinces them of their need for Christ, and when they repent of their sin and place their faith in Jesus, converts their souls (John 3:5–6; 15:26; 16:8–11; Titus 3:5).

THE METHOD OF THE GREAT COMMISSION

The method, or strategy, God has chosen to employ in order for the Great Commission to be accomplished is the evangelistic witness of his followers in his church. According to the Great Commission passages, God's method of communicating the gospel to the world is through both the personal witness and the public proclamation of the gospel of his beloved Son by those who know him. The word "witness" appears in two of the Great Commission passages and is implied strongly in two others; whereas, the words "preach" or "proclaim" appear in two of the passages as well. One of the Great Commission passages contains forms of both words. The object of proclamation is the gospel revealing that mankind through repentance of sin and faith in Jesus can receive forgiveness and enter a right relationship with the Father (Acts 20:21).

Jesus Christ fully accomplished all that was necessary for the redemption of mankind. Jenkins explains,

> (W)hat remained was that the good news concerning it, the gospel, had to be carried and proclaimed to the ends of the earth. Hence the Great Commission—given first to the apostles and through them to those who would succeed them in faith and work. . . . In this Great Commission, then, we see the mammoth and momentous task assigned by Christ to his apostles and inevitably those who follow in their train. . . . (T)he Lord's plain words in the commission—clearly meant that the mandate given the apostles was intended also for all who would follow them in every succeeding generation.[15]

Through the Great Commission the Lord Jesus gave the monumental task of communicating the availability of redemption to all those who would become his followers in the church throughout the ages. God's method

---

15. Jenkins, *The Great Commission*, 22–29.

for delivering the message of salvation since the ascension of Christ back to heaven once the final commission was given to his disciples has been through the personal and public proclamation of those who have experienced the saving grace of Christ. The Lord left the greatest message ever to be proclaimed in the hands of imperfect human beings, as represented by the first disciples and all subsequent followers of Christ. Until Christ comes again his plan is, as it always has been, for someone who trusts Christ for salvation to tell someone else how he or she can be saved.

THE MESSAGE OF THE GREAT COMMISSION

All of the Commission passages make clear what believers are to do to fulfill the Great Commission. These passages set forth the mandate that believers are to bear witness of Christ in order that nonbelievers will be converted to him and become his disciples. Two of the five commission passages specifically identify the saving message that is to be shared with the lost. In Mark 16:15, Jesus commanded his disciples to "preach the Gospel to every creature." The object of proclamation in this passage is the gospel, the good news of Jesus Christ. Clearly the particular message of the Great Commission that believers are to share is the gospel. Jesus revealed more specific aspects of this gospel message in the Lukan commission, "Thus it is written, that the Christ would suffer and rise again from the dead the third day, and that repentance for forgiveness of sins should be proclaimed in his name to all the nations, beginning from Jerusalem" (Luke 24:46–47). The focus of the gospel message as Jesus related it is his substitutionary sacrifice on the cross of Calvary for the sins of humanity and his victorious bodily resurrection from the grave for the salvation of mankind (Rom 4:25). Further, the message includes the requirement for salvation and response from the hearers, which is repentance for the forgiveness of their sin and trust in the person and work of Jesus Christ, indicated by the phrase "in His name" (Acts 20:21).

In keeping with these Great Commission passages, the Apostle Paul summarized the content of the gospel when he addressed the believers in Corinth to whom he had preached. He specifically identified the message of the gospel as the life, death, burial, resurrection, and post-resurrection appearances of Jesus Christ (1 Cor 15:1–11). The gospel is God's plan of salvation for sinful mankind and it is found exclusively in Jesus Christ. Many methods exist for communicating the gospel but there is only one plan of salvation and it is Jesus! Today, some people refer to the gospel in such broad terms that they indicate it encompasses all the truths of Scripture. Without maintaining the biblical definition and focus of the gospel on the saving work of Jesus Christ, the gospel can become whatever the theologian or preacher deems it to be. The result is that without the "razor focus" which Jesus and Paul gave concerning the gospel as salvation in Jesus Christ, the theologian or preacher can lay claim that he is teaching or preaching the gospel when he essentially is proclaiming various religious truths and even a doctrinal system. The gospel is about how someone can be saved through Jesus Christ. The message of the Great Commission is simply that Jesus will save anyone and everyone who will come to him in repentance and faith (1 Tim 2:4; 2 Pet 3:9; Rom 10:13–17). The good news is that sinful mankind can come into right relationship with the holy God of the universe when individual sinners acknowledge their sin and accept Jesus as their Savior and Lord. As the Bible declares, "Whoever will call on the name of the Lord will be saved" (Rom 10:13).

THE MAGNITUDE OF THE GREAT COMMISSION

The magnitude of the Great Commission is directly stated or strongly implied in all five of the biblical passages. Common to all of the passages is the extent to which the Great Commission is to be implemented. Jesus made it clear through his language when delivering the Great Commission to his disciples that it encompassed a world-wide dimension. In the Great Commission passage in Matthew, Jesus commanded his followers to "make disciples of all the nations" (Matt 28:19), which meant all the people groups (literally, ethnic groups) on the face of the earth. The universal scope of the Great Commission was delineated by Jesus in the commission passage in Mark when he commanded, "Go into all the world and preach the gospel to all creation" (Mark 16:15). Luke recorded that Jesus commissioned his disciples to proclaim the message of "repentance for forgiveness of sins . . . to all the nations" (Luke 24:47). In John's Gospel, Jesus declared that as he had been sent on mission to this earth by the Father, he was sending his disciples on mission to share the message of forgiveness with the whole world (John 20:21, 23). In the last words of commission from Christ to his disciples before he ascended to heaven, he told them they were to be his witnesses, "both in Jerusalem, and in all Judea and Samaria, and even to the remotest part of the earth" (Acts 1:8). The disciples were to give witness for Christ to every person possible in every possible place beginning locally and progressing globally throughout history (Matt 28:20).

The magnitude of the Great Commission indicates God's desire for all people throughout the entire earth to hear and to respond to the message of salvation. Since Christ died for the sins of all mankind, the offer of salvation is available to all who will call on the name of the Lord in repentance and faith (John 3:16; Acts 20:21; Rom 10:13; 1 Tim 4:10; Titus 2:11; 1 John 2:2; 4:14). God's will is that all people come to salvation through his Son. This truth is stated explicitly in two verses, one from the writings of the Apostle Paul and the other from those of the Apostle Peter. Paul wrote to Timothy that the Lord "desires all men to be saved and to come to the knowledge of the truth" (1 Tim 2:4). Peter wrote that the Lord does "not wish for any to perish but for all to come to repentance" (2 Pet 3:9). Therefore, the responsibility of the church is to fulfill the mission to which Christ has called her, and that mission in obedience and cooperation with the Lord—hence the term "commission"—is to proclaim the message of salvation to all peoples on the face of the earth so that all who believe will be saved.

MISTAKES RELATED TO THE GREAT COMMISSION

Mistakes have been made throughout Christian history related to the Great Commission. Some people have claimed that the Great Commission was given only to the original apostles and as a result should not be the basis for the church's mission. Others have concluded that the task of spreading the gospel to all nations has been completed; therefore, the Great Commission should not set the agenda for the thrust of the ministry of the church. Further, some have rejected the Great Commission as the priority of the present day church, believing it to be an outdated command that is culturally-conditioned. Pluralism has influenced these adherents to this view to value tolerance to such a degree that they believe no one should attempt to convert another person to his or her religious faith as mandated by the Great Commission.[16]

Probably the most prevalent mistake made currently concerning the Great Commission is by those who adhere to a deterministic theological system which causes some of them to diminish or even dismiss the vital role that the witness of the church plays in the fulfillment of the Great

---

16. For an expanded discussion of these objections to the Great Commission see Plummer, "Great Commission," 35–37.

Commission.[17] Their almost exclusive focus upon the sovereignty of God in evangelism and missions causes some of them to forget that the task of evangelizing the world was given to the church to be fulfilled in cooperation with Christ himself. That is why it is called the "Great Commission!" The prefix "co–" at the beginning of a word means "together with." Together with Christ, under his authority and by his power, the church is commanded to take the salvation message of the gospel to the entire world and make disciples of all nations for the expansion of God's kingdom and for the exaltation of Christ among all the peoples of the earth.

CONCLUSION

The means of fulfilling the Great Commission is the power of the Holy Spirit. The method God in his sovereignty has chosen is the evangelistic witness of his own people who have experienced his redemption and are obedient to proclaim the availability of his salvation to all who will repent of their sin and by faith receive Christ as their personal Savior and Lord. What a phenomenal privilege it is for believers to be called to partner with Christ in carrying out the Great Commission! What an awesome responsibility it is for believers to be tasked with proclaiming the most precious yet most powerful story known to mankind, the gospel story of God's offer of forgiveness through the sacrifice of Christ which is the message of the Great Commission. May the church of the living God be ever faithful to the "marching orders" delivered by her Lord and Master Jesus Christ, and carry out the mandate of the Great Commission to make disciples of all peoples on the earth in order that those who receive his gift of salvation will be among that innumerable multitude in heaven "from every nation and all tribes and peoples and tongues, standing before the throne and before the Lamb" (Rev 7:9–10; also 5:9–10) giving praise, honor, and glory to Jesus Christ forever and ever! Amen!

---

17. By contrast, Steve Gaines, senior pastor of Bellevue Baptist Church in Memphis, Tennessee, boldly declares that "when we share the Gospel with lost people, God saves people that He would not have saved had we not shared Jesus. Our sharing Jesus/witnessing/evangelism/soul-winning *does* matter!" (emphasis his). Gaines, *Share Jesus*, xii–xiii.

BIBLIOGRAPHY

Arias, Mortimer, and Alan Johnson. *The Great Commission: Biblical Models for Evangelism.* Nashville: Abingdon, 1992.

Ascol, Thomas K. "The Great Commission Tension: God's Work and Ours." In *The Great Commission Resurgence: Fulfilling God's Mandate in Our Time*, edited by Chuck Lawless and Adam W. Greenway, 149–76. Nashville: B&H Academic, 2010.

Bailey, Waylon. *As You Go: Biblical Foundations for Evangelism.* New Orleans: Insight, 1981.

Banks, William L. *In Search of the Great Commission.* Chicago: Moody, 1991.

Boice, James Montgomery. *Foundations of the Christian Faith: A Comprehensive & Readable Theology.* Rev. ed. Downers Grove: InterVarsity, 1986.

Coleman, Robert E. *The Great Commission Lifestyle: Conforming Your Life to Kingdom Priorities.* Grand Rapids: Revell, 1992.

Gaines, Steve. *Share Jesus Like it Matters.* Tigerville, SC: Auxano, 2016.

Glasser, Arthur F. "My Last Conversation with Donald McGavran." *Evangelical Missions Quarterly* 27.1 (January 1991) 58–62.

Hobbs, Herschel H. *The Baptist Faith and Message.* Nashville: Convention, 1971.

Jenkins, T. Omri. *The Great Commission.* Durham, England: Evangelical, 1997.

Johnston, Thomas P. *Evangelizology: A Biblical-Historical Perspective on Evangelism.* 2 vols. Liberty, MO: Evangelism Unlimited, 2011.

———. "Unleashing the Power of Matthew's Great Commission." In *Mobilizing a Great Commission Church for Harvest*, edited by Thomas P. Johnston, 1–13. Eugene, OR: Wipf & Stock, 2011.

Leavell, Roland Q. *Evangelism: Christ's Imperative Commission*, revised by Landrum P. Leavell II and Harold T. Bryson. Nashville: Broadman, 1979.

Plummer, Robert L. "The Great Commission in the New Testament." In *The Challenge of the Great Commission: Essays on God's Mandate for the Local Church*, edited by Chuck Lawless and Thomas Rainer, 33–48. Crestwood, KY: Pinnacle, 2005.

Is the Traditional Statement Semi-Pelagian?

Adam Harwood

SHEDDING A FALSE CHARGE can be difficult. Consider as an example McCarthyism in the 1950s. A person publicly accused of belonging to the Communist Party had difficulty shaking the accusation. "You're a Communist. Prove you're not!" How does one disprove such an accusation? Those who affirm the Traditional Statement (TS) find themselves in a similar situation. Claims have been made that the TS is, or appears to be, semi-Pelagian. This chapter seeks to disprove the charge in four ways. First, historical and theological definitions of semi-Pelagianism will be provided and will be shown to be contradicted by claims in the TS. Second, it will be demonstrated that the theological claims made at the Second Council of Orange (529) fail to indict the TS as unbiblical. Third, the historical-theological context of fifth-century semi-Pelagianism suggests that the historical debate has no connection to the current conversation among Southern Baptists regarding the TS. Fourth, errors will be exposed in an early assessment of the TS.

HISTORICAL AND THEOLOGICAL DEFINITIONS OF SEMI-PELAGIANISM ARE CONTRADICTED BY THE TRADITIONAL STATEMENT

According to *The Oxford Dictionary of the Christian Church*, semi-Pelagians "maintained that the first steps towards the Christian life were ordinarily taken by the human will and that grace supervened only later."[1] The TS explicitly argues against this view. Consider this line from Article 2: "While no one is even remotely capable of achieving salvation through his own effort, no sinner is saved apart from a free response to the Holy Spirit's drawing through the gospel." Article 2 is clear that sinners are saved through a free response to the Holy Spirit's drawing through the gospel. This drawing of the Holy Spirit described in the TS occurs *prior* to the response of the sinner. In this way, the TS *prohibits* the semi-Pelagian understanding of a sinner taking the first steps toward the Christian life.

The *Evangelical Dictionary of Theology* explains that the term semi-Pelagian first appeared in 1577 to describe the fifth-century view which rejected Pelagian theology and respected Augustine but rejected some of the implications of his views. Fifth-century semi-Pelagians "affirmed that the unaided will performed the initial act of faith." The "pivotal issue" in semi-Pelagian theology is "the priority of the human will over the grace of God in the initial work of salvation."[2] Article 4 of the TS contradicts this view, "We affirm that grace is God's generous decision to provide salvation for any person by taking all of the initiative in providing atonement." The TS states that God takes "all of the initiative in providing atonement." The TS in no way prioritizes "the human will over the grace of God in the initial work of salvation."

Lewis and Demarest's *Integrative Theology* explains, "The semi-Pelagians claimed that sinners make the first move toward salvation by choosing to repent and believe." Also, "The semi-Pelagian scheme of salvation thus may be described by the statement 'I started to come, and God helped me.'" The idea that sinners initiate their salvation apart from God's grace is ruled out by the words of the TS. Consider again Article 2, "While no one is even remotely capable of achieving salvation through his own effort, no sinner is saved apart from a free response to the Holy Spirit's drawing

---

1. *The Oxford Dictionary of the Christian Church*, 3rd ed., s. v. "Semipelagianism."
2. *Evangelical Dictionary of Theology*, 2nd ed., s.v. "Semi-Pelagianism."

through the gospel."[3] Also, this sentence from Article 4 bears repeating, "We affirm that grace is God's generous decision to provide salvation for any person by taking all of the initiative in providing atonement." The TS is clear that sinners do not "make the first move toward salvation." Rather, God takes *all* of the initiative in providing atonement. Article 8 explains that "God's gracious call to salvation" is made "by the Holy Spirit through the gospel." Sinners are saved by responding to the drawing of the Holy Spirit through the gospel.

One more definition, this one from a Reformed perspective, will be provided to reinforce the argument that there is a broad consensus on the term semi-Pelagianism. *The Westminster Dictionary of Christian Theology* defines semi-Pelagianism as follows: "A term which has been used to describe several theories which were thought to imply that the first movement towards God is made by human efforts unaided by grace."[4] This definition is consistent with those already provided and is contradicted by statements in the TS as demonstrated above. The following tables illustrate the research:

Definitions of Semi-Pelagianism
Semi-Pelagians "maintained that the first steps towards the Christian life were ordinarily taken by the human will and that grace supervened only later." - *The Oxford Dictionary of the Christian Church*
Semi-Pelagians "affirmed that the unaided will performed the initial act of faith" and "the priority of the human will over the grace of God in the initial work of salvation." - *Evangelical Dictionary of Theology*
"The semi-Pelagians claimed that sinners make the first move toward salvation by choosing to repent and believe." Also, "The semi-Pelagian scheme of salvation thus may be described by the statement 'I started to come, and God helped me.'" - *Integrative Theology*
"A term which has been used to describe several theories which were thought to imply that the first movement towards God is made by human efforts unaided by grace." - *The Westminster Dictionary of Christian Theology*

---

3. Lewis and Demarest, *Integrative Theology*, 3:20–21.
4. *The Westminster Dictionary of Christian Theology*, s.v. "Semi-pelagianism."

Semi-Pelagianism Contradicted by the Traditional Statement
"While no one is even remotely capable of achieving salvation through his own effort, no sinner is saved apart from a free response to the Holy Spirit's drawing through the gospel." - Article 2
"We affirm that grace is God's generous decision to provide salvation for any person by taking all of the initiative in providing atonement." - Article 4
"God's gracious call to salvation" is made "by the Holy Spirit through the gospel." - Article 8

THE DECISIONS OF THE SECOND COUNCIL OF ORANGE WHICH FAIL TO INDICT THE TS AS UNBIBLICAL

Immediately after the release of the TS, there were online accusations that the TS affirmed semi-Pelagian views. Some of those online essays included appeals to the Second Council of Orange (529).[5] The appeal to this council to support the accusation of semi-Pelagianism will be addressed in two ways. First, the decisions from the council will be compared to the TS. Second, the thesis of an historical study of the fifth-century controversy will be considered. In both cases, it will be demonstrated that the decisions of the Second Council of Orange fail to indict the TS as unbiblical.

The decisions of the council compared to the Traditional Statement

At the outset, it is important to understand that the Second Council of Orange is not authoritative for Southern Baptists. The decisions of the council addressed differences between western and eastern theology on the exercise of the will in the context of monastic life (see the next section in this chapter) one millennia before the birth of the Baptist tradition. Even if the decisions at Orange were considered binding for Southern Baptists, then the question arises as to which decisions were violated by the TS and

---

5. See, as examples, Jeph, "My Response," par. 8, who links The Canons of the Second Council of Orange; and Carter, "Southern Baptists," who cites Roberts, "Is the Statement Semi-Pelagian?" Roberts ends his essay, "I do not see how the Statement can avoid being rightly called semi-Pelagian."

Is the Traditional Statement Semi-Pelagian?

in what way? The decisions were finalized as a list of canons.[6] In comparing the Canons of Orange to the TS, it will be demonstrated that there is both agreement and contradictions between the two documents. Further, the contradictions between the two documents are theological differences which result from the fidelity of the TS to the BFM. Below are five replies to this charge of semi-Pelagianism based on the Canons of Orange.

1. Southern Baptists reject baptismal regeneration (salvation via water baptism). But baptismal regeneration was affirmed by this council. Canon 5 refers to "the regeneration of holy baptism." Also, Canon 13 states: "The freedom of will that was destroyed in the first man can be restored only by the grace of baptism." The Canons of Orange are not consistent with the BFM. For that reason alone, the council should be regarded as non-binding for Southern Baptists.

2. Canon 4 requires an admission of the working of the Holy Spirit. Article 2 of the TS states: "(W)e deny that any sinner is saved apart from a free response to the Holy Spirit's drawing through the gospel." That sentence clearly affirms the work of the Holy Spirit, who draws the sinner through the gospel.

3. Canon 5 denies that faith "belongs to us by nature and not by a gift of grace." The TS makes no claim that faith belongs to us by nature. Rather, Article 4 states that by God's grace, we are united "to Christ through the Holy Spirit by faith." This means that a person's union with Christ is by God's grace (a gift) and through the Holy Spirit. These claims remove any idea that faith could "belong to us by nature."

4. Canon 6 affirms that God's mercy is a gift of God's grace. So does the TS. Consider Article 4 of the TS, "We affirm that grace is God's generous decision to provide salvation for any person by taking all of the initiative in providing atonement." Article 4 of the TS is clear that salvation is a gift of God's grace and he takes the initiative in providing atonement.

5. Canon 6 states, "(I)t is by the infusion and inspiration of the Holy Spirit within us that we have the faith, the will, or the strength to do all these things as we ought." Canon 7 emphasizes this by stating that no one can be saved by "assent to the preaching of the gospel through our

---

6. The Canons of Orange (529) can be found in Pelikan and Hotchkiss, *Creeds & Confessions*, 1:693–98.

natural powers without the illumination and inspiration of the Holy Spirit." The ministry of the Holy Spirit must be acknowledged in one's understanding of a sinner's regeneration. The TS repeatedly refers to the ministry of the Holy Spirit in bringing a sinner to repentance and faith in Christ. Consider these claims in the TS:

1. Article 2, "(W)e deny that any sinner is saved apart from a free response to the Holy Spirit's drawing through the gospel."
2. Article 4, "We affirm that grace is God's generous decision to provide salvation . . . in freely offering the gospel in the power of the Holy Spirit, and in uniting the believer to Christ through the Holy Spirit by faith."
3. Article 5, "We affirm that any person who responds to the gospel with repentance and faith is born again through the power of the Holy Spirit. He is a new creation in Christ and enters, at the moment he believes, into eternal life."
4. Article 8, The call to salvation is made "by the Holy Spirit through the gospel."

The TS clearly acknowledges the necessity of the ministry of the Holy Spirit in the work of God to bring a sinner from death to life. It is unclear how a charge could be sustained that the TS teaches otherwise.

These comparisons demonstrate that it is neither helpful nor accurate to charge the TS with semi-Pelagianism based on the Canons of Orange. In the next section, the historical-theological context of fifth-century semi-Pelagianism will be considered to see if its views are consistent with the TS.

The historical-theological context of fifth-century semi-Pelagianism

Rebecca Harden Weaver published her PhD dissertation through the North American Patristic Society under the title *Divine Grace and Human Agency: A Study of the Semi-Pelagian Controversy*. Weaver's careful historical-theological analysis makes a compelling case that the decisions of the Second Council of Orange (529) wrongly characterized the views of the opponents. In other words, the fifth-century semi-Pelagians did not teach the views they were accused of teaching. If this is the case, then this renders impotent any appeals to the Canons of Orange against the TS.[7]

---

7. Weaver, *Divine Grace and Human Agency*.

Is the Traditional Statement Semi-Pelagian?

The semi-Pelagians, whose views are best illustrated in the writings of John Cassian, understood salvation as the struggle for perfection within the monastic disciplines. Which group of Southern Baptists defines salvation in terms of eastern monasticism? None. The fifth-century, eastern monks questioned how God would judge and reward spiritual life apart from the exercise of the human will. The Augustinian reply (and the later decision by the Second Council of Orange) was a reply to this question about this monastic struggle for perfection, not a reply to contemporary Southern Baptists who differ over Calvinism.

Conclusion Regarding the Second Council of Orange

Contemporary Southern Baptists who view the Second Council of Orange as a model for discussing Calvinism within the SBC will be disappointed. First, the council affirmed baptismal regeneration (salvation via water baptism), which is inconsistent with the BFM. Second, the council did not resolve the question of whether certain people are predestined by God to salvation. Third, if Weaver is correct in her reconstruction of historical events, then the council addressed the semi-Pelagian view of the perfection of saints, not the salvation of sinners. In those three ways, the canons against semi-Pelagianism do not apply to the TS.

AN EARLY ASSESSMENT OF THE TRADITIONAL STATEMENT

Less than one week after its public release, Roger Olson, professor of theology at Truett Seminary in Waco, Texas, commented on the TS. In the blog post, he made three errors before concluding that certain statements in Article 2 "can be interpreted in a semi-Pelagian way."[8] First, he begins with a false premise which ends in a wrong conclusion. Second, Olson links the TS with people who deny an important claim which the TS affirms. Third, Olson wrongly regards the non-use of an Arminian phrase as a denial of divine initiative. Each of those errors will be detailed below. If Olson erred

---

8. Olson, "Thoughts," par. 10. Olson concludes his article with this comment, which reveals his position on this issue prior to reading the TS: "For a long time I've been stating that most American Christians, including most Baptists, are semi-Pelagian, not Arminian and not merely non-Calvinist."

in his assessment of the TS, then his claim that the TS can be interpreted in a semi-Pelagian way should be considered inaccurate.

Beginning with a false premise leads to a wrong conclusion

Olson moves from a false premise to a wrong conclusion in order to charge the TS with semi-Pelagianism. First, he wrongly assumes that Southern Baptists are limited to only two biblical options for addressing the issues in Article 2: Calvinism and Arminianism. Next, Olson notes the failure in Article 2 to include two theological concepts which are used in debates between Calvinists and Arminians. Arminians acknowledge the bondage of the will and counter it with prevenient grace. Because Article 2 fails to acknowledge both the problem (bondage of the will) and the solution (prevenient grace), Article 2 should be regarded as neither Calvinist nor Arminian. Olson's error is that he regards the only other option to be semi-Pelagianism. Must one choose between Arminianism or Calvinism in order to affirm Christian views? According to Olson, yes.

Olson was wrong to require this Arminian-Calvinist theological grid. Article 2 failed to engage the bondage of the will because such a view belongs to a philosophical-theological system which obstructs a clear reading of Scripture.[9] Such doctrines are neither helpful nor necessary for Article 2. The TS summarizes a biblical view of the impact of sin on people without importing the bondage of the will. How? Doctrinal statements which reject the Calvinist-Arminian framework are not obligated to employ doctrines belonging uniquely to that system, such as bondage of the will. It is not enough to argue that the TS fails to employ the terms bondage of the will and prevenient grace. In order to make a case against the TS as unbiblical, it must be demonstrated that the views are *required* by the words of the Bible. Olson did not attempt to make such a case.

Olson's false premise is that the TS, a distinctively Southern Baptist doctrinal statement, must employ an Arminian doctrine (prevenient grace) to answer a doctrine belonging to Calvinist-Arminian debates on the will. Otherwise, he wrongly concludes, the Southern Baptist document is semi-Pelagian. Advocates of the TS reject the notion that Baptists must borrow from Arminians to defend against Calvinists.

---

9. For more on this view, see Allen et al., "Neither Calvinists" and Hankins, "Beyond Calvinism," 87–100.

Wrongly linking the Traditional Statement with people who deny an important claim it affirms

Olson links the TS with people who deny divine initiative in salvation, but the TS explicitly affirms divine initiative. In his blog article, Olson writes,

> (T)he statement's mention of "the Holy Spirit's drawing through the gospel" . . . can be interpreted in a semi-Pelagian way. Semi-Pelagians such as Philip Limborch and (at least in some of his writings) Charles Finney affirmed the necessity of the gospel and the Holy Spirit's enlightening work through it for salvation. What made them semi-Pelagian was their denial or neglect of the divine initiative in salvation (except the gospel message).[10]

Olson claims that "the Holy Spirit's work of drawing sinners to salvation through the gospel . . . can be interpreted in a semi-Pelagian way." How so? Olson explains that Limborch and Finney, whom he labels as semi-Pelagians, affirmed the need for the Holy Spirit and the gospel. At this point, Olson has only established that any doctrinal statement which affirms the need for the Holy Spirit to use the gospel in order for sinners to be converted should be regarded as semi-Pelagian. That would include both the TS and the BFM. But Olson continues, "What made them semi-Pelagian," and it is unclear to whom was Olson referring. Olson was probably referring not to advocates of the TS but to Limborch and Finney. Thus, "What made [Limborch and Finney] semi-Pelagian was their denial or neglect of divine initiative in salvation." Even so, Olson implies that if the TS denies or neglects divine initiative, then it should be regarded as semi-Pelagian. But the TS *affirms* divine initiative in salvation. In that way, the TS is innocent of Olson's charge.

Wrongly regarding the non-use of an Arminian phrase as a denial of divine initiative

In his blog post on Article 2, Olson writes,

> The problem with this Southern Baptist statement is its neglect of emphasis on the necessity of the prevenience of supernatural grace for the exercise of a good will toward God (including acceptance of the gospel by faith). If the authors believe in that cardinal biblical truth, they need to spell it out more clearly. And they need to

---

10. Olson, "Thoughts," par. 10.

delete the sentence that denies the incapacitation of free will due to Adam's sin.

Leaving the statement as it stands, without a clear affirmation of the bondage of the will to sin apart from supernatural grace, inevitably hands the Calvinists ammunition to use against non-Calvinist Baptists.[11]

Olson identifies "(t)he problem with this Southern Baptist Statement" as "its neglect of emphasis on the necessity of prevenience of supernatural grace (. . .)." Previously, Olson noted the problem with Limborch and Finney was their "denial or neglect of the divine initiative in salvation." Olson has not established that the TS denies or neglects divine initiative in salvation. But Olson apparently thinks this is the case since the TS does not mention "the prevenience of supernatural grace."

It is true that the TS does not use this Arminian phrase "prevenience of supernatural grace." But any concern that Article 2 neglects an emphasis on God's grace should be assuaged by the following declarations in the Statement:

> ". . . no sinner is saved apart from a free response to the Holy Spirit's drawing through the gospel."—Article 2, sentence 4

> "We affirm that grace is God's generous decision to provide salvation for any person by taking all of the initiative in providing atonement . . . ."—Article 4, sentence 1

The language of the TS comforts neither Calvinists nor Arminians because Article 2 fails to mention either the bondage of the will or prevenient grace. The reason the theological language of Calvinism and Arminianism is not employed is simple. The TS describes the theology of Southern Baptists who identify with neither of those theological systems.

Olson's dedicated and intense study of the Calvinist-Arminian framework over a prolonged period of time has resulted in both help and hindrance. The help is found in Olson's recent books. One is a masterful explanation of Arminianism. The other is a devastating critique of Calvinism. These books are outstanding.[12] Unfortunately, the help is accompanied by a hindrance. Olson now places all doctrinal blocks into one of only three holes: Calvinism, Arminianism, and Unbiblical. Because the preamble of the TS explains it was prompted by the rising influence of Calvinism within

---

11. Ibid.

12. Olson, *Arminian Theology*; Olson, *Against Calvinism*.

the SBC, Olson skipped the Calvinism hole. Next, he tried to fit the TS into the Arminian hole. When the TS mentioned neither the bondage of the will nor prevenient grace, Olson knew it would not fit in the Arminian hole. Olson reasoned the TS must fit into the third hole. But, as argued above, that would only be the case if one accepts the premise that there are only three options: Calvinism, Arminianism, and Unbiblical. The TS reflects a fourth option, Southern Baptist theology which maintains faithfulness to the Bible but disregards certain commitments of both Calvinism and Arminianism.

SUMMARY

The claim made by Olson was then echoed by an SBC seminary president, who wrote that the TS appears to affirm semi-Pelagianism.[13] This chapter attempted to disprove the charge in four ways. First, standard definitions of semi-Pelagianism were provided which are contradicted by claims in the TS. Second, the decisions of the Second Council of Orange fail to indict the TS as unbiblical. Third, the historical-theological context of the fifth-century debate suggests no connection to the current discussion regarding the TS. Fourth, particular errors were exposed in an early assessment of the TS.

The aim of this chapter has been to defeat a false charge. It has been demonstrated in several ways that the TS does not affirm semi-Pelagianism. Perhaps those who were accused of semi-Pelagianism for affirming the Traditional Statement will one day be exonerated like those who were wrongly accused of Communism in the 1950s.

---

13. Two days after Olson's article was posted online, R. Albert Mohler, president of The Southern Baptist Theological Seminary, commented on the TS in an article on his blog, "Some portions of the statement actually go beyond Arminianism and appear to affirm semi-Pelagian understandings of sin, human nature, and the human will—understandings that virtually all Southern Baptists have denied." See Mohler, "Southern Baptists," par. 8. Mohler offered no support for his claim. At the time of this writing, he has neither rescinded nor repeated the charge.

BIBLIOGRAPHY

Allen, David L., et al. "Neither Calvinists nor Arminians but Baptists." White Paper 36. The Center for Theological Research (September 2010). http://www.baptisttheology.org/white-papers/neither-calvinists-nor-arminians-but-baptists/.

Carter, Joe. "The FAQ's: Southern Baptists, Calvinists, and God's Plan of Salvation." http://thegospelcoalition.org/blogs/tgc/2012/06/06/the-faqs-southern-baptists-calvinism-and-gods-plan-of-salvation.

Hankins, Eric. "Beyond Calvinism and Arminianism: Toward a Baptist Soteriology" *Journal for Baptist Theology & Ministry* 8.1 (Spring 2011) 87–100. http://baptistcenter.net/journals/JBTM_8-1_Spring_2011.pdf.

Jeph (no last name). "My Response to 'A Statement of the Traditional Southern Baptist Understanding of God's Plan of Salvation.'" http://righteousbutnotyet.blogspot.com/2012/06/response-to-statement-of-traditional.html.

Lewis, Gordon R., and Bruce A. Demarest. *Integrative Theology*, three volumes in one. Grand Rapids: Zondervan, 1996.

Mohler, R. Albert. "Southern Baptists and Salvation: It's Time to Talk." http://www.albertmohler.com/2012/06/06/southern-baptists-and-salvation-its-time-to-talk/.

Olson, Roger. *Against Calvinism*. Grand Rapids: Zondervan, 2011.

———. *Arminian Theology: Myths and Reality*. Downers Grove: IVP Academic, 2006.

———. "Thoughts about 'A Statement of the Traditional Southern Baptist Understanding of God's Plan of Salvation.'" http://www.patheos.com/blogs/rogereolson/2012/06/thoughts-about-"a-statement-of-the-traditional-southern-baptist-understanding-of-gods-plan-of-salvation-"/.

Pelikan, Jaroslav, and Valerie Hotchkiss, eds. *Creeds & Confessions of Faith in the Christian Tradition*. 4 vols. New Haven: Yale University Press, 2003.

Roberts, Chris. "Is the Statement Semi-Pelagian?" http://sbcvoices.com/is-the-statement-semi-pelagian-by-chris-roberts/.

Weaver, Rebecca Harden. *Divine Grace and Human Agency: A Study of the Semi-Pelagian Controversy*. Patristic Monograph Series 15. Macon, GA: Mercer University Press, 1996.

Five Theological Models Relating Determinism, Divine Sovereignty, and Human Freedom

Steve W. Lemke

SEVERAL OF THE CLAIMS in the Traditional Statement (TS) involve the interrelation of divine sovereignty and human freedom. This question is addressed in several chapters in the present book, but this chapter provides an overview of different perspectives on this important subject. Although there is a broad spectrum of views on this question, there are five basic perspectives held by evangelicals to describe the relationship of divine sovereignty to human freedom—hard determinism, soft determinism, Molinism, soft-libertarian freedom, and strong-libertarian freedom. This article seeks to survey each of these perspectives, particularly because each of them has its own vocabulary that can be confusing or misunderstood. These topics are controversial, and are discussed in many settings, both in person and online. All Christians should be able to articulate where they stand on this important subject. It is very important for church leaders to understand these terms and be able to discuss them intelligently. I will also provide some commentary on the viability of each of these models from a Traditional Southern Baptist perspective.

Anyone Can Be Saved

HARD DETERMINISM/CAUSAL DETERMINISM

The strongest challenge to personal human freedom is *hard determinism* or *causal determinism*, the view that everything we are and do is determined or caused by prior events. So, though we think that we have a choice in what we eat for lunch or whom we marry, in fact we are deceived. These apparent choices are but an illusion. We had no choice but to eat a particular lunch or marry a particular person—it was imbedded in our DNA or brain cells. In fact, all of what we call "choices" are just an illusion—everything is determined by prior events and causes. Determinism is popular among many materialists, New Atheists, and postmodernists because it portrays the world as a closed system in which everything is completely determined by natural causes. For example, note how postmodernist thinker Richard Rorty's determinism is expressed in his view of the radical contingency with which each person's life is shaped by previous events and causes: "Our language and our culture are as much a contingency, as much a result of thousands of small mutations finding niches (and millions of others finding no niches), as are the orchids and the anthropoids."[1] So, for Rorty, "for all we know, or should care, Aristotle's metaphorical use of *ousia*, Saint Paul's metaphorical use of *agape*, and Newton's metaphorical use of *gravitas*, were the results of cosmic rays scrambling the fine structure of some crucial neurons in their respective brains. Or, more plausibly, they were the result of some odd episodes in infancy—some obsessional kinks left in these brains by idiosyncratic traumata."[2]

In a Christian reading of hard determinism, however, it is not physical causes but God's decrees which determine everything that happens. Not many evangelicals endorse this (hard) theological determinism, but some such as Paul Helm, Paul Helseth, and John Feinberg are willing to insist that God ordains all things that happen in order to assure a perspective that God is totally in control of the universe, even at the most detailed level.[3] So, again, in hard determinism we have no real choices; everything is

---

1. Rorty, *Contingency*, 16.
2. Ibid., 17.
3. Helm, *Providence of God*; Helm, "Classical Calvinist," 5–52; Helseth, "God Causes," 25–77; Feinberg, *No One Like Him*, 677–776; and Feinberg, "God Ordains," 17–60. Feinberg's view is more nuanced than Helm's, and at points he could also be described as advocating the compatibilist view, but fundamentally, as the title of his article suggests, he affirms that "God ordains all things."

predetermined and caused by prior events, and in a Christian hard determinism, God ordains everything that happens; we really have no choice or freedom.

SOFT DETERMINISM/COMPATIBILISM

Hard determinism is so out of touch with our own experience of life, however, that many feel that it does not give an adequate account of human freedom. This problem has led to the affirmation by many of *soft determinism* or *compatibilism*, which asserts that freedom is in some sense compatible with determinism.[4]

Having defined what compatibilism *is*, we must also note what it is *not*. Unfortunately, some theologians have profoundly confused what compatibilism is, and this confusion greatly muddles the discussion of this topic. They have described compatibilism not as the compatibility of determinism and human freedom, but the compatibility of divine sovereignty with human freedom.[5] However, the compatibility of God's sovereignty and human freedom is noncontroversial. Even an Open Theist, an Arminian, or a Pelagian would affirm the compatibility of human freedom with divine sovereignty. Nor does compatibilism refer to the compatibility of human freedom with God's will. Again, even an Open Theist, an Arminian, or a Pelagian would affirm the compatibility of human freedom and some sense of God's will. So the compatibility of God's sovereignty and/or God's will with human freedom is not at issue. The issue is whether or not Christianity is compatible with hard determinism, or whether God exercises his sovereignty in such a way that allows for meaningful human freedom.

Genuine compatibilists, then, believe that human freedom can be reconciled with determinism in some way. However, they do so only at a great price—what they call compatibilist freedom is not what we normally mean when we use the word freedom. By compatibilist freedom, the soft

---

4. *Routledge Encyclopedia of Philosophy*, s.v. "Free Will"; *The Oxford Dictionary of Philosophy*, s.v. "Free Will"; *The Cambridge Dictionary of Philosophy*, 2nd ed., "Free Will Problem"; *Encyclopedia of Philosophy*, 2nd ed., s.v. "Determinism and Freedom"; *A Dictionary of Philosophy*, s.v. "Compatibilism"; *Stanford Encyclopedia of Philosophy*, s.vv. "Compatibilism," "Arguments for Incompatibilism."

5. For examples of this confusion, see Carson, *How Long*, 200-204; Ware, *God's Greater Glory*, 73-85; and Ware, "Modified Calvinist," 98-99. Paul Helm points out Ware's inconsistent use of these terms in Helm, "Classical Calvinist," 44. An example of a compatibilist who avoids these confusions is Feinberg in *No One Like Him*, 635-39.

determinist says that we always act according to our greatest desire. In other words, we are always ruled by desire. We never make a choice between two options, but we do what we do willingly because we are ruled by desire.

In a Calvinist account of compatibilism developed by Jonathan Edwards,[6] divine determinism is compatible with humans doing things by their own volition. In Edwards's view, our wills are so dominated by our sinful natures that we are incapable of doing anything but our greatest desire. We never really have a choice—we are sinful from birth due to the inherited guilt of original sin. And yet, people are held accountable for their sins despite the fact that they never had a choice because they participated in their sins willingly. In salvation, God changes our wills and desires through irresistible, enabling grace as the Holy Spirit regenerates our spiritual life. However, this enabling grace is given only to those whom God has already predestined and elected; the majority of the human race will never have this opportunity to respond to God. The elect then genuinely desire to trust Christ. We do so willingly, even though we did not have the ability to choose or do anything else. Again, compatibilist freedom is not really freedom at all—it is *voluntary* but not *free*. Just being willing to do something does not mean that a person is free. If you were being robbed at gunpoint, you might be willing to hand over your wallet to the robber, but your decision is not really free because you have no real choice. To truly be free, there must be a choice between at least two alternatives.

All Traditionalists would agree that all have sinned and come short of the glory of God (Rom 3:23, 5:12–18, Isa 53:6), that there are none who are righteous (Isa 64:6, Jer 17:9, Rom 3:10), and that we have depraved sinful natures (Jer 17:9). However, most Traditionalists do not agree that persons inherit *guilt* for Adam's sin. As the Baptist Faith and Message (BFM) 2000 affirms:

> Through the temptation of Satan man transgressed the command of God, and fell from his original innocence whereby his posterity inherit a nature and an environment inclined toward sin. Therefore, as soon as they are capable of moral action, they become transgressors and are under condemnation.[7]

---

6. For Edwards's argument for compatibilism, see Edwards, *Freedom of the Will*. Among other Reformed thinkers, John Piper adopted Edwards's view most closely. See Piper, *God's Passion*.

7. BFM 2000, Article 3 ("Man").

Five Theological Models

So, although we inherit a nature and environment *inclined* toward sin, we do not actually become guilty of sin until we *choose* to do so ourselves after we reach the age to be accountable for our moral actions. Also, the BFM insists that we have the ability to make a *choice* to respond to God's invitation to salvation through Christ. It affirms that divine election is "consistent with the free agency of man,"[8] and that salvation "is *offered freely to all who accept* Jesus Christ as Savior and Lord."[9]

Compatibilism presents a rather negative view of human nature in which not only are all persons seen as spiritually depraved sinners (a point with which almost all evangelical Christians would agree), but we are never able to rise above mere desire to dream or aspire to things which transcend desire. While we are not conscious of being "forced" to do something, in fact we are not free to do anything but what we have been programmed to do. Since it is our greatest desire we do it willingly, but our minds can never override desire—we really have no choice. Therefore, compatibilism really does not qualify as a variety of freedom, since freedom requires the ability to choose between alternatives. In compatibilism, we act willingly according to our greatest desire, but we do not choose freely.

MOLINISM/MIDDLE KNOWLEDGE

Another proposed solution to the dilemma of free will and determinism was proposed by Luis de Molina in the sixteenth century, and has gained popularity among many evangelical scholars in the last few decades.[10] Molinism affords a conceptual framework in which both God chooses everything that happens and humans have genuine freedom. Although space does not permit a more thorough discussion of Molinism, let us delineate in brief several aspects of God's knowledge which are fundamental to this perspective. God knows not only all the myriad possibilities of what *could* happen (his *"natural knowledge"*), but he also conceives (by his own omniscience,

---

8. BFM 2000, Article 5 ("God's Purpose of Grace").

9. BFM 2000, Article 4 ("Salvation"), emphasis mine.

10. For more details on Molinism, see Craig, "Middle Knowledge View"; Craig, "No Other Name," 172–88; Craig, *Only Wise God*; Flint, *Divine Providence*; Keathley, *Salvation and Sovereignty*; MacGregor, *Luis de Molina*; and Plantinga, *God, Freedom, and Evil*. Some infralapsarian Calvinists have applied some insights from Molinism to their view of divine permission. See Tiessen, *Providence and Prayer*, 289–364; and Tiessen, "Why Calvinists," 345–66. Tiessen clearly identifies himself as a middle knowledge Calvinist, and finds Molinist beliefs in Calvinists such as Bruce Ware and John Frame.

not by his perception of future human choices) what persons *would* actually do in every possible situation (his *"middle knowledge"*). Based upon his natural knowledge and middle knowledge of all the "possible worlds" (i.e., each different future series of events in which there is at least one choice that is different from all the other series of events), God actualizes the possible world of free human choices that he desires (his *"free knowledge"*).[11] Molinism thus allows for both genuinely free human choices and God determining which possible world he desires. As one might expect of a view that attempts to take a middle position between two extremes, Molinism has faced criticism from both Calvinists and those affirming a high view of human freedom.

Calvinists challenge the notion that God can foreknow the genuinely free decisions (with libertarian freedom, not just compatibilist volition) of human beings.[12] Persons from a libertarian freedom perspective challenge whether persons are genuinely free if God has predetermined the one future world in which they functionally have no choice, since God has determined to actualize this particular possible world in which they cannot make any different choices than what God has chosen. Some Traditionalists and other conservative evangelicals have found Molinism a good compromise in expressing the tension between divine foreknowledge and human freedom, but it is still a minority perspective.

DECISIONISM/CONGRUENTISM/SOFT-LIBERTARIAN FREEDOM

While the somewhat technical term soft-libertarian freedom is unfamiliar to many people, it is a commonsense view broadly held by many people, as well as nationally known philosophers and theologians. Libertarian freedom simply means that in every key decision we have a choice between at least two alternatives, even if the only alternatives are "yes" or "no." It may be labeled decisionism in that we always have a choice, or a decision. It is named *soft* libertarian freedom in order to distinguish it from any who

---

11. For an excellent discussion of these three moments in God's knowledge in Molinism, see Keathley, *Salvation and Sovereignty*, 39–41.

12. This challenge is often described as the "grounding objection." Molinists have provided thoughtful responses to this challenge, but these discussions go beyond the subject of this article.

Five Theological Models

would hold to absolute or total freedom.[13] In soft libertarianism, limited choices are available in almost every aspect. While our decisions are not *determined* by prior causes and events, our decisions are definitely *impacted* by forces outside ourselves. We do not make decisions in a vacuum; we often face profound pressures which weigh heavily on our choices. However, at the end of the day, we are still able to decide freely. In Leibniz's famous phrase, a prior event "inclines the will without compelling it."[14] Our choices can be powerfully impacted without being determined.

Soft libertarianism affords at least two significant advantages over determinism and soft determinism:

(a) Soft libertarianism squares with our experience of decision making in real life. As we make decisions, we believe that we are genuinely making a decision between real alternatives, not just doing what we most desire. Most of us picture our decision making as being like a president and his cabinet of advisors. The advisors may argue with each other about what choice should be made, just as our emotions, desires, and rational judgment may cry out for us to act in a particular way. In the end, however, it is the president who decides what will be done. Likewise, in our own lives, though our desires are a powerful force, it is the *self* or *person* who decides what we will do, not just our desires.

(b) Do we always do what we desire the most, as compatibilism claims? In fact, we often do what we do not want to do. As Paul confesses in Rom 7:15–16, we sometimes do what we do not want to do, and at other times we do not do the good things that we desire to do.

How then does a decisionist, or the soft libertarian view, interact with determinism? Soft libertarianism rejects hard or causal determinism, and thus is sometimes described as *indeterminism*.[15] Soft libertarianism

---

13. For more discussion of the soft libertarian perspective, see Kane, *Contemporary Introduction*; Kane, *Oxford Handbook*; Kane, *Significance of Free Will*; Keathley, *Salvation and Sovereignty*, 69–100; Lemke, "Soft Libertarian"; Lemke, "Moral Accountability"; McCann, *Works of Agency*; Mele, "Soft Libertarianism," 251–64; Mele, *Free Will and Luck*; and O'Connor, *Persons and Causes*.

14. Leibniz, *Theodicy*, 327.

15. By "indeterminism," I mean only that what we do is not necessarily determined by prior events or causes, but may be chosen by a personal free agent. It does *not* mean that events are uncaused or random, but that free moral agents can originate a decision by choosing options that were not causally determined by other factors.

also denies that human freedom is compatible with determinism, so it is described as *incompatibilism*. However, soft libertarianism is compatible with God's will and sovereignty, since both are affirmed in Scripture. Divine sovereignty and human freedom must be held in tension, or what might be described as *congruentism*. Just how human freedom and divine sovereignty are reconciled is bound up in God's transcendence over our finite lives. Most Traditionalists simply note that the Bible affirms both a high view of divine sovereignty and of human freedom, and thus these two scriptural truths must be held in tension in the realm of *mystery*. Although they may not be familiar with technical language such as soft-libertarian freedom, most Traditionalists believe in a perspective such as this that maintains the scriptural tension between strong divine sovereignty and genuine libertarian human freedom.

STRONG-LIBERTARIAN FREEDOM/SELF-DETERMINATION

Although soft libertarianism advocates a creaturely freedom that takes into account the limitations of human existence and the powerful forces that bear down on our decisions, a strong view of libertarian freedom accords a more unfettered version of freedom. Often associated with Openness of God theology, this view asserts that God does not know with certainty the future decisions of persons.[16] Therefore, although God can predict the future with a high degree of probability due to his immense knowledge, he cannot know with certainty what humans will do. As noted in the earlier discussion in this article on omniscience, the BFM and most evangelical Christians understand Scripture to deny this view because it portrays God's omniscience and foreknowledge of future human choices as limited.

What is the right perspective on these issues? I affirm the soft libertarian/decisionist perspective, and I explained my reasons in the article. Individuals must search the Scriptures for themselves and decide their own perspective on these important issues.

---

16. Representative presentations of Openness of God theology can be found in Boyd, *God of the Possible*; Pinnock et al., *The Openness of God*; Pinnock, *Most Moved Mover*; Sanders, *God Who Risks*.

Five Theological Models

BIBLIOGRAPHY

Boyd, Greg A. *God of the Possible: A Biblical Introduction to the Open View of God.* Grand Rapids: Baker, 2000.

Carson, D. A. *How Long, O Lord? Reflections on Suffering and Evil.* Grand Rapids: Baker, 1990.

Craig, William Lane. "The Middle Knowledge View." In *Divine Foreknowledge: Four Views*, edited by J. K. Beilby and P. R. Eddy, 125–36. Downers Grove: InterVarsity, 2001.

———. "'No Other Name:' A Middle Knowledge Perspective on the Exclusivity of Salvation through Christ." *Faith and Philosophy* 6.2 (April 1989) 172–88.

———. *The Only Wise God.* Grand Rapids: Baker, 1987.

Edwards, Jonathan. *Freedom of the Will.* 1754. Reprint, New York: Cosimo, 2007.

Feinberg, John. "God Ordains All Things." In *Predestination and Free Will: Four Views of Divine Sovereignty*, edited by David Basinger and Randall Basinger, 17–60. Downers Grove: InterVarsity, 1986.

———. *No One Like Him: The Doctrine of God.* Foundations of Evangelical Theology. Wheaton: Crossway, 2001.

Flint, Thomas P. *Divine Providence: The Molinist Account.* Ithaca, NY: Cornell University Press, 1998.

Helm, Paul. "Classical Calvinist Doctrine of God." In *Perspectives on the Doctrine of God: 4 Views*, edited by Bruce A. Ware, 5–52. Nashville: B&H Academic, 2008.

———. *The Providence of God.* Downers Grove: InterVarsity, 1994.

Helseth, Paul Kjoss. "God Causes All Things." In *Four Views of Divine Providence*, edited by Dennis W. Jowers, 25–77. Grand Rapids: Zondervan, 2011.

Kane, Robert. *A Contemporary Introduction to Free Will.* Oxford: Oxford University Press, 2005.

———. *The Oxford Handbook of Free Will.* Oxford: Oxford University Press, 2011.

———. *The Significance of Free Will.* Oxford: Oxford University Press, 1998.

Keathley, Kenneth. *Salvation and Sovereignty: A Molinist Approach.* Nashville: B&H Academic, 2010.

Leibniz, Gottfried W. *Theodicy: Essays on the Goodness of God, the Freedom of Man and the Origin of Evil*, edited by W. Stark. London: Routledge & Kegan Paul, 1951.

Lemke, Steve W. "Agent Causation, or How to Be a Soft Libertarian." http://www.nobts.edu/Faculty/ItoR/LemkeSW/Personal/libertarian%20agent%20causation.pdf.

———. "Agent Causation and Moral Accountability: A Proposal of the Criteria for Moral Responsibility." http://www.nobts.edu/resources/pdf/ETS%20Agent%20Causation%20and%20Moral%20Accountability.pdf.

MacGregor, Kirk R. *Luis de Molina: The Life and Theology of the Founder of Middle Knowledge.* Grand Rapids: Zondervan, 2015.

McCann, Hugh J. *The Works of Agency: on Human Action, Will, and Freedom.* Ithaca, NY: Cornell University Press, 1998.

Mele, Alfred. *Free Will and Luck.* New York: Oxford University Press, 2006.

———. "Soft Libertarianism and the Flickers of Freedom." In *Moral Responsibility and Alternative Possibilities: Essays on the Importance of Alternative Possibilities*, ed. David Widerker and Michael McKenna, 251–64. Burlington, VT: Ashgate, 2003.

O'Connor, Timothy. *Persons and Causes: The Metaphysics of Free Will.* Oxford: Oxford University Press, 2000.

Pinnock, Clark, et al. *The Openness of God: A Biblical Challenge to the Traditional Understanding of God*. Downers Grove: InterVarsity, 1994.

Pinnock, Clark. *Most Moved Mover*. Grand Rapids: Baker Academic, 2001.

Piper, John. *God's Passion for His Glory: Living the Vision of Jonathan Edwards*. Wheaton: Crossway, 1998.

Plantinga, Alvin. *God, Freedom, and Evil*. Grand Rapids: Eerdmans, 1977.

Rorty, Richard. *Contingency, Irony, and Solidarity*. New York: Cambridge University Press, 1989.

Sanders, John. *The God Who Risks: A Theology of Providence*. Downers Grove: InterVarsity, 1998.

Tiessen, Terrance. *Providence and Prayer: How Does God Work in the World?* Downers Grove: InterVarsity, 2000.

———. "Why Calvinists Should Believe in Divine Middle Knowledge, Although They Reject Molinism." *Westminster Journal of Theology* 69 (2007) 345–66.

Ware, Bruce A. *God's Greater Glory: The Exalted God of Scripture and the Christian Faith*. Wheaton: Crossway, 2004.

———. "A Modified Calvinist Doctrine of God." In *Perspectives on the Doctrine of God: 4 Views*, edited by Bruce A. Ware, 76–120. Nashville: B&H Academic, 2008.

Subject Index

A

accountability, 85–86
  age of, 44, 51
Anabaptist, 49, 68
apostasy, 22, 132, 133n1, 134, 138–39
Arminian/Arminianism, ix, 10, 12n8, 12n10, 74, 97, 136, 138, 163–67, 171
atonement, 20, 37, 54–63, 65, 158–61, 166
  general/universal, x, 57, 61, 63, 96
  limited, 5, 7, 12, 16, 38, 57–64, 124
  penal substitutionary, 20, 54–55, 61

B

baptism, 9n1, 49, 143, 149, 161, 163
  infant, 41
Baptist Faith and Message (BFM), ix, 2, 17, 40–41, 43, 50–51, 63, 73, 92–93, 103–4, 109–10, 114, 129–30, 134–35, 161, 163, 165, 172–73, 176
born again, 20, 38, 76–78, 84–85, 87, 115, 162

C

call
  effectual, 22, 83n14, 84, 118, 125, 130, 137
  general, 22, 84, 118, 125, 130
  gospel, 63
  to repent and believe, 79n9, 82, 140
Calvinism/Calvinist, ix–x, 1–8, 10–13, 16–17, 31–34, 38–39, 51, 55, 57–63, 74, 77–87, 91–93, 97–98, 100, 112, 115, 120–21, 123–25, 128, 130, 134–40, 163–64, 166–67, 172, 173n10, 174
  hyper-, 16
  New, 16
  Non-, x, 12, 77, 79, 82, 84, 87, 93, 128, 136, 138, 163n8, 166
Canons of Dort, ix, 58
causation, 33, 105
choice
  God's, 34, 91–99
  human, 30, 41, 56, 73, 77, 81–86, 93, 95, 98, 104–6, 113, 120, 126, 129, 137, 170–76
  libertarian, 85, 125
compatibilism, 7, 13, 39, 56, 86, 93, 120–26, 130, 171–73, 175
concurrence/congruentism, 97, 99, 112–13, 174, 176. *See also* election, concurrent.
condemn/condemnation, 7, 19, 21, 30–34, 36, 40–42, 47, 49–51, 70, 89, 91, 94n9, 102, 114, 129, 172
contingency, 83, 106, 121, 170
conversion, 38, 60, 85, 134, 137–40, 148
creation
  God's, 26, 31, 42n10, 93–95, 110–11, 113, 119, 128–29, 147, 153
  new, 20, 76, 87, 162
cross, the, 37, 55, 60, 62, 68, 141, 152

179

Subject Index

D

decisionism, 174
decree(s), divine, 31, 33, 56, 74, 83n14, 92, 100, 104, 107, 111, 134n4, 170
depravity, 30, 42, 50, 81n13, 172–73
   total, 5n3, 6, 38, 51, 81, 115
determinism (divine), xi, 13, 31–32, 56, 77, 81n12, 85–86, 93, 96–97, 104n5, 111, 113, 120–21, 130, 138, 169–76
   hard, 169–71
   soft, 13, 120, 169, 171, 175
double-talk/double-speak, 85, 91n1

E

elect, the, 11n7, 29, 31, 32, 34n17, 56–63, 77n2, 78–79, 86, 96, 98, 100, 107, 114–15, 125, 135, 137, 140, 172
election, xi, 6, 12n10, 21, 34–35, 57, 79, 89–100, 104, 107–9, 114–15, 123, 130, 135, 138, 173
   of Christ, 96, 98
   conditional, 114
   congruent, 105n6. *See also* concurrence.
   corporate, xi, 97–99, 123
   of Israel, 94, 96–98, 107
   unconditional, 5n3, 31, 34n17, 38, 79–80, 82–84, 86, 96–97, 104, 115, 137, 140
evangelism, 3, 13, 62–64, 73, 120, 125, 134, 146, 155
evil, 13n12, 26, 44, 46, 67, 112–13, 126–28, 130, 137

F

faith, 2, 6–7, 10–11, 16–18, 20–23, 28, 30, 33, 37–38, 46, 51, 54–56, 61–63, 65, 67–74, 76–87, 89–90, 94–96, 98–100, 102, 104, 106–8, 114–16, 118, 122, 128, 132, 134–42, 144, 146–51, 153–55, 158–59, 161–62, 165
fall, the, 19, 32, 36, 41, 72, 81, 127
foreknowledge, 83n14, 92, 103–8, 115–16, 127, 174, 176

foreordain, 13, 32, 91–93
free agency/agent, 92, 114, 128, 130, 162, 173, 175n15
freedom, xi, 7, 41, 56, 84, 86, 93, 96–97, 100, 104–5, 108, 111, 113, 120–22, 125
   compatibilist, xi, 171–72
   genuine, 7, 56, 185
   hard-libertarian/strong-libertarian, 122, 169
   libertarian, 39–40, 56, 77n3, 121–22, 125–27, 130, 169, 174–76
   soft-libertarian, xi, 122, 126, 128–29, 169, 174–76
free will, 19–20, 22, 36–41, 49, 54–57, 68, 73–74, 81, 83n14, 86n20, 93, 97, 112, 118–30, 134n4, 136–37, 166, 173

G

Gentiles, 29, 59, 66, 82, 95, 98–99, 108
glorification, 22, 114, 132
gospel, the, x, 2, 5, 10–11, 13, 17, 19–31, 33–36, 38, 41, 60, 62–65, 67–68, 72, 76, 79–81, 86–87, 90–91, 93, 95n13, 96, 99–100, 106–8, 118–22, 124–25, 131–32, 134, 138, 140, 142–44, 146–49, 151–55, 158–62, 165–66
grace, x, 2, 11, 13, 17–18, 20, 27, 35, 37–38, 41, 46, 61, 65–70, 72–73, 78, 80–84, 87, 91n1, 96–98, 121, 128–30, 134–36, 138, 140–41, 143, 152, 158–62, 165–66
   "doctrines of," 16, 82, 134
   enabling, 79n7, 80–83, 87, 172
   irresistible, 5n3, 7, 12, 38–39, 56–57, 70, 72–74, 83, 104, 115, 124
   monergistic, 38
   overcoming, 128
   prevenient, 164, 166–67
   resistible, 39, 129
   saving, 11, 84, 143, 152
Great Commission, xi, 3, 23, 63, 142–55

Subject Index

H

heaven, 22, 27, 66, 68, 79n7, 100, 132, 140, 145, 152–53, 155
hell, 13, 19, 24, 31, 34–36, 41, 61, 91, 93, 121, 125, 146
Holy Spirit, 8, 10–11, 20, 22, 38, 46, 65, 68, 72, 76, 80–81, 83n14, 87, 90, 96, 100, 106–8, 116, 118, 121–22, 124, 128, 131–32, 134, 137, 149–51, 155, 158–62, 165, 172
  conviction of the, 68, 72, 80, 114, 116
  drawing work of the, 19, 36, 38, 41, 72, 158–61, 165–66
  enabling power of the, 131
  enlightening work of the, 165
  internal calling of the, 38
  resisting the, 39, 72

I

incompatibilism, 176
indeterminism, 175
inerrancy, biblical, 2, 6, 10n3
Institutes of the Christian Religion, 32, 111n12
Israel, 29, 43–44, 72, 94–96, 98–99, 107–8

J

judgment, 34, 37, 41, 43–45, 51, 67, 73, 134, 146
justification, 22, 38, 47, 51, 107, 114, 132, 138

K

knowledge
  God's, xi, 21, 73, 102–6, 114–15, 173–74, 176
  middle, 97n14, 173–74. *See also* Molinism.
  moral, 44

L

lordship of Christ, 2, 62, 99, 140
love, 3, 63, 146

God's, 10–13, 26, 28–30, 34, 38, 67–68, 72–73, 79, 81, 87, 91, 96–97, 100, 126

M

mercy, God's, 32, 81, 87, 99, 148, 161
Messiah, 29, 94, 99, 109
mission(s), 3, 10n3, 11, 13, 16, 37, 143–44, 150, 153–55
Molinism, 169, 173–74. *See also* knowledge, middle.
monergism/monergistic, 38–40, 51, 77n2, 78, 83, 85–86, 115

N

New Hampshire Confession of Faith, 30, 135

O

omnicausality, 111
omnipotence, God's, 108–11
omniscience, God's, 103, 105, 128, 173, 176
Open Theism/Openness of God theology, 104–5, 128, 171
orthodoxy, Christian, 41, 82, 128

P

Pelagian, 49, 112, 122, 158, 171
perfection, Christian, 163
perseverance of the saints, xi, 5n3, 134n4, 135–37, 139
pluralism, 154
predestine/predestination, 19, 21, 24, 32–33, 35, 83n14, 89, 91, 96, 98, 106–8, 114–16, 123, 163, 172
  double, 16, 33–34, 91
  single, 33–34, 91
providence, 32, 111–12

R

rebellion, human, 10, 26, 37, 98, 100
reconciliation, 62, 121
redemption, 11, 26–27, 67, 81, 95, 110, 124–25, 151, 155
Reformation, Protestant, 5, 48, 58

Subject Index

regeneration, xi, 20–21, 38–39, 51, 56–57, 76–87, 92, 114–15, 130, 138, 162, 172
  baptismal, 161, 163
  precedes faith, 77–80
responsibility, human, 47–48, 56–57, 72–73, 83–86, 90, 97, 100, 121–22, 130, 155
resurrection, 19, 24, 68, 96, 120, 149–50, 152
righteous/righteousness, 38, 44, 97, 108, 172

S

sacrifice, 20, 28, 54–55, 68, 152, 155
salvation, ix–xi, 1–2, 7, 10–11, 12n8, 16–31, 33–39, 41, 47, 54–57, 60–66, 68–70, 72–74, 77–84, 87, 89–102, 105n6, 106–8, 110, 113–16, 118, 121–23, 124–25, 128–29, 132–34, 136–44, 146–48, 152–55, 158–63, 165–66, 172–73
sanctification, 22, 114, 132, 135, 138, 148
Satan, 26, 41, 82, 110, 129, 172
savable/savability, 9–13, 25, 33, 35, 141
Scripture, 2–6, 8, 12, 27–30, 32–33, 39, 43, 48, 50, 55–57, 59–62, 69–72, 74, 77–81, 83, 85, 87, 90–91, 93–94, 97–98, 100, 104, 108, 114, 121–22, 128, 130, 135, 138, 140, 143–47, 150, 153, 164, 176
Second Council of Orange, 46, 157, 160–63, 167
semi-Pelagianism, xi, 122, 157–65, 167
sin, x, 4, 12, 19–20, 22, 25–26, 31–34, 36–51, 54–55, 57–64, 67, 73, 78–79, 81–82, 84–87, 114, 116, 122–24, 126, 128–30, 132, 134, 138, 141, 144, 149–55, 164, 166, 167n13, 172–73
  Adam's, x, 19, 36–40, 42–44, 48, 51, 166, 172
  original, 46, 49–50, 172
sinful nature, 40, 41n7, 43, 46, 172

Sixteenth Council of Carthage, 46
soteriology, 10–13, 17, 27, 31, 119, 128
  Calvinistic, 2, 12, 17, 77n2, 83
  Southern Baptist, xi, 11–13, 17, 135
Southern Baptist Convention (SBC), ix–x, 1–4, 6, 8–10, 12n9, 13n13, 40, 50, 63, 143–44, 163, 167
sovereignty, divine, xi, 6, 12, 21–22, 35, 56–57, 72, 74, 82, 90, 94n10, 97, 99, 102–3, 108–15, 118–19, 126, 128–30, 143, 145n8, 145n9, 155, 169, 171, 176
substitution, penal, 20, 54–55

T

theodicy, free will, 126–27
theology, ix, 4–5, 7–12, 16, 55–56, 59, 134, 158–60, 166
  Baptist, 3, 10, 41
  biblical, 5
  Calvinistic, 2–4, 7
  Southern Baptist, 9–10, 12, 166–67
  systematic, 5, 10–11, 43, 47–48, 50, 94
Tridentine Council, 46
truth, 3–4, 11n7, 28–29, 33–34, 69, 79, 85–86, 106, 123, 150, 154, 165
TULIP, 5, 16, 123n6, 136

U

unity, x, 2–3, 8, 13n13
universalism, 62, 124

W

Westminster Confession of Faith, 83n14, 93, 111, 134n4
will, God's, 31, 113, 115, 154, 171, 176
  hidden/secret, 34, 84, 99
  revealed, 34, 99
  universal saving, 62
works, human, 66–70, 86, 108, 135, 137–40
worship, 95, 149
wrath, God's, 19, 36, 41, 46, 55, 61–62

Name Index

A

Akin, Daniel L., 3
Allen, David L., vii, x–xi, 1, 55, 57n5, 58n7, 164n9
Amyraut, Moïse, 58
Aristotle, 170
Ascol, Thomas K., 120, 137–38, 145n9
Augustine, 31–32, 41, 158

B

Baxter, Richard, 58
Blomberg, Craig, 72
Boettner, Loraine, 31
Boyce, James P., 12n10, 32
Boyd, Greg A., 176
Brainerd, David, 58
Broaddus, William, 12n10
Bunyan, John, 58

C

Calvin, John, 32, 58, 70–71, 111
Carson, D. A., 59, 171n5
Cassian, John, 163
Chafer, Lewis Sperry, 79n6, 80
Chapell, Bryan, 9n1
Charnock, Stephen, 58
Chrysostom, John, 48
Coleman, Robert E., 145n5, 145n8
Conner, Walter Thomas, 11
Craig, William Lane, 13n11, 120, 173n10
Criswell, W. A., 10n3, 11

D

Dabney, Robert Lewis, 58
Dahood, Mitchell, 46
Dalglish, Edward, 45
Davenant, John, 58
Delitzsch, Franz, 45
Demarest, Bruce A., 158
Dockery, David S., x, 9n3, 10n5, 50
Draper, Jimmy, 10n3
Duncan, J. Ligon, 9n1
Dunn, James D. G., 47, 67

E

Edwards, Jonathan, 38n1, 56, 58, 172
Eppling, Christopher J., 40n6
Erickson, Millard, 10n4, 47, 50–51, 97n16, 134, 136n10
Evans, Jeremy A., 57n5, 78n5, 105n5

F

Feinberg, John, 111n14, 170, 171n5
Finney, Charles G., 50n26, 165–66
Fitzmyer, Joseph, 46
Flint, Thomas P., 173n10
Frame, John M., 9n1, 112, 173n10
Fuller, Andrew, 38n1, 58

G

Garrett, James Leo, Jr., 50
Geisler, Norman, 80
George, Timothy, 29, 50
Gottschalk of Orbais, 58

Name Index

G
Goulder, Michael, 46
Gregory of Nazianzus, 48
Gregory of Nyssa, 49
Grudem, Wayne, 10n4, 91n2, 112, 139–40
Guthrie, George, 139n13

H
Hankins, David, vii, x, 25
Hankins, Eric, vii, ix–xi, 9, 16, 48n19, 49n23, 90, 164n9
Harwood, Adam, vii, ix, 37, 41n7, 48n20, 50n27, 157
Helm, Paul, 111, 170, 171n5
Helseth, Paul Kjoss, 111, 170
Himes, Paul, 13n11, 122
Hobbs, Herschel H., x, 10n3, 11, 73, 144n2, 145n4
Hodge, A. A., 38n1
Hodge, Charles, 58
Horn, Steve, vii, xi, 133
Howe, John, 58
Hubmaier, Balthasar, 68
Humphreys, Fisher, x
Hunter, Braxton, vii, xi, 119

I
Inwagen, Peter van, 13n11

J
Jenkins, T. Omri, 151

K
Kane, Robert, 175n13
Keathley, Kenneth, 13n11, 34n18, 70, 94n10, 97, 106n7, 128, 133n2, 135–36, 173n10, 174n11, 175n13
Keller, Timothy J., 9n1
Kraus, Hans-Joachim, 46

L
Lamb, James W., 13n11
Leavell, Roland Q., 146
Leibniz, Gottfried W., 175
Leland, John, 12n8

L (cont.)
Lemke, Steve W., viii, xi, 39, 57n5, 103, 115n33, 169, 175n13
Lewis, Gordon R., 158
Limborch, Philip, 165–66
Little, Bruce A., 13n12, 112n18
Lombard, Peter, 58
Luther, Martin, 49
Lutzer, Erwin, 136–37

M
MacArthur, John, 44, 91n3
MacGregor, Kirk R., 173n10
McCann, Hugh J., 175n13
McGavran, Donald, 145n7
Mele, Alfred, 175n13
Mohler, R. Albert, ix, 167n13
Morden, Peter, 58n7
Mounce, Robert, 67
Mullins, E. Y., x, 11, 50, 73
Murray, John, 42

N
Nettles, Tom, 11n7
Nix, Preston, viii, xi, 143

O
O'Connor, Timothy, 175n13
Olson, Roger, ix, 31n8, 38–39, 163–67

P
Parker, T. H. L., 31–32
Picirilli, Robert E., 106n7
Piper, John, 84–85, 91n2, 135, 172n6
Plantinga, Alvin, 13n11, 173n10
Polhill, John, 66
Preston, John, 58

R
Reynolds, Brad, viii, x, 66
Robertson, Paul, x
Rogers, Adrian, x, 8, 10n3, 11, 73–74
Rogers, Ronnie, viii, x–xi, 77
Rorty, Richard, 170
Ryken, Phillip G., 9n1
Ryle, J. C., 58

Name Index

S

Scotus, Duns, 40
Shedd, William G. T., 38n1, 58, 62
Sproul, R. C., 9n1, 84, 124n8
Spurgeon, Charles, 33–34
Stanley, Charles, 10n3, 133
Swinburne, Richard, 39

T

Tertullian, 49
Tiessen, Terrance, 173n10
Turretin, Francis, 112

V

Vines, Jerry, 10n3

W

Walker, Mark Thomas, 13n11
Walls, Jerry, 13n11, 56n4, 126
Waltke, Bruce, 45
Ware, Bruce A., 34n17, 56n3, 171n5, 173n10
Warfield, B. B., 111
Weaver, Rebecca Harden, 162–63
Weinfeld, Moshe, 44
Wills, Gregory A., 12n10

Y

Yarnell, Malcolm, 123

Z

Zwingli, Ulrich, 49–50

Scripture Index

Genesis
1:1	21, 102
1:26–28	21–22, 89, 95, 118
3:15	19, 24
3:15–24	19, 36
6:5	19, 36
6:5–8	21 102
12:1–3	21, 89, 95
12:2–3	29
17:1	108
18:16–33	21, 102
22	21, 102
35:11	108

Exodus
1:22	43
6:3	108
19:6	21, 89
30:14	44

Numbers
1:3	44
14	43
14:29	44
14:31	44
21:8–9	22, 118

Deuteronomy
1	43
1:39	19, 36, 44
29:14–21	95n12
29:18–21	95n12
29:19–21	96
30:12–14	99
30:19	22, 118
32:4	72

Joshua
24:15	22, 118

Ruth
2:12	72

1 Samuel
8:1–22	22, 118

2 Samuel
12	42
24:13–14	21–22, 102, 118

2 Kings
5:1–14	116

1 Chronicles
29:10–20	21, 102

2 Chronicles
7:14	21, 102

Ezra
9:8	20, 65

Esther
3:12–14	22, 118

Scripture Index

Psalms

2:1–12	19, 24
22:1–31	20, 54
23	21, 102
36:7	72
51:4	21, 102
51:5	45–46
51:13	23, 142
58:3	45
139:1–6	21, 102
139:1–10	103

Proverbs

3:34	20, 65
11:30	23, 142
15:3	21, 102
20:24	74

Isaiah

6:5	19, 36
7:15	44
7:15–16	19, 36
31:5	72
49:6	29
52:7	23, 142
53:1–12	20, 54
53:6	19, 36, 172
55	74
55:9	74
64:6	172

Jeremiah

17:5	19, 36
17:9	19, 36, 172
31:29–30	19, 36
31:31–33	21, 89

Ezekiel

18:19–20	19, 36
18:20	44
18:23	19, 24
18:32	19, 24
33:11	83

Joel

2:32	21, 39, 102

Zechariah

12:10	20, 65

Malachi

1:2–3	68n5

Matthew

1:16	43
4:1–11	110
4:17	79n7
6:10	113
7:13–14	22, 118
7:21–23	19, 36
7:24	39
9:2	70
9:22	70
9:29	70
10:32–33	39, 115–16
11:6	39
11:20–21	79n7
11:20–24	22, 83, 118
11:28	39
11:28–30	74
12:50	39
13:1–23	39
15:28	70
17:20	110
18:14	39, 116
19:16–30	20, 65
19:26	110
21:28–32	39
21:32	71
21:33–44	39
23:37	20, 39, 65, 72, 83
23:37–39	125
24:31	21, 89
24:36	79n7
25:34	21, 89
27:37	115
27:42	74
28	144
28:18	145
28:18–20	144n1, 145
28:19	147–48, 153
28:19–20	23, 142
28:20	149–50, 154

Scripture Index

Mark

2:5	70
5:19	148
5:34	70
6:12	38
9:24	71
9:42	71
9:42–49	125
10:17–22	22, 118
10:27	110
10:45	37
10:52	70
16:15	144n1, 147, 152–53
16:15–16	115

Luke

1:37	110
2:10–11	26
4:1–13	110
5:20	70
5:32	79n7
7:30	115
7:50	70
8:48	70
9:23–24	22, 39, 118
9:35	96
10:1–12	20, 65
12:4	125
12:14–21	79
13:34	22, 115, 118
14:23	147
14:26	68n5
15:7	79n7
15:17–20	22, 118
15:24	21, 76
17:1–2	128
17:5	71
17:19	70
18:18–23	39
18:42	70
19:10	19, 24, 37
22:32	70
23:34	83
23:35	96
24:45–49	19, 24
24:46–47	150, 152
24:46–48	144n1
24:47	79n7, 82–83, 87, 153
24:49	150

John

1:1–18	19, 24
1:7	39, 116
1:9–14	87
1:11–12	114
1:12	71, 80
1:12–13	78n5, 84
1:29	38, 59
3:3	21, 76, 78
3:5–6	151
3:12	71
3:14–17	115
3:15–16	39, 78
3:16	19, 24, 26, 28, 38, 59, 87, 91, 154
3:16–17	116
3:18	30
3:36	38, 78
4:13–14	39
5:18–30	96
5:24	78
5:40–47	83–84
6	97
6:29	71
6:40	39, 78, 115
6:44	21, 80, 102, 124
6:51	39
6:70	21, 89
7:17	39, 84
7:37	39
7:37–39	21, 76, 78
8:24	78, 87
8:34	123
8:51	39
10:10	21, 76, 87
10:28–29	22, 132
11:26	39, 115
11:42	83
12:32	20, 54, 80, 124
12:36	78n5, 84
12:46	39, 115
14:1–4	22, 132
14:6	20, 23, 54, 142
15:16	21, 89

15:26	151	16:30–32	20, 54
16:7–11	80–81	16:30–34	82
16:7–14	21, 76, 78	17:2–4	82
16:8–11	80, 151	17:11	4
20:21	144n1, 153	17:11–12	82
20:21–22	150	17:12	80
20:23	153	17:17	82
20:31	78	17:30	38, 79n7
		17:30–31	79, 82, 87
		18:1–18	60

Acts

1:8	23, 142, 144n1, 150, 153	18:4–8	82
2	60	18:19	82
2:1–13	150	18:27–28	82
2:21	39, 115–16	19:8–9	82
2:23	105	19:18	82
2:27–30	115	20:21	79n7, 82, 151–52, 154
2:37–39	21, 76	20:24	20, 65
2:37–40	114	22:18	82
2:37–41	82	26:14	115
2:38	38, 60, 79n7, 82–83, 87	26:16–18	82
3:19	62, 79n7	26:17–20	82
3:19–26	82	26:20	79n7
3:26	60	27:25	71
4:12	23, 142	28:23–24	82
5:31	82		
7:51	39, 72, 82, 115		

Romans

8:6–14	82	1:1–6	19, 24
8:22	79n7	1:8	70
8:22–23	82	1:16	23, 30, 68, 80, 142
8:27–39	114	1:18–32	19, 36
8:36–37	82	2:7	67
9:35	82	2:10	67
9:42	82	3:3	71
10:34–35	82	3:9–18	19, 36
10:39–43	20, 54	3:9–20	38
10:42–43	23, 142	3:10	172
10:43	39, 82, 115	3:21–26	20, 22, 54, 132
11:18	82	3:22	71, 80
11:21	82	3:23	67, 80, 172
13:8–13	82	3:24	20, 65, 67, 80
13:38–41	79, 82	3:27–28	20, 65, 69
13:46–47	82	4:13–25	95n13
14:1	82	4:25	152
15:11	20, 65–66, 71	5	46, 51
15:19	82	5:1	46, 82
16:14	81	5:1–2	46
16:30–31	114–15	5:3–5	46

Scripture Index

5:6	20, 65	10:14	21, 71, 76, 81, 99
5:6–8	46	10:21	99
5:8	19–20, 24, 65, 67	11:1–2	107
5:9	46	11:2	103, 105
5:9–11	46	11:3	21, 102
5:12	19, 36, 46–47	11:7	21, 89
5:12–18	172	11:11–15	99
5:12–21	47	11:16–24	99
5:14	47, 49	11:25–26	99
5:15	80	11:32	99
5:15–21	20, 65	16:27	103
5:18	47, 80		
5:19	47		

1 Corinthians

6:4–11	21, 76, 87	1:1–2	21, 89
6:15–26	138	1:18	68
6:23	19, 36, 42, 80	1:17–21	23, 142
7	56	1:18–25	19, 36
7:9	19, 36	1:21	71
7:16–16	175	2:5	70
8	42	6:9–10	19, 36
8:29	96, 98, 104–5	10:13	122
8:29–30	21–22, 89, 103, 107, 116, 125, 132	10:27	71
		15:1–11	152
8:30	135	15:3	60, 64
8:33	21, 89	15:3–11	60–61
8:34	19, 24	15:11	60
8:35–39	22, 132	15:14	70
9	99	15:17	70
9–11	98–99, 107, 114	15:22	19, 21, 36, 76
9:6	99		
9:6–8	21, 89, 107	### 2 Corinthians	
9:6–29	99	1:24	70
9:13	33, 68n5	4:17	22, 132
9:17–18	99	5:10	19, 36
9:30–33	108, 114	5:17	21, 76, 87
9:30–10:16	99	5:17–21	19, 24
9:33	39, 115	5:18–21	62
10:5–17	99	5:19–20	62
10:6–8	99	5:21	20, 54
10:8–13	108, 114	6:18	109
10:9	71	10:15	70
10:9–10	22, 118		
10:9–11	115	### Galatians	
10:9–13	99		
10:11	39	1:6	20, 65
10:13	116, 153–54	2:20	21, 61, 76, 87
10:13–15	23, 142	2:21	20, 65
10:13–17	148, 153	3:8	95n13

3:10–14	20, 54	2:13–17	20, 65
3:26	82, 84		
4:4–7	19, 24	\multicolumn{2}{c}{**1 Thessalonians**}
5	20, 65		
6:15	21, 76, 87	1:8	23, 70, 142
		3:2	70

Ephesians

		3:5	70
1:4	96	3:6	70
1:4–6	21, 89	3:7	70
1:5	96	3:10	70
1:11	96, 123	4:14	71
1:13	70, 73		
1:13–14	22, 132	\multicolumn{2}{c}{**2 Thessalonians**}
1:15	70	1:3	70
2	70		

1 Timothy

2:1–3	61–62	1:16	71
2:5–7	69	2:3–4	19, 21, 24, 28, 91
2:8	128	2:4	39, 62, 116, 153–54
2:8–9	37, 82	2:4–6	59
2:8–10	20, 65, 69, 115	2:5	23, 142
2:9–10	69	2:5–6	20, 54
2:11–22	21, 89	4:10	71, 154
2:12	62		
2:14	29	\multicolumn{2}{c}{**2 Timothy**}
3:1–11	21, 89	1:12	22, 140
3:7–9	23, 142	2:13	71
4:4–13	21, 89	4:1–5	23, 142
6:19–20	23, 142		

Philippians

		\multicolumn{2}{c}{**Titus**}
1:6	22, 132	2:11	154
1:12–14	23, 142	2:12	22, 118
1:29	71	3:3–7	21, 102
2:5–11	20, 54	3:5	151
2:9–11	62		
2:17	70	\multicolumn{2}{c}{**Philemon**}
3:2–9	20, 65	6	70
3:12	22, 132		

Colossians

		\multicolumn{2}{c}{**Hebrews**}
		1:1–3	19, 24
1:4	70	2:1–4	138
1:13–20	20, 54	3:7–19	138
1:19–20	62	4:11–16	138
1:21–22	22, 132	4:12	81
1:21–23	19, 24	4:14–16	19, 24
1:26–27	29	4:16	20, 65
2:13	21, 76, 87		

Scripture Index

6:1–6	80	**1 John**	
6:4–12	138–39	1:7	20, 54
9:12–15	20, 54	2:2	20, 38–39, 54, 116, 154
9:24–28	20, 54	2:19	22, 132
9:27–28	19, 36	2:23	39
9:28	20, 65	3:2	22, 132
10:1–18	20, 54	4:8	67
10:19–39	138	4:14	154
10:23	70	4:15	39
11:6	21, 82, 102	4:19	20, 65
12:2	70	5:1	39, 78, 115
12:28	21, 102	5:4	70, 78
13:5	22, 132	5:13	141
13:7–19	79	5:13–15	22, 132

James

1:3	70
1:12	22, 132
1:13–15	21, 102
2:18	70

Jude

24–25	22, 132

Revelation

1:8	109
2:13	71n10
3:20	39
4:8	109
5:9–10	155
7:9–10	21, 89, 155
11:17	109
15:3	109
16:7	109
16:14	109
19:6	109
19:15	109
20:11–15	19, 36
21:22	109
22:17	22, 39, 87, 116, 118
22:20	79

1 Peter

1:1–2	21, 89
1:2	105
1:7	70
1:9	70
1:17	21, 102
1:20	96
1:21	70–71
1:23	78
2:4	96
2:6	96
2:9	21, 89

2 Peter

1:5	70
3:9	19, 21, 24, 28–29, 39, 62, 79n7, 83, 87, 89, 91, 116, 153–54

www.ingramcontent.com/pod-product-compliance
Lightning Source LLC
Chambersburg PA
CBHW071230170426
43191CB00032B/1221